Art In The Blood

Art In The Blood

SEVEN GENERATIONS OF AMERICAN ARTISTS
IN THE FULLER FAMILY

Blair Fuller

CREATIVE ARTS BOOK COMPANY

Berkeley ～ California

For information contact:
Creative Arts Book Company
833 Bancroft Way
Berkeley, California 94710
1-800-848-7789

For my children Mia, Anthony, and
Whitney, with love

ISBN 088739-305-5 (cloth)
ISBN 088739-304-7 (paper)

Library of Congress Catalog Number 99-64936

Printed in the United States of America

Table of Contents

Preface

In 1984 a letter came for me from John Dryfhout, curator of the Augustus Saint-Gaudens National Historic Site at Cornish, New Hampshire. He was looking for paintings and sculptures by members of the Cornish Colony for an exhibition he was planning to open the following summer. My sisters and I and our first cousin were the grandchildren of the painters Lucia Fairchild Fuller and Henry Brown Fuller (HBF), Colony members, and Dryfhout was contacting us to find out what paintings of theirs we possessed.

The Colony had been made up of successful, Beaux Arts trained, neoclassicist, mostly New York artists who had followed the lead of sculptor Saint-Gaudens and had set up their summer studios in the failing-farm properties in Cornish, to which Saint-Gaudens had first come in 1885.

Like their neighbor, Maxfield Parrish, Lucia and HBF were year-round Cornish residents, "Chickadees," so named for the hardy birds who do not migrate south away from the harsh New England winters. Lucia and HBF lived there from 1897 to 1908, most of the fifteen years that they stayed together, and these were the formative years of my father's and his sister Clara's lives.

The Cornish artists created their own exclusive society with its own customs and pleasures, and my father had imitated them in our family life to the extent that he could. Dryfhout's letter made me think of those features of my early years, and I remembered the summer when I was seven that we had spent in Lucia and HBF's Cornish house, an exciting time deeply disturbed by HBF's death far away in New Orleans.

I sent Dryfhout snapshots of the three rescued–from–attics HBF paintings that I owned. He did not choose any of them, but he invited me, sisters Sage Cowles and Jill Fox, and cousin Lucia Taylor Miller to attend the exhibition's opening, which would feature the reenactment of a mock-Olympian pageant entitled "A Masque of Ours." Colony members had produced and performed it eighty years before to honor the twentieth anniversary of Saint-Gaudens's coming to Cornish and the completion of his new, grandly-proportioned studio designed by Stanford White.

I felt dazzled at the opening. The expansive spirit and sure-handedness of the visual art and of the "Masque," in which the artists had unshyly impersonated Zeus and other deities, was both impressive and fun. Far from least among the paintings were HBF's large, symbolic *Illusions*, which customarily hangs in the Renwick Gallery of the Smithsonian Institution in Washington, and Lucia's miniature self-portrait of an artist at truly serious work, *In the Mirror*.

Much of the art was dated, certainly, in its use of dramatic mythological characters and situations, but how excellently finished, how coherent, how successful in the creation of emotionally transporting scenes this art was!

Reacting to my enthusiasm, Dryfhout told me that a collection of letters and documents in the names of Lucia and HBF existed as a Special Collection in the Dartmouth College Library. Perhaps I would like to have a look?

When curiosity took me there some months later I was astonished by the collection's extent. There are about ten thousand items, most of them letters written by Fairchilds to Fairchilds, but also included are hundreds of HBF's and my father's and my aunt's letters. While I was marveling that all this material had been saved I was told of a much larger collection of Fuller-Higginson papers and Negus papers at the Memorial Hall Library in Deerfield, Massachussets.

I knew Deerfield as the site of the family farm, The Bars. My great-grandfather, the painter George Fuller (1822–1884), had grown up on it and had had to work it during a long, crucial period of his adult life. His children, including HBF and his artist brothers Spencer, Robert, and Arthur Fuller, had been born in the farmhouse, and cousins of mine continued to own it.

When I reached Deerfield, more months later, the librarian told me that the Negus-Fuller-Higginson papers counted at least thirty thousand items. Where did I wish to start?

Using the contents inventory and sampling, I learned there had been two Negus generations of artists before George, Negus being the family name of George's mother, and that George's older half-brother, Augustus, had become an artist by an unexpected route—as a student in America's first school for the deaf. All these artists had had to travel as itinerants or settle in distant cities to find work. They had written home frequently, home had responded as often, and everyone had kept their correspondence. They even cautioned one another—"Remember to keep my letters!"

I was fascinated. I knew that HBF's brothers and brother-in-law had been painters, that there were others in the generation of my children. What accounted for this heritage? I nibbled indecisively at the collections on several trips, and worked at other projects.

Then I fell ill. Tests showed coronary obstructions, but while heart disease had been fatal to HBF and other male Fullers, by 1989 a surgery existed that produced for me a life that felt fundamentally new. Feeble as I was, recuperating, everything in my house looked just arrived. Every dawn was a revelation. What would I do with this extraordinary gift of life?

As I grew stronger I came to realize that what I was choosing to do led me to more knowledge of the family artists. In Los Angeles for another purpose, I inquired at the County Museum if there were Fullers in the collection. Yes, two of George's paintings. The curator told me that in 1917 one of them, *Girl Driving Turkeys*, had got the highest price ever paid at auction for a painting by an American artist. In Portland, Oregon, I found another good George, and I began to plan trips to find certain things.

I drove to the Southeast in 1991 and spent a month looking for family work and traces of the painters' lives. I found the site of the Dixie Tourist Court in New Orleans where HBF had died, and the riverbank spot of the slave auction that George had witnessed in 1850 in Hamburg, South Carolina, about which he had written vividly. I found the newspaper ads placed by Nathan Negus in 1820 in Savannah, and his portrait of U.S. Army General and Creek Nation Chief "Chilly" McIntosh. And more.

Then in San Francisco I learned that through the Archives of American Art much of the Memorial Hall Library's material was available to me on microfilm at the De Young Museum . . .

Seven consecutive generations of artists in one family—if not unique, it must be nearly so. There are famous artist families—the Della Robbias, the Peales, the current Wyeths. None, I believe, are seven generations long.

A few of the Negus-Fuller artists' lives have in some way resembled the lives of their parents but most have not, either in aesthetics or personal history. They have all had to start fresh. Yet here is a history of what it has been like to be an artist in this country from our beginnings to the present, one history which includes several partial ones:

◦a history of how women artists have fared—there are women artists in five of the seven generations, starting with the second;

◦a history of art training;

◦another of American artistic taste;

◦one of how African-Americans have been perceived and affected white America;

◦and another of the problems American artists have faced in surviving.

I have tried to see through these artists' eyes as well as my own. Whatever the degree of my success or lack of it, the effort has produced different—clearer, I think—perspectives on my own life and times. I am grateful for the heritage they have given me, one that comes alive each time I see one or another of their works.

In researching this book I am particularly grateful for the help of my cousins, Joan and Richard Arms, Mary and Herb Marsh, who manage The Bars, Jeffrey Legler, whose family genealogy has been invaluable, and Lucia and Harry Miller who have kept a foothold on Monhegan Island and have kept, particularly, Lucia Fairchild Fuller's work and history alive.

Suzanne Flynt and the staff of Deerfield's Memorial Hall Museum have been immensely helpful, as have the librarians of the adjoining library, as well as Abby Kennedy. Curators across the nation have given their knowledge, and opened their storage rooms to show me out-of-sight works, and directors of historical societies have turned up facts of which I could not have dreamed. Friends of the artists have contributed, and I especially thank the three living artists for telling me their stories and showing their work.

Thank you all!

September 1999
Tomales, California

Art In The Blood

Chapter One

THE NEGUSES

My great-great-great-grandfather, Joel Negus, (1768–1816), painted signs and standards—the emblems of a variety of enterprises, some commercial, some not. He ran a ten-acre farm, was a justice of the peace, a surveyor, a school teacher during the winter months, a captain in the Petersham, Massachusetts militia, and sometimes the town clerk. He was the inventor of a formula for the manufacture of paint, which he attempted to patent, and the father of fourteen children, twelve of whom survived infancy.

The older people of the town called him Captain, or Squire, meaning surely that his energy and command were plain to them, and a portrait of him by his son Nathan shows him to be ruddy, confident, and lively. What he most cared about was not command or wealth but art, the fine arts.

Joel liked to say, "Whatever comes from the hand of Joel Negus is a work of art," and there seems no doubt he believed it, although none of his work has survived as evidence. He carried with him a notebook with a list of "proper materials for drawing and the manner of using them," and a sheet of "rules for drawing the human figure at length."

All of his children were touched by Joel's passion, which must have been rare for a man who grew up in a small, north-central Massachusetts town in Revolutionary times. Four of the children became practitioners of the arts—two of them were among the best professionals of their time—and the others helped the artists as they could.

The town of Petersham stands off from any much-traveled route, then and now, quite apart from any other town, and is unique in its design and personality. It is exceptionally beautiful, which suggests that Joel's passion had its antecedents in Petersham's creators.

The town's center is not a square but a half-moon-shaped park planted with oak and maple shade trees and with a tall flagpole at its middle. On the park's curved side stand the church and the town's finest Colonial and Federal houses, and on the straight side are the graveyard, the town hall, the general store, and a commons pasture.

The scene is a quiet one today. The Petersham Lions Club publishes an annual calendar with the names of many of the town's residents printed on their birth dates, a suggestion of the population's intimacy. In the earliest years of the nineteenth century, however, when there were some twenty-three hundred residents, the children of the large families must have kept the scene noisy. Hay rides were frequently organized for them in the summer and sleighing on moonlit winter nights.

As a teenager my great-great-grandmother, Fanny Negus, the seventh child of Joel and his wife, Basmeth, became locally famous for having jumped from a sleigh in which she was riding to avoid the attentions of an interested young man on a particularly cold and dark night. She refused to reboard, walked several miles home through the snow, and never expressed either regret or anger about the incident.

One of Fanny's nephews, Benjamin Howe, wrote an unpublished family memoir to which I am indebted for much of the material on the Neguses. In it he describes Fanny as "remarkable for her gaiety, light-heartedness, and quick temper." Apparently she liked to say, "Love would go where it was sent, even if it were into a fiddler's elbow." Love and its opposite, too, perhaps.

She was a great dancer, Howe wrote, and had a way later of turning the work she required of her own and other children into pleasure. "What was the power she possessed to make us useful, and still leave us with the impression it was part of a play?" The atmosphere she created surely reflected her own upbringing in Petersham.

Next born after Fanny was Nathan in 1801, the child for whom Joel had been hoping. Nathan's visual talents were such that Joel took him to Boston at age thirteen and apprenticed him for some months to the portrait painter Ethan Allen, and then to the "decorative painter" John Ritto Penniman, with whom Nathan would remain for five years.

Although Nathan was sometimes resentful of his subservient position with Penniman, he had had great luck. Only a few months after Nathan's placement in Boston Joel was thrown down an embankment in a sleighing accident. He never recovered and died in 1816.

The oldest boy, Joseph, then nineteen, was sufficiently equipped to fend for himself but not to assume the support of the large family. Basmeth and the younger children soon were scattered into the houses of relatives.

While Nathan had a safe harbor with the Pennimans he

worked hard for it. He painted ornaments on fire buckets, made drawings for patent applications, painted signs, and decorated Masonic aprons. At some point during these years Nathan became a "most excellent master" in a Masonic order and later, as an itinerant, the painting of Masonic emblems would be important to his income.

In 1819 Nathan painted a large canvas of Boston's Exchange House being consumed in a fire, basing the work on a drawing by Penniman. When the painting was exhibited at Boston's Gallery of Fine Arts it met with "great applause," but Penniman took all the credit, and Nathan chafed.

Thus, when a pulmonary illness in May of 1819 was severe enough so that Nathan left Boston to recuperate at the house of friends in Fitchburg, Massachusetts, he used his disability to end the apprenticeship. His independent career began when he was well enough to work.

Nathan was then tall, dark, and wavy-haired, handsome, something of a dandy and something of a salesman. By way of promoting himself he made gifts of the ink sketches he drew of the subjects he painted, and the tactic succeeded. During his eight weeks in Fitchburg he painted nine miniatures and seven full-scale portraits on commission. When he departed he carried a recommendation of himself as a painter and "as a man" signed by "most of the prominent men of the community." (I am quoting a letter from Nathan to his sister, Fanny.)

From Fitchburg he went to Deerfield at Fanny's invitation. She had married Aaron Fuller earlier that year and was living at The Bars, which Aaron had bought in 1808. He was a widower, thirteen years older than she, and she became stepmother to his five children, two of them deaf-mutes.

Fanny's letter to Nathan told him to "bring his paints,"

that she had commissions lined up for him.

Fanny had attracted a number of suitors over the past few years, some of them championed by one or another of her relatives. She behaved with them in such a way that an uncle wrote to remind her of the dangers of "walking out" with young men in the evenings, and of the fragility of a young woman's reputation. She rejected all those suitors decisively, and the same uncle was upset that she should then accept Aaron, who, having heard of her, turned up one day to call looking "travel-stained and dusty, and older than his years." He proposed forthwith—still on the doorstep, it was said. Fanny accepted immediately.

Aaron had grown up in Fitchburg and had married the same year he acquired The Bars. The farm was so named because carts and carriages passing it on Mill Road had to remove and then replace fence bars that kept sheep on the higher ground of the perhaps fifteen-foot-high bluff above the Deerfield River's flood plain.

The Bars' then-substantial acreage was nearly all bottom-land and the gambrel-roofed house was large by the standards of the time—four rooms upstairs and four down surrounding a wide central hall and a staircase with a solid and ornamental bannister and newel post. The town of Old Deerfield, founded in 1669, had survived Indian raids and a "massacre" in its early history and had developed a tradition of building handsomely, and to last.

Aaron's first wife, Elizabeth, had died in 1818 and he had clearly been struggling to run the farm and raise his children with hired help. Fanny wrote a sister soon after her marriage that when she first saw the Fuller family they were eating "only codfish tongues and sounds for dinner."

Fanny may have been touched by Aaron's difficult situation, but he was an attractive man. According to Benjamin Howe's description Aaron had a "dark, superb manly figure, eyes that could beam like a benison, or flash fire." He was "reticent, calm, quiet, world wise." Whatever Aaron's qualities, Fanny never expressed any doubt of the rightness of her decision to marry him.

Nathan came and went from The Bars in the summer of 1819 working on portraits in Deerfield and the nearby towns. In all probability he also painted the striking self-portrait that now hangs in the Memorial Hall Museum. In it his chin is raised and his gaze is forthright. Long hair is pushed back over his shoulders, and a handkerchief curls out of his breast pocket.

It was fitting that Nathan should see himself so proudly, for he was in love with his best friend's sister and he was asking her to wait for him until he accumulated enough money to provide a family home. He wanted to look like a catch worth waiting for to Martha Childs.

For some months Nathan had been getting letters from his brother Joseph, written from Georgia where he had gone the year before to seek his fortune. He proposed that Nathan join forces with him. "I think we would make money very fast in the southern states." After the South, they would travel "to all the most considerable places in the U.S., working in each place as we found encouragement."

They would be partners, Joseph wrote. Portrait and decorative painters were in demand in Savannah and elsewhere. Joseph could do the easier and heavier work—stretching the canvases, painting the backgrounds, and so on. He would run the business, and Nathan could concentrate on his art.

Perhaps for selfish reasons, but also, I think, sincerely, Joseph expressed great admiration for Nathan's talent. "It is your object to immortalize your name. . . . You may with propriety exert yourself to procure a name that will live for ages after you have left this stage of action, because the knowledge you have of your art . . . is sufficient to prompt you to the greatest exertion."

If his brother and his sister were perhaps more enthusiastic than knowledgeable about Nathan's skills, Nathan himself had a quite clear idea of his contemporary competition and his own standing. While a Penniman apprentice, Nathan and a few others had formed the Pennimanic Society, a group that went together to see what works of art were available in Boston at a time when there were no museums. Members of the group would analyze and discuss what they saw, judging "the drawing, the likeness, the trueness of the colors." There were no competing "schools" of art or theories to complicate the paths to their opinions.

His observations had convinced Nathan of his own worth, but before glory could be thought of he must make some money. He said yes to Joseph's proposal.

Nathan paid a farewell visit to Martha Childs and later wrote to Fanny, "Heaven grant that I may live to possess that hand, that she may live to inspire me to virtuous action and to crown my happiness in this world."

Joseph had sent $141 to buy paints, brushes, gold leaf, "ivories," on which to paint miniatures, and some other things that would be impossible to find in Georgia. Nathan then entrusted his earnings from that summer's work to his "most sincere and beloved friend, Shubael Childs"—

Martha's brother—and sailed from Providence on the brigantine Eagle November 20th, 1819.

The length of the voyage made Nathan impatient. At the mouth of the Savannah River he transferred to a smaller boat to get more quickly upstream to the city and then was keenly disappointed. Joseph was not there to greet him, and what Nathan saw was sand and shacks and grubby, slave-worked docks.

Not only did little please his eye, Nathan's advertisement in the newspaper, *Savannah,* offering his services as a portrait and miniature painter, did not bring work immediately. He wrote a lonely letter to Fanny on New Year's Day. Nothing good for him was yet in sight.

Joseph returned to Savannah in early January. He had been scouting out towns in Georgia's interior as prospective markets for Nathan's talents, and looking for deals in other commodities and services. Joseph thought there might be buyers for New England-made furniture, for example. But now he focussed on Nathan and soon found many portraits and a mosaic floor for him to do.

In March of 1821 the brothers moved westward and settled in Eatonton from which they made frequent business trips to nearby Milledgeville, then the capital of the state, and to Madison and other towns.

Nathan noted in his journal that the people of Milledgeville looked "sickly," but it was his own poor health that was the problem. It incapacitated him for weeks at a time despite bleedings and the use of a number of recommended remedies.

In the same edition of a Milledgeville newspaper in which Nathan advertised "N. Negus, portrait painter, offers professional services," an item reported a negro being "condemned to receive 150 lashes on his bare back," and there were several notices in the classified section of rewards offered for runaway slaves. Nathan mentioned the flogging in a letter, and in others he would sometimes make disdainful comments about the uncouthness of the white society in which they moved. Neither brother courted a southern woman, apparently, although they did some partygoing and attended a ball in Madison.

Besides portraits, the brothers collaborated on the "decoration" of Eatonton's Masonic Hall and painted scenery for the Milledgeville and Eatonton thespians, and in August they had an extraordinary adventure.

According to Nathan's journal, "Immediately after finishing some scenes for the Eatonton Thespians we started for Indian Springs for the purpose of painting General McIntosh's portrait." They traveled on horseback as far as Monticello in Jasper County where, Nathan wrote, "We slept out by the side of a hut with a fire at our feet; the soft side of planks was our bed, a cloak our covering, and a bull's hide our roof. . . . The next day we traveled on through wilderness. At sunset we arrived at our place of destination"—Indian Springs, Georgia, near the Alabama state line. "General McIntosh was too full of business to attend to his portrait, and of consequence we waited several days without doing anything. Here we saw about two hundred Indians."

Creek Indian Chief and U.S. Army General "Chilly" McIntosh was the son of a Scot and a Creek woman. As a chief he had led the Creeks onto the American side in the war of 1812 and in the war against the Seminoles in 1817, and for these important services General Andrew Jackson had commissioned McIntosh a general. McIntosh had profited from his choices and had accumulated large holdings of land, both at Indian Springs and near Carrollton, Georgia.

Nathan's journal continues, "During our stay at this place we painted the General's portrait in full-length and his daughter, head-size. After remaining there about two weeks we returned to Eatonton."

The daughter's portrait has been lost, but the general's portrait hangs today in the Museum of the State of Alabama in the Archives Building in Montgomery. It is an extraordinary painting and in excellent condition.

On a canvas approximately four feet wide and eight feet high, McIntosh is standing, posed imperiously, and indicating by his outstretched arm his lands behind him—a rocky cliff, a lake, and a forest. He is wearing a ruffled white European shirt and a dark stock at his throat, but his loose, knee-length cloak bears a Creek symbol in its pattern and is cinched by an Indian-woven belt. He wears Creek leggings and moccasins. Nathan worked his own initials into the moccasins' beadwork. McIntosh's hair is black and short, his face elegantly lean and white-skinned, and his expression is one of dignified pleasure touched by amusement. It is a grandly flattering portrait in the aristocratic tradition.

Nathan's journal becomes again quotidian. "Returned to Eatonton ... went to Milledgeville to finish a miniature for Mr. Hopper . . . being sick with the liver complaint I resolved to undergo the operation of salvation and bleeding for which purpose I put myself under the care of Dr. Rogers and declined doing much work for the present."

Four years after his portrait was painted, "Chilly" McIntosh was assassinated by some one hundred men of the Hillibee branch of the Creek Nation. Two months earlier he and other Creek chiefs had signed the Second Treaty of Indian Springs, which had ceded the last of the Creek lands to the government of Georgia. It was McIntosh's point of view that the whites would take the land in any case, and that the Creeks should at least be paid for it. The Hillibees and other opponents argued the sacredness of their land and then, having lost the argument, picked up their rifles.

Perhaps McIntoch foresaw the Trail of Tears, the action in which all southeastern Indians, including the Creeks, were forced to march to Oklahoma in 1832, many thousands dying along the route.

For many years after McIntosh's death the whereabouts of his portrait were unknown. It hung in Kivlin's Tavern in Columbus, Georgia from some time in the late nineteenth century until the 1920s, when it was sold to the Alabama museum by a Mr. Edson May of the Acton Coal Company. New York's Metropolitan Museum made an offer to buy it from Alabama in the 1950s, which Alabama turned down.

McIntosh hangs now in a museum which is historical-anthropological and includes natural history as well as the arts. All school children brought to visit their state capital walk by it as part of their tour.

McIntosh has been joined by other fallen heroes and symbols of lost causes in Montgomery—by the Confederate flag flying atop the capital's dome, by the nearby shrine of the house in which the Confederate secession was proclaimed by Jefferson Davis, and by the recently created monument to civil libertarians of all times and places. The names of Abraham Lincoln and Martin Luther King, Jr. are prominent there, as well as those of Schwerner, Goodman and Cheney, the civil rights workers who were murdered in neighboring Mississippi in the 1960s while attempting to establish the "one man, one vote" principle.

By the autumn of 1821 the Negus brothers were planning another westward move. Joseph went ahead toward Cohaba, Alabama, a new town on the Alabama River that had recently been named the state capital, hauling some miscellaneous merchandise he hoped to sell along the way. The brothers wanted to use the funds from the sale of these goods to go to Cuba for their health in the early months of 1822, and then to visit New England in the spring.

Nathan was still in Eatonton, however, on the first day of 1822, and he wrote a depressed letter to his mother saying that Joseph had had difficulty selling his goods, although he had reached Cohaba. Nathan wrote, "The fireside of home frequentlly occurs to me, those pleasures afford me most pleasing reflections. How do all those pretty girls that adorned the village party? Half, I imagine, are secured by the bonds of matrimony. I ought not to think of love, but then it will sometimes cross my brain. I have scarcely spoken to a female these twelve months, nor do I expect to till I return to the North."

Nathan promised to send money to pay for his younger sisters' schooling and added, "A share of my love to all." In fact, neither of the brothers would get to Cuba or leave the South in any direction that year.

When he wrote to his mother Nathan had some portrait commissions yet to fulfill and some debts to collect. These accomplished, he moved on, first to Montgomery and then in late July to Cohaba, where Joseph had not only found quarters and started a carriage-building business but had married a Massachusetts woman, Elizabeth Filcont, whom he had persuaded by correspondence to join him.

Cohaba sits on a pretty bend of the river some twenty miles south of Selma and was then a booming town making every effort to become a capital Alabamans would take pride in. Nathan immediately found work painting scenery for the thespians, and he had the leisure to write letters to a sister in Petersham asking for gossip that would have "much weight and interest" with him, a "poor, lonely fellow, off here in the wilds of Alabama."

He did not want to appear too sorry for himself, however, and told her he was more contented than he had been since leaving the North, and that he was studying anatomy.

He wrote also to Fanny's husband, Aaron: "Cotton, corn, and yellow fever are all familiar with us here. Our crops are flourishing. We are just commencing harvesting which is (to the planter who works a hundred slaves) an annual fortune. Cotton was never known to yield more. High bilious fevers continue to rage and carry many of its victims to the realm of Pluto. Brother Joseph has been brought to death's door twice this season. His first attack lasted twenty days, the second about a week; since then he has had two attacks of the fever and Ague, but that is laughed at here. (If I die, I will write and let you know by the first mail.)

"This country is certainly too sickly for white folk to live in. Notwithstanding the richness of the lands, 'tis only fit for Indian hunting grounds. This is my opinion and, please God I live, early in the Spring I shall bid adieu to it, and return to the 'land of steady habits,' get married and settle down where I can again have intercourse with good society. Tell Fanny I anticipate much pleasure in seeing her boy." That was George Fuller, her firstborn. "I shall commence a series of paintings from him."

Nathan found portraits to do. His health had improved so much that he could "draw a long, searching breath without occasioning pain, which is a thing I have not been able to do these three years."

From memory and, perhaps, sketches, Nathan painted a portrait of his father, Joel, now six years gone. In it his artistic impulse seems wholly down to earth and affectionate, and the portrait is without pretension. Nathan's letters of this time show that fame has disappeared from his mind, that survival has become his only strong objective. He wrote, "It makes me curse the whole concern to see how inhumanely the sick are neglected. A man here, unless he has a family of his own to tend upon him when he is sick, stands a slim chance. For a female to visit a patient of the other sex is sufficient to ruin her reputation, so you may judge."

Before the end of the year Nathan moved downriver to Mobile. Letters reflect a hint of disagreement between the brothers, but the move may well have been made simply for commercial reasons.

The port of Mobile was the liveliest city in Alabama. Held by the Spanish until 1813, it was a Creole mix of brick and ironwork buildings and teeming, cobbled streets. Much French was spoken as well as Spanish and English, and every sort of business was being done.

Nathan set up shop at the Masonic Hall on Dauphin Street and offered through a newspaper advertisement not only his skills in portraiture, miniatures, and scene painting, but lessons in drawing and painting. To demonstrate his talents he displayed a large panorama of The Canoe Fight, a crucial settler-against-Indian battle in early Mobile history. The painting was described in the press but has been lost.

In relative good health and with his services in demand, Nathan soon had an enthusiastic following. He collected testimonials from his patrons, as he had in Fitchburg, and made enough money so that by late spring he could respond to Fanny's advice to come home and think of marrying. Fanny had become something of a mother to all her siblings. Some stayed with her for long periods at The Bars, and others were freely advised by mail.

Nathan reached Boston by ship in June of 1823. He was eager to settle down but it soon became clear that Martha Childs would not marry him. At first he pretended that he, rather than Martha, had made this decision, saying that he could not ask a woman to marry him when his health was so precarious. The rupture had, however, been her doing, and something almost as hurtful came to light simultaneously. Martha's brother, Shubael, had squandered Nathan's savings.

To begin his life anew Nathan conceived of a plan to open an art school in Charleston, South Carolina, a port he had visited on his voyage home. To settle accounts with Shubael and to add to his repertoire as a teacher, Nathan arranged to study perspective with a teacher in the town of Milton, and that Shubael should pay the bill for his tuition. Shubael failed to do so and disappeared. The baliff was called and, in flight, Nathan took a ship bound again for Mobile.

Putting the best face on the situation that he could, Nathan wrote to Fanny and others of the family that he had commissions to complete in Mobile, but he was a bit-terly discouraged and depressed man. Eventually, he wrote that if his health were better he would like to dedicate what remained of his life to "the patriot army of South America"—the army led by Simon Bolivar that was chal-lenging colonial regimes.

Still another blow now hit him. On arrival in Mobile he learned that Joseph had died in Cohaba and that he, sickly Nathan, was the last male member of the Negus family, a "child of misfortune," as he called himself.

While in Boston, Nathan had received a letter from Joseph saying that after a brief period of success he, Joseph, was once again in trouble. "I left home full of ambition to make money without the aid of other men, but my fortune in this particular has fallen much short of my ambition. I have this satisfaction—I am confident that I have made every laudable exertion agreeable to my judgement that any poor devil could make in my situation, while for many others there is 'no honor but in riches.'" Joseph's death made Nathan feel "at the very climax of human wretchedness."

Joseph's was far from the only early death in Cohaba. The toll taken by yellow fever was such that the capital was abandoned in 1824, and today it is an unusual state park. There is no official entrance, no ranger, and no commer-cialization. Brush and trees have been cleared away from a grid of streets in which stand forlorn chimneys and frag-ments of brick walls and foundations. Few stones in the graveyard have survived and Joseph's, if he had one, is not there. The river flows swiftly around a bend into which docks once jutted. On the day I visited, the only sounds were of birds and wind and the singing of an elderly black man washing his car beside a solitary house across the street from the park.

In November of 1823 Nathan advertised in the *Mobile Commercial Register*: "To the Patrons of the Fine Arts. Negus and Codman are ready to execute in the finest style portraits, miniatures, military standards, transparencies, Masonic paintings, signs." I know nothing of his partner, Codman.

Patrons responded, but Nathan's health once again stopped him. On July 27, 1824, he wrote Fanny from a friend's country place at Bayou that he was recuperating on a diet of "milk and rye mush." He was sensing his own doom and wanted to be honest with her. He had consumption. His "pecuniary concerns" when he had been in the North had been "very embarassing." Martha Childs had rejected him—he had not, in truth, had the opportunity to be gallant about his health. He was grateful for the hospitality and care his southern hosts were providing him. "I receive every attention that ingenuity and opulence can invent."

When Nathan was well enough to move on neither Mobile or New England attracted him. He traveled across southern Mississippi to New Orleans, then a city of twenty-seven thousand, one census claimed. Nathan thought it would soon become America's "greatest port." The Anglo side of the city was growing fast across Canal Street to the west of the French Quarter, and an important part of the new culture's upsurge had been the opening of an English-language theater on January first of that year.

James Caldwell, an English actor whose company had previously played in Charleston and in Richmond, Virginia, had brought the company to New Orleans for the first time in 1819. Then it had shared the facilities of the existing French theater, but in 1823 American investors had been found to build a new Camp Street theater which seated eleven hundred in a "pit, parquet, and three rows of galleries"—an enormous auditorium, considering the city's population.

The theater's facade was "in the Doric order." Marble steps led from the board sidewalk to the entrance, and within was a system of gaslight stage illumination and a "drop" system for the storage of scenery which were extraordinarily sophisticated for their time. Here, Nathan designed and painted scenery while, in a single season, Caldwell "made Shakespeare New Orleans' most popular playwright."

Half the people of the city were "colored," many or perhaps most of them "freed," and the theater's seating policy reflected the accepted social stratifications. The second gallery was for colored only, the third for "women and the mob." One night per week "quadroons" and their escorts were welcome. No white women would attend on these nights.

For the respectable sum of fifty dollars a week Nathan did his last work as a painter for Caldwell's theater. The season ran from the first of the year until June, when the company departed to play the inland cities of Natchez and Nashville, thus avoiding New Orleans's yellow fever season. Nathan took ship for home.

His wretched luck continued. The ship was becalmed for many days in the Gulf of Mexico. Nathan did not reach Petersham until July, and he died there five days later. He is buried near his father in the graveyard.

An account of Nathan's life to which I am indebted was

written early in this century by Mary Williams Field Fuller. It is entitled *A Youth to Fortune and to Fame Unknown,* but now Nathan has some reputation. In 1992 an ambitious exhibition, "Meet Your Neighbors: New England Portraits, Painters, and Society, 1790—1850," was curated and presented in Old Sturbridge Village, Massachusetts, the re-created historic village that incorporates a research library and a museum.

Four of the eighty-two paintings included in the exhibition were Nathan's—virtually all his surviving work apart from the McIntosh portrait—and they show him to be artistically equal to anyone of his time and place. Two of the other paintings were by Nathan's fourteen-years-younger sister, Caroline Negus Hildreth, one of those being used as the Exhibition's catalogue cover. Seven of the paintings were by Augustus Fuller, one of Fanny's deaf-mute step-sons—Nathan had only known Augustus as an unruly eight-year-old, and Caroline at six, but he had nonetheless inspired them.

An unexpected and affecting family reunion was on those walls. Nathan's portrait of Joel was there, as well as his Deerfield self-portrait. One of Caroline's paintings was of her sister Laura, and the catalogue's cover was of another sister, Mary Angela Spooner, with two of her children. Augustus had painted his grandmother, Aaron Fuller's mother, Mercy Bemis Fuller, and—with extraordinarily visible affection—his step-mother Fanny with her infant twin sons, Frank and John Fuller, in her arms.

Chapter Two

AUGUSTUS FULLER

While Nathan's talent had been recognized at an early age and his career fostered in every way Joel could imagine and afford, Augustus Fuller's childhood was dominated by the crippling problem of his deafness.

Born in 1812, the third son and the second deaf child of Aaron's first wife, Elizabeth, Augustus and his four siblings experienced scarcities of everything—affection most importantly. Elizabeth died when Augustus was five, and it was two years before Aaron found and married Fanny, who began to put some order and happiness into life at The Bars.

Fanny and Aaron soon started a new family. George was born in 1822, and Joseph two years later. In all, Fanny would bear seven children and, in addition, she brought several of her younger sisters into the household for long visits. One, Caroline, arrived in 1824 at age ten and remained into adulthood. Two years younger than Augustus, Caroline became his fast friend and, eventually, his fellow art student and artist.

In the fall of 1824 Aaron took his two deaf sons, Aaron

Jr. and Augustus, to Hartford, Connecticut, and enrolled them in America's first school for the deaf, the American Asylum, which had been founded in 1817 by a group of Hartford men inspired by the need of one of their daughters, Alice Cogswell, a clearly bright and vigorous deaf child.

The group had financed a trip to Europe by an educator, Thomas Hopkins Gallaudet, to recruit a teacher of the sign language which had recently been invented in France and bring him to Hartford to found a school for all deaf children.

On a fifty-three-day homeward-bound Atlantic crosssing from Le Havre, Gallaudet taught English to Laurent Clerc while Clerc taught him sign language. When they reached Hartford they were thus prepared to open the school in a grand-looking colonnaded hotel that had been bought for the purpose.

Due to the wealth and determination of the founders and the novelty of the school's intent no course of instruction that might conceivably prove valuable to the deaf went untried. Communication was the essential problem that the deaf faced, and thus reading, writing, and sign language were at the core of the curriculum, but many skills and trades were also taught. There were sewing and dressmaking classes for the girls, for example, and cabinetmaking, shoemaking, and harnessmaking for the boys. An instructor was brought to the Asylum to teach drawing and painting to Augustus and three others who showed some aptitude, and from the experience of this class it came to be believed in America that the deaf often possessed a special visual acuity.

Because it was Alice Cogswell's deafness that had brought about the creation of the school that so changed and enabled Augustus's life, he came to think of her as a sort of saint. He expressed his gratitude to her in many of his letters.

Today in Hartford's Asylum Place, the site of the colon-naded hotel, now a downtown square surrounded by offices, there stands a life-size, bronze memorial sculpture by Frances Wadsworth of Alice and the men who sent Gal-laudet to Europe. Alice, perhaps aged eight, stands looking confidently ahead while the mass of the ten men behind her, grouped tightly to suggest their mutual concern and effort, makes an impression both somber and affecting.

In the collection of Hartford's major museum, the Wordsworth Atheneum, there is a small oil portait of Clerc that may be by Augustus. It is unsigned and, by his own later standards, it is primitive work. But after five years at the Asylum Augustus's skills were considered to be professional. The portrait was certainly given to the Atheneum with pride.

When Augustus left the Asylum in 1829 he began im-mediately to do commissioned portraits in and around Deerfield, and by 1832, when Augustus was twenty, he was often traveling in search of work, sometimes with his father as agent, guide, and protector.

Benjamin Howe, who wrote so affectionately of Fanny, thought Augustus "was a painter though hardly an artist," that he was capable only of making "excellent burlesque like-nesses." But this seems to me a harsh and faulty judgement.

Augustus was undisciplined and inadequately trained. The backgrounds and secondary features of his paintings are often cursorily and poorly done. But at his best he ren-dered the essentials of expression and emotion with a truly interesting talent.

Howe wrote that Augustus himself was "rapid, impulsive, genial." Caroline, remembering Augustus as a young man, wrote that he was "the born gentleman. I often dwell with delight on those old days when Augustus was as gay and graceful as a faun; and he was admitted by all to be the most fascinating of boys—I never cease to regret his being deaf and dumb."

In adulthood, however, Augustus was erratic, troubled, and sometimes despairing. He soon became a heavy drinker.

On his first solo painting trip in 1832 Augustus wrote home from Chatham, Connecticut, that the people of the town "have much money," and that he could do five to seven portraits there at no less than ten dollars each. As in many later letters he found some local gossip to titillate his readers at The Bars. "I understand Mr. Cordelia was caught with amazement in New York and loose (*sic*) his money very freely."

That summer Augustus and Aaron headed west on a por-trait-painting tour beyond the Berkshire Mountains into New York State. They soon discovered a demand for por-traits, but success at any given place was by no means cer-tain. In Utica Aaron wrote to Fanny that a portrait painter had already been there, and, Aaron added, it should be understood that finding sitters for Augustus took some time. "The people have a great curiosity to examine Au-gustus. They think there is some witchery in him" (prob-ably because he uttered unexpected and unintelligible sounds as deaf people are likely to do) "and they must take time to investigate that first." Thus, despite the quality of Augustus's samples, a couple of days might pass before cus-tomers came forward.

A letter from Aaron and Augustus written September third from Fort Plain, Montgomery County, said six portraits had been finished, and there were eight or ten more to do, and some, perhaps, could be bartered for winter clothes. Further traveling was in doubt, however, due to a cholera epidemic in Utica. Augustus added a postscript that a local woman had eloped, leaving her husband and three children. The young man with whom she had gone was "the son of a judge whose wife weighs two hundred and thirty pounds." This woman was to sit for an Augustus portrait.

During this and other trips Aaron kept an eye out for a tavern or inn he could afford to buy. He wanted to quit farm life, but he could not find an affordable property he thought could be made profitable.

The next letter from Augustus was written November 7th and was addressed to "Mr. Aaron Fuller, my best father and family, and brother and sister," and was mailed from New York City. He wrote, "Perhaps you thought I ran away."

Augustus had found work as a lithographer in a shop located at Nassau and Wall Streets. He could do "a stone a day, easy," he claimed and he was boarding cheaply, for two dollars per week, so they should not feel worried about him. In a following letter he wrote, "I live for nothing but money," and, incidentally, "I am informed that Mr. William Smith sold horse and wagon of Polly Stebbins and ran away."

Augustus moved frequently during the years that followed. He periodically returned to The Bars where efforts were sometimes made to induce him to stay or, alternatively to send family members with him on his trips. When he was gone his letters increasingly were evidence of his alcoholism.

In 1838 Augustus wrote his half-brother George, then sixteen and working with a team surveying the railroad line to be built between Terre Haute, Indiana and Alton, Illinois, that "I am quite low from bad habits and bad company. . . characters full of money and pleasure-hunting every day except Sunday."

In 1842 he wrote, "I have pledged cold water temperance," but shortly thereafter he claimed he had drunk "no ardent spirits" but was drinking ale.

During one of his visits to The Bars Augustus's younger half-sister, Harriet wrote to another sibling, "Augustus is going to leave home. I dislike to have him go but he says he shall look out and not get into bad company. He has said the same before, and I feel afraid to trust him again away from home. Father has talked with him, but I do not think he could be persuaded to give up the idea of going, as he has nothing to do at home, and thinks he should be earning a little money."

Unlike Augustus, older brother Aaron Jr had returned from The Asylum trained as a cobbler. He had had the good fortune to have met a deaf girl at the school who wrote to him, once his business was established in Deerfield, "I shall let you was (sic) engaged to me, I am very happy to have you, I should like to let you be married with me next fall, I am much happy to live with you." Indeed, she was an irrepressibly happy soul, and their happiness together was much admired during their long lives.

Augustus had not found a woman to love among the deaf, and he did not easily succeed with others. His longings for women often burst through in his letters:

"Pittsfield, old and stingy place (but) I like old maids there which are always honest and flattery." And, "I like to see many girls—poor souls they are—5,000 in number and will not like to be married but are often deceitful and cheating beaux."

Another, written in mid-winter: "Silk! Good for girls to

walk in their own legs—glorious heroes! But I am sorry to say that their toes are prettily frozen and dangerous of getting better lovers. Upon my word I will take care of them if they give me a sweet kiss."

Augustus's letters grew wilder as his life approached a crisis. In early 1850 he wrote George, "Trees, grass, birds, and circus come again to sing more sweet songs, and all girls crazy to death and get married like buckshots."

I most clearly feel Augustus's lust in his *Portrait of a Lady Wearing a Red Pompom*, a life-size oil in the collection of the Springfield Art Museum. His subject is dark-haired with large dark eyes, exceptionaly full lips, and an exaggeratedly long neck. The young woman's expression is faintly amused, wary, and provocative all at once—surely in reaction to the painter.

When I visited the museum the painting was brought out of storage and propped against a curator's desk for me to see. As I studied it, an employee passing through the room asked facetiously, "Where'd we get the Modigliani?"

Modigliani would have done better painting the pompom on top of her head, her shoulders, and her dress, but he could not have bettered the play of feeling across her features.

Like virtually all portraits executed at that time most of Augustus's were straightforward attempts at likenesses of his subjects in dignified poses, costumes, and settings—attempts to make records of their subjects of which their posterity could be proud. In the portraits and double-portraits of men and their wives that Augustus painted of people he had known at the Asylum, the inclusion of good clothes and good furniture seems especially important.

There are two portraits in addition to the Pompom lady

in which dignity is of little or no importance. One is of a young man who is probably Augustus himself. He has a square, rather flat-featured face, and he is looking at the viewer with an expression both reticent and soulful. It is a snapshot in feeling, rather than something posed for.

The second is of Fanny holding in her arms the two last children that she bore, the twins John and Francis, born in 1838. They are thin-looking infants wearing the skirts male children customarily wore then. One of them is holding a toy whip in his hand.

Fanny is looking at the painter, and thus the viewer, with visible affection and at the same time, a barely suppressed urge to laugh. It appears she thought it would be a good idea to have a dignified picture of herself and her twins, and she put on her lace cap and good clothes for the occasion, but because it is dear and comic Augustus who is attempting the task she cannot be truly serious about it.

Fanny's cap is not painted very well, and the position in which the boys are held is awkward and untrue, but the painting is as alive as any American work of the period.

Howe wrote that Fanny was remarkable in treating the children of Aaron's first marriage with the same amount of affection as her own. Indeed, Augustus had written to George that she was "cheerful and kind, not mad to kill all rats in barns"—a striking metaphor for someone who could live with the faults of others, notably Augustus's own.

They were a deeply loving family. None of the members turned on or despised another, according to the thousands of letters in the Memorial Hall Library collection. Augustus would put them to the test, but none would turn his back on him.

Augustus's letters became more melancholic. One in

1841 includes his only known poem, whose refrain is, "We are hastening away, we are hastening away." In it, friendship is described as an "antipast of Heaven." His letters to George, however, were often enthusiastic and facetious, particularly in their salutations: "Everlasting Brother Eagle George," "Captain Fuller, Doctor, Sir," "Emperor George the III of the World for Fine Arts!" and "Reverend Mr. Fuller, Proven Artist."

In these letters he bragged about the progress of American Art and vaunted America itself: "American! We are proud of being unconquered with foreign countries!" Once—only once that I can find—he offered the younger George advice on painting: "Study your nature! Open your ears to heavenly bliss and new speeches if you will paint a beautiful picture!"

Alone among all the family painters, Augustus spoke of his talent as a gift from God. He believed that George had more of this gift than he, and he refers to "Cousin Caroline Negus, the splendid miniature painter," and to others with whom he had no family connection as his "betters" in art.

One of his letters lists in prideful, elaborate penmanship every school for the deaf that had opened in America, ending with the exultantly capitalized "GALLAUDET COLLEGE!" after it opened in Washington, D.C. As the years passed, Augustus felt increasingly cursed by his deafness. "God pity the poor ignorant deaf mute for the world is sin, suffering, and death."

He complained of being cheated on payment for his work, and perhaps the communication problem was most painful for him with those he loved. During Ausgustus's visit to George in 1844, George wrote to The Bars that "Augustus in the goodness of his heart sends I don't know exactly what, but *(he)* thinks you will find out."

In 1849 Augustus wrote George from Springfield that he had not heard from anyone in the family for more than a year, excepting George himself. Fanny had died several years before. Perhaps at George's urging, Augustus went to The Bars to help pick the apple crop and, returning to Springfield, wrote George, "All Indians will advise sun smiling every day of your noblest natures and inspiring truth and love."

But Augustus's euphoria was brief. More and more often he railed against figures in the international political scene ("Down with the Pope!"), against immigrants crowding into industrial cities like Springfield, and against "miserable and idle niggers."

In early December of 1850 the *Greenfield Gazette and Courier* reported that the grand jury of nearby Hampden had indicted Augustus for selling "obscene prints," and before the year's end he was tried, convicted, and sentenced to six months in jail. Whether Augustus had made the prints himself or was selling the work of others is unclear. After his release sister Harriet again tried to persuade him to end his itinerant career, but by 1852 he was working again in Connecticut.

Augustus stayed out of trouble until 1857, when he was arrested and jailed in Springfield. One historian has it that Augustus was charged with "drunk and disorderly conduct," but the fact that he was tried by jury and sentenced again to six months suggests a more serious charge.

From jail Augustus wrote George that his lawyer had

induced him to plead guilty, and that he should not have done so. "This trial was not correct. God pity the deaf mutes of the world." To add insult to injury, Augustus reported that he and his fellow prisoners were made to work "hard like a slave in the south" as shoemakers and basketmakers.

Aaron came to visit Augustus in prison, bringing the twins Augustus had painted ten years before. Augustus included this news in a letter to George, who by then was successfully making his way as a painter in New York and living in Brooklyn, New York's first suburb.

"We are portrait painters, inspired of God," Augustus wrote, but he had been thoroughly humiliated now, with permanent effects. On his release Augustus returned to The Bars, and this time he would remain there. He wrote few letters and he signed them, "A. Fuller, cranberry cultivator."

Twenty years after his second trial and imprisonment Augustus wrote a wild letter to a "dear friend" he had known at the Asylum. The text contains murky references to Queen Victoria and Napoleon Bonaparte, and it talks of "genius workmen," whom he presumes to be dominating the world. At one side of the page Augustus made a drawing of a standing, rumpled-looking man smoking a pipe. Augustus wrote that he was sixty years old. "My hair is gray. The wind is bad and kills all."

Augustus died in 1872 at a time when George's career as a painter had apparently been thwarted. George had been forced to leave New York and undertake the management of The Bars not long after both Aaron and George's younger brother, Elijah, had died in 1859. Sister Harriet was there, still unmarried, and John and Francis were not yet launched on their careers. The farm had to be made to provide for them, as well as Augustus, and, soon, for George's own family. Virtually all of George's energies were absorbed by this work.

Caroline had died in 1867 and during Augustus's last years it must have seemed to him that the family's ventures into the fine arts had come to an end.

Five of Augustus's portraits were included in the Sturbridge "Meet Your Neighbors" exhibition, a greater number of works than by Caroline or Nathan or, for that matter, any other painter in the show. In all of his paintings one feels Augustus's struggle with technique, his impatience with details that do not interest him, and what seems his pleasure in the things he got right. Above all, however, the emotional keenness of his difficult vitality and perception are there. His most dignified subjects never look complacent, and look alive today.

Chapter Three

CAROLINE NEGUS HILDRETH

Caroline was born in 1814 and was the next to last of Joel and Basmeth Negus's fourteen children. Joel died two years later.

Basmeth was soon forced to give up the family home, a two-story house on two acres bordering the Petersham Commons Pasture. She moved herself and her younger children into the house of her eldest daughter, Arethusa Negus Howe, and as her childen grew up some were moved on into the houses of other relatives. In 1824, aged ten, Caroline was sent to The Bars to live with Fanny and the Fuller family.

That same year Joseph Negus died in Cohaba. Fanny wrote to Nathan, "I give vent to some tears to suppress the pangs that rend my heart." There were many pangs for them all yet to come. Nathan's life was already doomed, and by 1830 seven of the Negus children would be dead, including all the boys.

Augustus, two years Caroline's senior, became her close friend. They drew and painted together, and the training Augustus received at The Asylum benefited them both.

Early in the 1830s Caroline attended Catherine Fisk's Female Seminary in Keene, New Hampshire, where the "ornamental arts" were taught, and during more than one brief period she and Augustus were both students of the established, itinerant painter Chester Harding. Caroline was also a regular-curriculum student at Deerfield Academy, and after graduation she became a teacher there.

Like Nathan, Caroline was tall and striking. She may well have been the strongest of the Negus children emotionally, for neither sexual attraction nor convention dictated her decisions. Not before she was thirty did she accept a proposal of marriage.

The proposal came from someone new and unexpected. Richard Hildreth was the son of the Academy's headmaster and he had come to Deerfield to visit his parents after spending several years in Guiana, working in the South American independence movement.

Caroline wrote the news of her impending marriage to her nephew, George Fuller, who was only eight years her junior and a dear friend: "You will say this is hasty, but my eyes are wide open and I am awake. I have only about three weeks, and I am afraid I shall not get ready. I am very desirous that we should all be together once more.

"O!" she continued, "Richard Hildreth is so good, so intelligent." She quoted what Hildreth had written to her: "'You shall have a husband who, if he is not such as you had hoped and such as you deserved, yet understands you, *loves* you, and will do all in his power to make you happy.'" She exulted to George, "I am going to marry a gentleman who wishes to spend some time traveling, and who wishes me to be a *great artist*, and will encourage me in every way."

No woman artist in this history—and there are three later generations of them—was made to feel so free to fulfill the potential of her talent, or was so heartened by the support given her.

Caroline concluded to George, "I am tired of being alone. I am glad of one to love who is worthy of it."

Seven years older than Caroline, Richard Hildreth was a man of passionate causes, energy, and talent. In 1836 he had published an anti-slavery novel, *Archy Moore, and Despotism in America,* which went through a number of printings. The 1852 edition contained chapters he had added to the original text, and the title was changed to *The White Slave, or Negro Life in the slave states of America.* The novel became a staple of Abolitionist argument and propaganda.

The book's long, episodic narrative tells the story of Moore, the son of a Virginia colonel and his "concubine," who had a "trace of African blood." Moore's slave mother and his father die in quick succession, and he is sold into a life of the most painful and degrading slave experiences. Moore's skin is as white as his owners.'

Principally because of the novel's fame, the Hildreths, once they were installed in Boston at 35 Essex Street, quickly became familiar figures among the city's intelligentsia. Toward the end of 1844 Caroline wrote George, who was in Pittsfield doing as many portrait commissions as he could find: "How much I wished you were here this winter. I must high *(sic)* to my lesson—I am just educating myself. I really feel my pent-up soul expand! I am studying German and French every day, taking lessons in singing of Mrs. Franklin and lessons on the piano of Mr. White. I also attend Miss Margeret Fuller's philosophical class every

Thursday—it consists of about twenty. It is truly an intellectual treat."

Margaret Fuller, then the editor of the transcendentalist magazine *The Dial*, was George's third cousin—so he had calculated although they did not know one another. Educated by her father to be the intellectual equal of any man, Margaret's fourth book, *Woman in the Nineteenth Century*, considered by many to be America's first "feminist" work, would be published the following year. Her philosophical class was for women only and was an attempt to provide women with the kind of background education Margaret's friends and colleagues, Ralph Waldo Emerson and Henry Thoreau, possessed.

Caroline ended her letter to George ecstatically: "Write, my dear little soul, *do,* and remember her who loves you, Caroline."

While her husband Richard had "an inability to harbor malice" and was loving to his intimates, he was often "caustic and disputatious" with his antagonists. He was a slim and wiry man and was usually seen with a hat balanced on the back of his head, prepared to challenge anyone with whom he disagreed. These characteristics endeared him to many in Boston, but hardly to those he targeted.

Over the years that followed, Richard published *A Science of Morality,* which concluded that a belief in God was unnecessary as an ethical foundation. Thus he angered the clergy on doctrinal grounds. And in pamplets he self-published he also wrote "with glee" of clergymen found out in adultery or thefts. He opposed Sabbath Laws, arguing that the clergy was not entitled to a monopoly of Sundays.

Another cause of Richard's was his opposition to the

political party, the Know-Nothings, that wanted to to stop further immigration into the United States. With perhaps the most serious consequences to himself, he selectively attacked the Boston rich, writing gossip about the scurrilous ways in which some of their fortunes had been made. When he was taken to task for publishing unsubstantiated hearsay he wrote that "one of the penalties of good fortune is to be an object of curiosity and public notice." Since he did not sign this attack he was accused of hypocrisy.

Eventually, Richard would be at odds with Emerson on political theory. Richard was an 1848 socialist who looked forward to "An Age of the People—of the working classes," while Emerson rejected socialism on the ground that it would reduce an individual's self-reliance, which Emerson held to be the highest human good.

Disagreements did not lessen the Hildreths' compatability with the transcendentalists, however, as Emerson defined that label: "What is popularly called Transcendentalism among us, is Idealism. The materialist insists on facts, on history, on the force of circumstances and the animal wants of man; the idealist on the power of Thought and of Will, on inspiration, on miracle, on individual culture. The Trancendentalist adopts the whole connection of spiritual doctrine. He believes in miracles, in the perpetual openness of the human mind to new influx of light and power; he believes in inspiration, and in ecstasy."

In the early years of the Hildreth marriage, Richard was writing the first two volumes of *A History of the United States,* which were followed by *Observations on Universal History.* He did research for these works in the private library of the Boston Atheneum, where he became known as "the spectre of the Atheneum, tall, gray, silent." Nathaniel Hawthorne, who often saw him there, marveled at the intensity and endurance of Richard's concentration.

While the books were being written (*A History of the United States* would grow to thirty volumes) Caroline helped and sometimes entirely supported the household, allowing no intrusions on Richard's time. Fortunately, she had found a ready and lucrative market for her crayon and miniature portraits, in part, it seems, due to an extraordinarily successful rapport with her subjects.

Emerson, who sat for a miniature in 1845, wrote that "'superb' was the word to describe [Caroline]." Her figure, he wrote, was "majestic," her "auburn hair, striking." She wore a "sweet and serene expression." In addition to the miniature of him, there is a life-size portrait of the two Emerson daughters hanging in the Emerson house in Concord that, although unsigned, I am certain is Caroline's work. The painting's technique is identical with that of the Bronson Alcott portrait that hangs in the nearby Alcott house, which is attributed to Caroline, and with the presumed self-portrait at the Petersham Historical Society Museum.

In these portraits she worked on tan-colored paper, and rather than using charcoal or pencil to shadow, she used white crayon to highlight outstanding features such as cheekbones. While the technique was not her invention it was not commonly used and is thus a kind of signature appearing in that time and place.

The Bronson Alcott portrait was his daughter Louisa May Alcott's favorite, and it hangs by the desk on which

Little Women and other works were written. Amy Alcott, Louisa May's younger sister, who later became a professional artist in Europe, was one of Caroline's students in drawing and painting.

Another of Caroline's sitters, the poet John Greenleaf Whittier, wrote a poem to her, parts of which read: "Maiden with the fair brown tresses/ . . . a serious soul/ is looking from thy earnest eyes."

For much of the information on Hildreth and the reactions of the transcendentalists to Caroline I am indebted to Donald Emerson's *John Hopkins University Studies in History and Political Science paper*, "Richard Hildreth," published in 1946.

Caroline's work was shown at the annual Atheneum exhibitions and at the National Academy of Design in New York.

Martha Saxton, in her biography, *Louisa May*, claims that Louisa May was disastrously in love with Henry Thoreau. Saxton writes, "Like Emerson and her father [Bronson Alcott] Henry offered principles without affection, morals without involvement or warmth. The self-doubt that he engendered [in Louisa] stirred up her earliest childhood disappointments, and she called this unfulfillable grief love."

It would seem that such emotional deprivation was common among Louisa May's Bostonian contemporaries. In the early 1840s the Boston sculptor William Wetmore Story wrote from Rome: "How shall I ever again endure the restraint and bondage of Boston? There is no such thing as flesh and blood [there]. We love nothing. We criticize everything. The heart grows into stone."

But although Caroline had also been emotionally deprived in some ways, even traumatically so, neither she nor

Richard fit this picture nor at all resemble the unfortunate Louisa May. Like the others in the Negus and Fuller households she had loved rather than criticized and had been enthusiastic rather than restrained.

Now in the 1840s a brief evolution began in the world around her that made "principles without affection" and the confusion of grief and love relics of the past. Whittier's poem to her, a married woman, and Emerson's uninhibited adjectives are indications of it. In Van Wyck Brooks's phrase "the flowering of New England" had begun.

The Hildreths' houses, the second one being at 3 High Street and the third at 15 Temple, were alive with music. Caroline's singing voice was much admired, and a number of instrumentalists were brought into the Hildreths' circle of friends both as accompanists and soloists. George Fuller, who was mostly in Boston from the mid to the late 1840s, had found for a studio-mate a sculptor, Thomas Ball, who was one of Boston's finest tenors, and they often went to the Hildreths for musical evenings.

Ball was one of the younger childen of a large and poor family. He had become a street urchin and had had the luck at approximately age ten to find a job janitoring a private, for-profit museum of "curiosities," where he could also sleep. Some of the attractions were works of art and from them Ball began his self-education as an artist. He discovered his singing voice in church, and it was trained in several church choirs.

At first Ball's reputation as a singer grew more quickly than his fame as an artist, but later on the appreciation of his talents would even out. He later lived for twenty-five years in Florence, singing opera with Italian companies and executing such sculpture commissions as the *Daniel Webster* which stands in New York's Central Park, and the *Emancipation Group* in Washington, D.C. which depicts Abraham Lincoln breaking slaves' chains with hammer and chisel.

In 1848, however, Ball and George Fuller were sharing attic rooms at 17 Tremont Row, doing what portrait work they could find, voraciously studying their craft, and enjoying themselves. Besides the more formal musical evenings in people's homes, they "often went serenading together" according to a letter Ball wrote to the *Boston Transcript* after George's death in 1884. "Though [George] was not musical himself, he had the highest admiration for my humble performances, and on many a summer night, when we could not sleep for the heat, we used to take my guitar and sally forth after midnight (dogs in the manger that we were!) to disturb those who could. I never declined to assist in paying that delicate compliment to anybody in whom he might recently have become interested, always having the most implicit faith in the truth of his description of her beauty, and merit. We used to say he went as my 'obligato accompaniment and protection'; and for these services he claimed any little flower that might by accident drop from above during the performance."

An atmosphere in which early morning serenades did not cause arrest was unlike Boston's before, or Boston's later on. In 1890 when George's son Henry Brown Fuller [HBF] was courting a fellow art student in Boston he was confronted by nightmares of Puritanical-Victorian prohibitions and required niceties.

During the twenty-year period prior to the Civil War, however, Boston was experimental and lively. Bostonians took strong positions, particularly on abolition and temperance, and they tried new concepts like Brook Farm, a community dedicated to making all the tools it used and the clothes worn, and producing everything its members ate.

Bostonians were open to difference and eccentricity. Unitarianism had won the day over Trinitarianism and had become known as the Church of Boston. Anything less inclusive than Unitarianism was made to seem primitive and constricting.

In Italy in 1847, Caroline's former mentor, Margaret Fuller, wrote in her journal, "Once I was almost all intellect; now I am almost all feeling. I feel all Italy glowing beneath the Saxon [her own] crust. This cannot last long: I shall burn to ashes if all this smoulders here much longer."

At that moment Margaret was, in fact, in love, something her brother Richard may have sensed when he wrote to her from Boston, "You ought not to confine your life to books and reveries. You have pleaded the liberty of women in a masculine and frank style. Live and act as you write. I have seen you, with all your learning and all your imagination, living in a bondage harder than that of a servant. The relationships which suit you are those which develop and free your spirit, responding to the legitimate needs of your body and leaving you free at all times. You are the sole judge of those needs."

Richard was telling Margaret, then in her mid-thirties, that she should lose her virginity, and the letter pleased her very much.

Perhaps she had lost it before the letter's arrival. If not, she was very soon to do so with the younger son of a noble Roman family, who had picked her up in Saint Peter's

Cathedral by offering her historical information on what was before her eyes. She may have been the first in a long line of educated American young women to have found attentions in Rome the lovely likes of which they had not found at home. In *Woman in the Nineteenth Century* Margaret had written that "Woman is born for love, and it is impossible to turn her away from seeking it," and now she would take her own chances on it.

Margaret became pregnant. She found it impossible to tell her mother of this before she and Giovanni Ossoli had obtained a flimsy "civil recognition" of their relationship. His family's disapproval (she was older, untitled, and a Protestant) prevented a genuine marriage. Tragically, Margaret, Giovanni, and their infant son died in a shipwreck off Fire Island as they were coming to America for a family presentation.

At the end of the 1840s Caroline was getting forty dollars per miniature portrait, and in addition to his *History* Richard was writing occasional potboilers to ease their financial strain. They and their friends read each other's works, criticized each other's pictures, and struggled forward.

The Hildreths were badly disappointed when Harvard did not appoint Richard to a Chair in the History Department. Apparently, he was thought to be too antagonistic to theocracy, too adamantly committed to the separation of church and state to be preferred by Harvard's Overseers, despite his extraordinary list of published works. Then, early in the 1850s two things happened to change their lives—Caroline bore a son, and Horace Greeley offered Richard a post as principal editor of *The New York Tribune*.

The Hildreths moved to New York. Since Richard was making a more than adequate salary, Caroline could confine herself to the chores of motherhood. She wrote to George in February of 1852: "I will yet show you what I can do [artistically, she meant] beyond the creation of a beautiful, blue-eyed boy." It is not clear if she returned to work, however, before her son died of a cause I cannot discover.

She wrote George in early 1857: "Often in the midst of my deep and impenetrable sorrow, dear, dear George, has my heart turned toward you in love and good faith. I have tried my eyes a good deal of late—drawing and reading and, more than all, weeping." But soon after, her energies were again going into the "soul-absorbing arts"—a phrase she used a number of times. In March she wrote, "Now I am hard at work in pastels, hope to paint a tolerable head before you read this."

Her Petersham Historical Society self-portrait was probably done at this time. It shows her head and shoulders, life size, rendered in dull colors and white highlights on tan paper. The face is that of a handsome and formidable-looking fortyish woman, hair held tightly under a plain, close-fitting bonnet whose strings are tied under her chin. Like her brother Nathan, she has a high forehead, a long straight nose, and a wide, full-lipped mouth. A line of concentration runs upward between her brows.

Caroline's right eye is in shadow and seems both introspective and compassionate, while her strongly-lit left eye looks forthrightly at the viewer. Her attitude seems challenging: "Here I am, take it or leave it. I won't put on my best clothes or smile for you." Then one is drawn in by the compassionate right eye.

Richard saved and invested his money. A bank crash in 1857 wiped out what he had put aside. Not long after that blow he suffered a breakdown of his health that brought his editorial and writing careers to an end and made it necessary for Caroline to return to doing commissioned portraits.

Richard's breakdown was not diagnosed in terms that are understandable today, but I believe he had suffered a stroke. Caroline sent him to the West Indies, where it was hoped the climate would help him to recover, but after a number of months he returned to New York in no better condition.

Apparently, Richard had doubted Caroline could support the household, but she did so, now getting fifty dollars per portrait. Happily, with the election of Lincoln to the presidency in 1860 she saw a possibility of finding some security for them both.

Caroline traveled to Washington and persuaded Senator Sumner of Massachusetts to speak with Lincoln and request a diplomatic post for Richard as a reward for his services to the abolitionist cause and thus to Lincoln's victory. Lincoln complied, appointing Richard to be the American Consul at Trieste, and the Hildreths took ship directly.

William Dean Howells, who later became a novelist and successively, editor of the *Atlantic Monthly* and *Harper's*, and who figures importantly in further family history, was then Consul at Venice, a reward for having written a Lincoln campaign biography. Howells had known Richard as principal editor of the *Tribune*, and he went to Trieste to see him. Howells was shocked by Richard's appearance and he described him as a "phantom of himself."

So far as Howells could see, Caroline was doing all the work of the consulate and doing it well enough, but Richard required a great deal of her attention. Howells thought Caroline was suffering acutely from loneliness.

Richard wrote a letter from Trieste to Howells in Venice

on June 20, 1862, that is mainly illegible but that certainly concerns consular business. Caroline added a postscript that reads in part, "How fares the Muse of Poetry with thee? Does she visit thee still in the form of home and mother— & Heaven? 'Mother, Home, & Heaven?'"

Richard officially retired in 1864. Perhaps some sort of government pension was due him, and help certainly came from Boston. Caroline wrote George from Parma: "The money which I draw upon has been collected for Richard's benefit by the friends of Richard (please keep it in the family)."

Caroline was then once again thinking of art: "I think that the works of the great masters have to be copied to be appreciated fully. I am not exactly wild, but I am very happy about the opportunity I have of examining their works of art." She had seen exhibitions of contemporary italian painting in Venice and Milan and thought that "it hardly compares with our own."

The Hildreths moved to Naples, then to Sorrento, then to Florence, where Richard died July 10, 1865. Caroline bore the pain and difficulty of it "as only a woman so noble as herself could bear so severe a trial," wrote a Boston friend.

Caroline stayed on in Italy and began again—and successfully—to make her living as a portraitist. There were a number of American artists working and studying in Italy, including Thomas Ball, and no doubt they made up a pleasant and invigorating society, but Caroline's new life and prospects were to be short-lived. She died in a cholera epidemic in Naples in 1867.

In the Sturbridge "Meet Your Neighbors" exhibition Caroline was as prominently represented as Nathan or Augustus, although there were only two of her works. One of them is on the cover of the exhibit's catalogue—a triple portrait of Caroline's sister Mary Angela Spooner with two of her children, one an infant in her arms and the other a boy of perhaps five. The other portrait is of another sister, Laura Negus Spooner, at perhaps eighteen. These sisters had married brothers.

Both paintings were made before Caroline's marriage and move to Boston, and both surely used family sitters for practical as well as affectionate reasons. In both the perspective is primitive. The subjects' clothing is suggested without an effort at trompe l'oeil, and the backgrounds are simply that—blank walls of crayon color. Caroline became a more accomplished artist during her Boston and New York years. The curator no doubt chose these two paintings partly for the feeling of loving intimacy that they project, as he did Nathan's posthumous portrait of Joel, and Augustus's portrait of Fanny and the twins.

Because Nathan was older and so little of his time was spent in Deerfield, he was an idol, perhaps a sort of myth to Augustus, Caroline, and George Fuller. To judge solely by the Sturbridge show, Nathan was the most skillful painter among them, but Caroline's later work at least equals his.

Among family artists her drawing is unsurpassed, witness the drawing presumed to be of Fanny during her last illness.

Emotionally Augustus and Caroline belong with George rather than with Nathan due to their years together. Caroline wrote her "darling friend" George in 1852, "Occasionally I allow myself to dwell on the iron chain that once bound together such warm hearts"—hers and George's and Augustus's.

By that time Caroline had felt or deduced a change in

the demand for art—away from the formal portrait to historical and allegorical works. She wrote George that Washington Allston was the painter to study and, if possible, to study with. Toward the end of his career, Allston was doing big allegorical canvases, sometimes "blowing up" the humans depicted in them to twice life-size, which then was a strikingly original idea. Ancient Roman sculptors had invented heroic scale to depict emperors, but Allston experimented with it as a magnifier of emotional display.

In 1990 one of the five miniature portraits by Caroline in the collection of the Boston Museum of Fine Arts was included in an exhibition organized by the Metropolitan Museum, entitled "Tokens of Affection: the Portrait Miniature in America." The show traveled to the National Gallery in Washington, and elsewhere.

Caroline's miniature of Mrs. James Page is deft and charming, probably exactly what both she and her subject wished it to be, but like the work at Sturbridge, I believe it does not show Caroline at her most impressive.

Caroline could imagine an art with broader objectives, and she could imagine, too, better-lived lives. Although many of those dearest to her had experienced disappointment and tragedy, she had felt, too, the liberating effects of the transcendentalists' ideas. Emerson had expressed optimism, enthusiasm for vigor and imagination—"Build a better mousetrap and the world will beat a path to your door," was one of his sayings. He declared the individual to be the sole relevant judge of self and accomplishment. Emerson's less bullish friend, Thoreau spoke for an idea of individual well-being created separately from the rewards that others, through organized structures such as corporations, could give or take away. Richard had spoken for the nation as commonwealth.

These were fresh visions, and in Caroline's 1852 letter to George she thought of possibilities that could not have been seriously considered in the Negus–Fuller family a generation before. She wrote, "I am looking here and there to find a nephew who will hold the reins of life with ease and eloquence. My eye is fixed *on you*."

Chapter Four

GEORGE FULLER

"Elegance" and "ease" are not the right words to describe George's life, but they are apt in how he held its "reins" once he had emerged from what must have been a tumultuous childhood.

George was born January 17th, 1822, at The Bars. The household then consisted of Fanny, Aaron, and the five children from Aaron's first marriage. Fanny's sister Caroline would soon become a permanent resident, their mother and several siblings would be frequent visitors, and Fanny would bear six more children. The farmhouse was evidently spacious enough for them all. The Negus family had, of course, been very large and perhaps the size of the crowd seemed natural to Aaron, too. His parents, Azariah and Mercy, had been innkeepers and had also run a bakery in Fitchburg.

The Bars did a considerable volume of business to support its residents. In the 1830s twenty to thirty men would be hired to help get in the cranberry crop, which came to about fourteen hundred bushels a season, and there were other crops and vegetables.

George was a big and healthy baby and he never lost his advantage in size and vitality. His schoolmates called him

Captain as their leader in games and adventures, and he was admired as well as loved in his emotionally volatile home. Benjamin Howe, who lived at The Bars for several years as a child, wrote of Fanny that "on a scale of one to twenty she would rate eighteen," her only major fault being her explosiveness. "She could scold frightfully, and show specimens of a temper hard to describe." Fanny and George were very close. Their only bone of contention arose in his later boyhood when he declared his wish to be an artist.

Presumably, George was impressed and delighted by Augustus's and Caroline's artistic skills, and paintings by his Uncle Nathan were also hung in the house. While it was to be expected that George would wish to emulate them, his parents did their best to discourage him.

The life of a painter was too uncertain and difficult— look at Nathan's tragic life! It was all right for Augustus to pursue such a career—he was disadvantaged and limited in his choices—and for a woman like Caroline to be able to exercise such a talent was certainly a plus. But George could and should do better.

When George reached age thirteen, Aaron took him to Boston to apprentice him not to a painter but to a grocer. That did not work well. After a few months Aaron moved George to a job in a Boston shoe store, but George was dreamy and absentminded, not sufficiently interested in his work to suit his boss. Aaron brought George back to Deerfield to continue school and to work on the farm. He became an avid reader through the Deerfield library.

In 1837 a prominent Deerfield man, Elihu Hoyt, organized a party of men to go west to survey a railroad line to be built between Terre Haute, Indiana, and Alton, Illinois, on the Mississippi River. It would be Illinois's first rail line.

Hoyt had helped persuade the government of Massachus-
setts to share in the cost of Aaron Jr.'s and Augustus's educations at The Asylum, and Augustus did Hoyt's portrait—perhaps simply out of gratitude—at around this time. Whether
or not George heard of the surveying party through this
connection is not clear, but at fifteen he and his closest friend
Richard Arms signed on for two years of work.

George and the others left Deerfield on a rainy May day.
According to legend, Fanny and Aaron missed George so
keenly that every day for many days thereafter they would
walk out from the house at sundown and quietly contem-
plate the bootprints George had left in the mud as he had
walked off down the road.

Sad though they were, they must have thought that
George was pointed in a good direction, toward a surveyor's
or an engineer's career, and they could not have been disappointed by the excited letters George wrote home:

"Terre Haute, June 11, 1837. We are all in good health
and good spirits. We took a steamboat at Hartford for New
York. I went into the museum there and saw many curiosities, among which was the arm and hand of a celebrated
pirate who was hung and his bones left to dry and rattle.
He had lost one finger in his last engagement."

From New York they went to Philadelphia, then to Pitts-
burg by train, and then by barge on the Ohio River to
Cincinnati. There, in a turn of fate, the party was joined by
an established sculptor of the time—and for the remainder
of the century—Henry Kirke Brown. Brown had been suffering what he thought to be heart troubles and wanted to
experience the open air of the prairies.

George's letter continues: "From Cincinnati we came to
Terre Haute. It is a pleasant town, situated on the Wabash

River, and on prairie ground. It is as bad a place for murder and thieves as New Orleans, in proportion to its size. . . . There has been a quarrel between two young men. Cutter met Watson in the street, and Watson struck at him with a cane; upon which Cutter drew a pistol, and they both ran into a grog shop filled with people, then let fly, but Watson at that moment turned into another room and escaped. No one was injured, although the pistol was loaded with buckshot. I mention this to show the character of the people. Similar occurences happen almost every day.

"We began our survey yesterday, and had a tough time as it lay through brush that had to be cut away."

By late August the surveying party was encamped on the Kaskaskia River opposite the town of Shelbyville, which, according to a letter from George, was home to about three hundred immigrants from Virginia and Kentucky. Those from Kentucky were "very human and hospitable to strangers," but they were "lazy," and "like everyone else in the state, great whiskey drinkers. Each town has a race ground. They also have shooting matches (but give me a Yankee rifleman)."

The surveyors continued westward. In a December 2nd letter George recounts an incident that became a family legend—the only anecdote I remember my father telling me about George. The party had taken a day off from their work and had struck out for a hunting ground some seven miles distant from their camp, through a "wilderness of alternate land and prairie. Night began to fall, and we became bewildered but at last we came in sight of a log cabin. We were informed by the owner of the cabin, who was chopping wood before the door, that we had arrived at our destination. He was in high glee, having just killed two deer, a doe and a faun. We asked for admittance for the night, and he, with all the hospitality so characteristic of his country, immediately complied, saying we were welcome if we would put up with what he had. His cabin consisted of one small room. After partaking of some corn bread and venison, we made a bed of a few blankets before the fire. The bed was not hard but we suffered from cold."

In the morning the hunters struck out in separate directions. George wrote, "As I was walking carelessly along, my attention was arrested by a crackling of twigs. Two very fine deer came bounding gracefully within ten feet of me, without seeing me, probably startled by some other in the party. I stood watching their graceful curving bounds until they were out of reach of my rifle. When I came to myself I found that I had firmly grasped and cocked my rifle but, alas, had forgotten to shoot!" But George had not "forgotten," he could not bring himself to fire. "On my return [toward the cabin] I saw a flock of wild turkeys, and while I was admiring the glossy black appearance of their feathers they also escaped me. Thus ended my day's hunt without killing anything."

As it turned out, none of his companions had killed anything either, and when they returned to their encampment as darkness fell they were made to eat possum as a punishment.

George often wrote home such sentiments as, "Tell mother that there is no place like Old Deerfield, and she will never be so happy as on the farm," but his experience on the frontier would be invaluable to him. While he remained strongly atttached to his roots, from this time on he would move with confidence wherever his work or travels took him. He had learned to cope not only with the wilderness but with strangers and with unexpected situations.

As the end of his contract approached, George debated with himself whether he should continue surveying at a raise in pay or return to Deerfield, but Deerfield won quite easily. He would finish his schooling.

Deerfield Academy was then presided over by Luther B. Lincoln, an educator with a strong regional reputation for "sympathy, gentleness, learning and the love of learning," and he inspired in George an interest in the classics. At eighteen George was, according to his younger cousin, Howe, "ardent and susceptible, falling in love right and left, and full of joyous life, at once buoyant and tranquil." Another friend of the time, Eliza Starr, later wrote of him that he was "never melancholy, but never as a schoolboy boisterous in mirth. There was a certain composure in his movements, so that if on a summer evening he pushed through the rose bushes before a neighbor's sitting room, and leaned his arms on the window to talk, no one was startled. Indeed, he seemed more at ease, more playful, than if he had come in at the door. His wit was always genial, never left a sting. I believe his companions from his earliest childhood would never recall an angry word or gesture, a cutting joke, or an ungentle action of George Fuller."

Howe wrote that in this period Fanny would sometimes, on the spur of the moment, "send out a two-horse wagon to round up eight or ten pretty girls" and have spontaneous parties. It seems likely that Fanny was looking for the right girl for George, perhaps because she had an intimation of what soon would become plain—she was suffering from consumption.

Henry Kirke Brown had left the surveying party when it was in the then-capital of Illinois, Vandalia, and had returned to his family and studio in Albany, New York. George had kept in contact with him, and after his studies at the Academy demonstrated to his parents that he was not the mathametician an engineer should be, George went with their blessing to Albany to become an apprentice to Brown.

He remained there three important months. Brown encouraged him, deeply and forcefully, and George found also a friend for life in his fellow apprentice, Larkin Mead, a sculptor as young and inexperienced as himself.

From Albany George went to Boston to try his fortune and believed almost immediately that he had found it in the newly invented daguerreotype machine. Painting was so entirely linked to portraiture in George's mind that he imagined, correctly, that when the camera became a commercial success painters' livelihoods would be threatened. He persuaded Aaron to lend him money and bought a camera for fifty dollars, believing he would quickly make the money back.

But George returned to Deerfield that fall disillusioned with the camera—there is no record explaining his change of heart—and he sold it at a considerable loss that winter.

During the spring and summer of 1841 George traveled with Augustus in upstate New York, acting as Augustus's business agent. He also painted his own first commissioned portrait—of a bartender in Rochester.

Augustus was getting fifteen dollars for a portrait, then twenty, and George wrote home that if they reached Niagra Falls, the westernmost city in the state, that he would ask for thirty. George had learned, he wrote, that for "the gen-

erality of people's judging of painting, I find it is more reg-
ulated by price than by merit."

George was not yet ready to make his living as an artist,
and he considered taking a railway job in New York, but as
the weather turned cold he and Augustus headed homeward. En route, in Newark, New Jersey, George wrote,
lamenting, "We are beset by Gamblers, Loafers, and Drunk-
ards but steer clear of them all. I never before saw total
depravity as is here exemplified." Augustus was not, of
course, entirely "steering clear," and perhaps George was
not either.

During the following few years George moved frequently between Deerfield, Albany, and Boston, always
studying and practicing his art but often taking other work.
As Thomas Ball wrote in his autobiography, *My Life,* "It
must be remembered that at that time there were no schools
or academies where the student could learn the technique
of his art; but each was obliged to dig one out for himself,
taking the works of those more fortunate artists who had
studied abroad for his models. The consequence was in my
case that each picture was a new experiment. Oh, how dear
old George Fuller and I used to labor in those days—
arguing, comparing, painting in, and scraping out while we
wrestled with color; appreciating and feeling in our hearts
all through us what we wanted to do; sometimes catching
a sunny glimpse of it on our canvas, only to see a cloud
come over it, bearing our souls down to the dust. He, dear
fellow! persevered," Ball wrote, while he himself became a
sculptor, having reluctantly recognized his own insuperable
difficulty with color.

George spent another nine months in Albany, partly with

the Browns and partly with some others who were left to use and guard the studio during a prolonged study trip to Rome that Brown took with his wife.

Before leaving, Brown wrote to George: "You ask my opinion in regard to your becoming an artist. You are already acquainted with it so far as pecuniary matters are concerned. You know the study it requires to become great in anything, and I know that by applying yourself you can accomplish wonders. In my opinion you need only ask yourself the question whether or not you like the art well enough to practice it with your whole soul and attention. It is a noble art, and worthy of any man's whole and undivided mind. It affords in its higher walks a vast and beautiful field for the imagination; it is a useful school for the mind, as it is continually upon the stretch, and as it grows in strength new and higher beauties delight it. Fear not to embark. Go ahead."

Three years later, on a second long trip, Brown wrote to George from Rome: "One of the first objects in all art is to conquer mechanical difficulties, such as drawing correctly, using colors with freedom and purity, and the general conduct of pictures. One needs constant practice and the utmost constancy, and let it be an object that, whatever you do, you do correctly; nature, to such a student, daily unfolds new secrets and beauties. Seek the truth. Let that be the object of your life.

"Look upon drawing and painting as your language, the medium through which you express to others your feelings, and learn to express thus your feelings, be they joy or sorrow, and the world will sympathize with you in all that you do. I am supposing you now have your eye on some-

thing beyond mere portrait painting, but don't despise that.
Look with open eyes, but let those eyes be all your own. . . .
I wish that you were here. I know you would improve very
fast, but I shall bring home much that will be useful to you.
I have had the compliment paid me of making a more correct drawing in crayon from an antique *bassorelievo* than the
best draughtsman in Rome."

In these years George kept a notebook in which to jot
down ideas and instructions to himself, such as: "From chin
to a point between the collarbones is two lengths of nose."

"The hand is the length of the face. Two faces from
shoulder to shoulder."

"From bottom of breasts to navel, one face."

"Whatever the local color of an object, be it white or
black, it must partake of the reds and yellows of the sun."

"There's a middle tone of color should be sought after."

For use during his travels, George painted a small sign,
"G. Fuller, Painter," which he hung outside the door of
whatever room he was living and working in. In central
and western Masschusetts he was now getting twenty-five
to thirty-two dollars for a portrait. In Boston, where the
competition was stiffer, he and Ball often worked quickly
from daguerreotypes of men and women who had just
died, making family mementos for less than twenty-five.
Sometimes they worked from the corpse if a daguerreotype did not exist.

George and Ball shared much laughter. George sometimes spoke pithily, but he mainly amused others with
ironic mimicry and droll timing. A line he was asked often
to repeat had been spoken at the funeral of President Benjamin Harrison in 1840. Harrison had caught pneumonia
delivering his inaugural address on a bitterly cold day and

had died a month later without having taken a single presidential action. An orator at Harrison's services had nonetheless proclaimed, "The death of President Harrison is the greatest calamity ever to befall this, *or any other,* Republic." George's rendering of this pomposity had an enduring popularity.

The Hildreth house gave George and Ball a stage and a sympathetic audience. When they met two young women there that George wanted Ball to serenade, George would say, according to Ball's autobiography, "Such subjects for pictures!" Ball would confess a weakness for blondes, and shoulder his guitar.

But there were certainly periods in these years when George felt he was paying a price for pursuing his art. One journal entry reads "I trust I love my Art more than myself, stern mistress that she is." Another, "My early friends are most of them living for others as well as themselves," meaning that they were married and producing children.

"My affections are as free as ever."

"I am becoming isolated."

There is a bit of yearning poetry:

"Oh, for a heart to be glad when we are glad!

Oh, for a heart to echo the thrilling of our own!"

By mid-1844 Fanny was clearly facing the end of her life. George wrote her to say he rejoiced that she felt resigned. He told her that in his memory of home and childhood "all is peace and happiness, friends to love and kind parents to watch over us." He went to Deerfield several times to visit her.

Fanny's death in 1845 affected George deeply. An entry in his journal that he crossed out—but not so completely as to make it illegible—ruminates about the possibility of existence after death. God's existence spoke to him "in the beautiful harmony of all nature."

However, he did not idealize or sentimentalize nature, then or later. The beautified, pristine landscapes painted by the Hudson River School painters, which were then beginning to appear, had no appeal for him. They lacked "truth."

Henry Kirke Brown returned to America in 1847, settled in New York City, and soon wrote George that he should join him. Brown was organizing classes that would draw from live models, and he believed George would find work in New York.

George asked Aaron for fifty dollars to help him make the move. In his letter he wrote that it must be obvious that, so far, his art had not been heaped with honors, but "nothing is more uncertain than public favor bestowed before the recipient is able to sustain himself and answer [the public's] expectations."

"Public favor comes but once," George wrote. "I wish you to believe I am laying the foundation on which I can stand when my time comes as it certainly will come."

Aaron sent the funds, and so began George's thirteen New York years, most of them lived in Brooklyn. For long periods in 1849–50, '54, and '56–57, George worked as an itinerant painter in Georgia and Alabama, and he made shorter painting stays in Philadelphia, Washington, and elsewhere, but for the most part he lived the life of a *slowly* up-and-coming artist in the cultural capital of the land.

He acquired a few collectors who believed in him— William Ames would be the most important. He accumulated recognition. In 1853 he was elected an Associate of the National Academy of Design, the most official sort of status that then could be achieved, and his work won public approval in the annual Academy exhibitions.

The Academy required that every artist it elected to membership supply a self-portrait for its permanent collection. George's shows a square-faced, handsome, intense-looking, dark-haired and dark-bearded young man who looks older than his thirty-one years. He is looking appraisingly from the corner of his eye at his own reflection.

The Academy self-portrait has deteriorated badly, as have a number of George's paintings. Like other painters of the same period, notably Albert Ryder, George often mixed bitumen with his paints, and much later these surfaces cracked and became distorted.

On March 15th, 1855, George wrote a description of that year's Academy show to his sister Harriet, Fanny's fourth child and ten years younger than he, who had taken charge of The Bars household after Fanny's death:

"This is 'Varnishing Day' at the Academy—this precedes the opening to the public which takes place tomorrow. Some [painters] actually 'varnish' their pictures, and [we all] see the result of the hanging committee's choices.

"I have but two things there—a sketch of a child's head and a portrait of [Henry Kirke] Brown. I have no cause to complain because both are in good light and in honorable places. The exhibition is generally better than I have ever known it.

"I am complimented today by all hands in the brethren of the brush on my success with it. Rec'd a letter from a Mr. Davis in Philadelphia offering $150 for Brown's portrait," and more work if George would go to Philadelphia.

"I cannot but consider myself very fortunate and feel a step taken against that adverse tide which I have contended against for so long—without *much* feeling of vanity. I am anxious for you all to know my good success, whom I have not forgotten, and who have remembered me when it was hoped for."

But before that year was out George would again be heading south in search of clients. An economic downturn had dried up commissions in New York and all his artist-friends were suffering.

Few of George's portraits from this period can be found, either in the Northeast or in the South. Many have no doubt deteriorated, and some may be lost in attics. A self-portrait in good condition hangs in the National Portrait Gallery, Smithsonian Institution, and a well-preserved portrait of George's friend, sculptor Larkin Mead, hangs in the William Dean Howells house at Kittery Point, Maine. Mead's sister had become Howells's wife.

Mead's portrait shows a clear-skinned, sensitive, and bright-looking young man's head against a dark background. I can imagine the family exclaiming over its likeness to its subject and the skill of the painter. The only criticism of it might be that the work could have been done by a number of other skillful painters. Unlike his later work there is nothing truly distinctive about it, nothing that identifies it easily as George's work.

Historical societies in Augusta, Georgia, and Montgomery and Mobile, Alabama, have made serious efforts in recent years to make inventories of antebellum, southern art but during my search of the region I could find no portraits I could definitely identify as being George's—this

despite the fact that I knew from George's letters and journals that he was sometimes completing two or three portraits a week, and that I also knew the names of many of
his sitters, familiar southern names like Carter, Ford, Wolfe,
and so on.

George returned to Deerfield only occasionally and
briefly during these years, but his presence there in spirit
was constant. He wrote hundreds upon hundreds of letters home.

The early ones to Harriet, or to John or Francis, were
often big-brotherly in tone and intention. He told Harriet
("Hatty") that he hoped she would apply herself seriously
to the study of music, "As at your age, the mind is capable
of the most basic and lasting improvements." And, later,
"Don't be alarmed about being 23, and don't run off and
get married for fear of being too old."

To the twins, sixteen years his junior, he wrote that at
Deerfield Academy he had learned both to swear and to
use tobacco, habits he hoped they would avoid.

The avuncular side of George gradually disappears from
the letters, but his affection and closeness does not. He wrote
to Aaron from Brooklyn while Augustus was staying with
him that Augustus had been "quite steady" for the past fort-
night. "But surrounded by such persons as he is here, I have
no confidence in his remaining so after I leave him." George
was about to travel south, and he suggested that Augustus
spend the coming winter at The Bars, which Augustus
seemed willing to do. "He must have some true friend near
him, or no one can answer what may be the final result. I
do not think that he has any strong love for drink, and I do
believe that by taking sufficient interest in him he may yet

become what he should be." George would "stand ready" to do whatever he could on Augustus's behalf.

In 1854 it became clear that George's younger brother by five years, Elijah, who had remained to work The Bars with his father, had become seriously ill, very likely with the disease that had killed Fanny. George wrote to Hatty, "the news makes me unhappy, but it is my wish to know the truth. You do right to tell me all. Make him some more of the cough medicines." The recipe for this medicine called for "bloodroot," one half-pint of gin, and several minor ingredients.

George wrote Elijah to say, "[I] fully endorse your intention of leaving home." Presumably George wanted this to avoid the spreading of the disease. He offered Elijah money, or any other help Elijah could think of. "Don't feel too anxious about business—the devil take it. It never helped man much in any way except to lord it over his fellows. Be jolly and comfortable as matters will allow."

George wrote Aaron that he was doing well financially and declared, "You know why this [giving Elijah help] should give me great satisfaction. My welfare is inseparable from home and all there."

Elijah came to New York in March of 1855, and George arranged a medical consultation with a Dr. Parker, who, looking at Elijah stripped to the waist, said, "I see the difficulty. The right lung is full and active. The left lung is diseased." Indeed, George's description suggests that the left lung had collapsed.

Dr. Parker proposed that Elijah go to the Rocky Mountains and "stay there," asssuring George that even cases worse than Elijah's were sometimes cured. He prescribed a regimen that included "cod liver oil three times a day with a spoonful of brandy," rubdowns all over his body with whiskey "night and morning," and that Elijah should sleep on a hard bed and *never* sleep in his daytime clothes.

Geroge called in some friends to help decide on the most promising destination for Elijah and how he might get there. One proposal was for him to go to Richmond, Virginia, buy a "moderate-priced horse," and ride over the Alleghenies via the Blue Ridge and Sulphur Springs through Kentucky to the west. The decision, however, was that Elijah should go to St. Louis by rail, and that his final destination should be California.

George wrote home that he and his friends had made Elijah's preparations thoroughly. He would be equipped with a letter of credit, letters of introduction to some people in St. Louis who might advise on his course from there, a prepaid ticket, and one hunded dollars in cash. "Everything has been done that could be done," George wrote. "Try to be resigned to whatever may come."

Not long after Elijah's departure westward George wrote Hatty, telling her, "I shall be obliged to work in my studio much of this summer to keep Elijah traveling." Elijah's need for funds was, in fact, a major reason for George's stays in Alabama in '55 and '56. But George was happy to help Elijah as one letter to him reflects: "You must feel entirely your own master," George wrote. "It is the pride of my life that I have been able to be of some assistance to you."

Elijah wrote letters from Chicago and then St. Louis. He felt a little better, then worse. In St. Louis he changed his plan and decided to buy a horse and ride west via the Santa Fe Trail.

"I wish I could be with you," George wrote back. "Keep a faithful record of all that you see.

"War is about to rage in the old world. Men are not satisfied with Nature, but must kill each other outright. Don't shoot a redskin without sufficient provocation."

In another letter and in a different mood George refers to Indians as "nature's noblemen. But remember the kind of scalp that Durand and I prefer." "Scalp" was a code word meaning woman bed partner.

John Durand, a fellow painter and the editor of the new and tiny but most important American art journal of the day, *The Crayon*, shared living and studio quarters with George at successive addresses, 137 Montague Place and 86 Clinton Street, both of them near Brooklyn's City Hall and the dock of the Manhattan Ferry.

The Crayon editorialized in favor of the aesthetics of John Ruskin, who argued that Nature was essentially good and should be represented without exaggeration or embellishment. The contemporary art critic Robert Hughes writes in his book *The Culture of Complaint* that Ruskin and *The Crayon* believed "it was within the power of the visual arts to change the moral dimensions of life." Durand, in fact, wrote, "The enjoyment of beauty is dependent on, and in ratio with, the moral excellence of the individual. We have assumed Art is an elevating power, that it has *in itself* a spirit of morality."

George seems always to have been respectful of these as ideas. The "spiritual" quality of his later paintings was often commented on, but not because either heaven or earth were glorified. His perceived spirituality came from his ability to express subtleties of human emotion and character in his portraits. George was not moralistic in work or in life, then or later.

Elijah kept in touch via mail that "crossed the plains"

twice a month, and he did keep a frustratingly sketchy journal. His ride to Santa Fe "with strong company" took two months. There, he felt at first better, then about the same. He complained that the tobacco smoke in "the fandango rooms" was bad for his breathing.

Instead of attempting to go on to California, Elijah joined a freebooting expedition to Chihuahua, Mexico. His journal is not explicit about what plunder was expected to be found, nor about the expedition's numbers of armaments, but it is clear they were heavily armed. As the party traveled south through the dry hills and plateaus of southern New Mexico they sometimes saw Indians, presumed to be Apaches or Comanches, but they were not attacked, nor were they after they had crossed the border. They half expected to be challenged by some remnant of the Mexican Army, which had been defeated a few years before in the Mexcan-American War, but instead of combat, the expedition's principal difficulty was in finding scarce water holes.

Elijah was exhausted when they reached Chihuahua. He found some like-minded companions in the company and they turned back without any trophies, wanting to return home. He reached El Paso and then San Antonio, Texas, where fatigue and illness brought him to a long halt.

By mail George and Elijah debated whether or not he should return to The Bars. It seemed to both to be accepting a death sentence to do so. George sent money to sustain him.

But after some weeks Elijah wrote that he was wasting his time in San Antonio. His health had not improved. "I cannot enumerate all the reasons I wish to go home, but the best are the wish to see you all."

George's reluctance that Elijah return came from his wanting to protect Hatty's health. He had been writing to her that too much responsibility had been put on her considering her age. It can be inferred that Aaron was not playing a strong role as a protective parent. George wrote Hatty that he wanted to but felt he should not give Aaron advice on running the farm, that Aaron would resent it.

Elijah returned to The Bars in 1856. One of the last letters that he wrote was addessed to a provisioner, and it complained in colorful language of the awful quality of a case of whiskey he had been sent. Not surprisingly, Elijah was not simply rubbing whiskey on his limbs.

During his years in Brooklyn, George felt he belonged to a "charmed circle" of artist friends. Their names are mainly unfamiliar now—Durand, T. Quincy Ward, S.W. Skillman, Larkin Mead, William Ames—but they had solid reputations then. As artists they were occasionally included in New York's formal receptions, but far more often they made their own amusements. They went on fishing and sketching trips together, attended "conversations" with Bronson Alcott, produced amateur theatricals, and put together dinner parties with their girlfriends to celebrate almost anything. There was a "brethren," and their letters give the impression of an excited, hopeful, and affectionate group of men who were often suffering money troubles. Typically, at George's moment of success in 1855, he raised his prices and soon had to head south to find work. He wrote Durand from Montgomery, "Give my best wishes to all our lady friends. How they must miss me!"

Clearly there were bohemian pleasures together with their competitive and money anxieties. Quincy Ward wrote George "important news" at this time. "Bridget has moved back in with us!"

George's letters occasionally show some professional envy of his friends. He reported to Hatty that Ames was being paid one thousand dollars for a full-length figure "for such pictures as he produces!" Perhaps he had to bite his tongue when he told her that Henry Kirke Brown was doing busts and equestrian statues of General Winfield Scott, Senator John Calhoun and other dignitaries for truly substantial commissions.

While George undoubtedly missed the Brooklyn girls and courted many young women on his travels, he fell in love only with New Englanders and not with the right one for many years. After a summer visit to the Berkshires he wrote to a Miss Estelle Ives of Great Barrington that he was "sitting before a grate of burning coals, without speaking, thinking of our lonely estate, building bright castles, or rather, recovering their ruins, feeling sadly the want of material to rebuild them."

The novels of Sir Walter Scott had opened "a romantic vista" to George, and he had to some extent adopted their vocabulary. In the same period, however, Dickens's *Bleak House* had impressed him, as had Carlyle's translation of Goethe's *Wilhelm Meister.*

Apparently the most serious of George's unrequited New England loves was Rebecca Williams, nicknamed "Becket," with whom he achieved a certain closeness, but not all that he desired.

Becket came to New York and attended a reception with him, and he wrote her afterwards that the gathering had presented "too true a picture, I fear, of New York life. All is dazzle and no substance. Wealth is becoming so very common we may hope soon for other things." He had vague hopes that something tending "to ennoble" might catch the public fancy.

He wrote Becket a Valentine poem. She signed her letters to him "ever your little friend," but a day arrived when George wrote to Elijah in San Antonio, lamenting, "She says she don't love me well enough to marry me, but should die if anything were to happen to me. Don't you think she had better take care of me?

"She has a nice little fortune which of course I do not consider, but only the girl herself, and she is enough to bless any man."

Soon after that letter George wrote to Hatty, "Tell father I am not in love, even if I do not write. That I am too busy for that complaint."

George showed a different side of his affectionate life when he wrote to Henry Kirke Brown and his wife (always "Mrs. Brown") that it had been sixteen years since they had first met and that "You have been kinder to me than you can remember, or I forget." And in a letter to Hatty he wrote, "I hope you have not much to regret. I often wonder what you are doing and if you are happy. We cannot tell our stories to one another fully, but the bond is strong that binds us, and it shall never be weakened."

Hatty eventually repaid George's devotion by recruiting a young woman to correspond with him during the last months of George's final sojourn in the South. She was Agnes Gordon Higginson, a twenty-year-old whose Boston-Brahmin family had bought a house on Deerfield's Main Street for summer use. Agnes was studying art and training to be a school teacher, and, four years after their correspondence began, she would become George's wife.

George's southern residencies not only better provided for him than did competitive New York, they made him reflect on and "see" humanity as he had not before. I think it is not too much to say that all the pictures he would paint between 1876 and 1884, the pictures that would make his fame and fortune, have something in them of his southern experience.

George went south for the first time in December of 1849, alone, aged twenty-seven, armed with one letter of introduction to a friend of a friend in Charleston, South Carolina. Perhaps he used the letter, perhaps not, but he soon left Charleston for Augusta, Georgia. He set up his studio there in the U.S. Hotel, which, he wrote, very much resembled the grand hotels of Saratoga Springs, New York.

George was soon doing portrait commissions at a fast pace. When he left Augusta after six months he wrote that, if he had stayed, "I could have made quite a little fortune but the weather became insufferably hot and I could stay no longer."

His success testifies that his work was as good as any competitor's, but no work of his can be found today in Augusta's museum or historical society, and none is reproduced in *Early Georgia Portraits,* a book that is a serious attempt to illustrate the state of art before the Civil War. To be sure, a great many things were destroyed during Sherman's march across Georgia "from Atlanta to the sea."

In Augusta George went calling socially with an eye to business, and went courting, too. He worked very hard and he seems to have been infatuated with one Ella Ford, who "excelled only in her inconstancy." Only one event of lasting importance occurred during those first six southern months.

From George's journal, January 26, 1850: "Going down Main St., a long, broad street, with Pease [a planter who had befriended George and commissioned a portrait from him] made a turn to the left by the market house and found ourselves at the bridge [which spanned the Savannah River from Augusta to Hamburg, South Carolina]. An old colored woman salutes 'Massa Pease' and would we like potato fries fresh? Not a bad idea—we take some for which we thank her very kindly. We press on over the river and we are in Hamburg, S.C. A low brown building up on the bank is the slave market.

"It has a wide portico. Marching forward and back upon it are about 150 negroes following the leader through a step somewhat intricate, keeping time to one of their chants and all joining in the refrain. A fellow with the bones [?] is their leader and manifests his superiority by an occasional extra shuffle. It is here that our negro melodists have gathered [illegible] but they suffer by comparison, falling far short of the original. Thus, during what would otherwise prove a wearisome day [they were] seeking and finding relief in exercise and song.

"To all appearances they could not be happier, young and healthy, well-clothed and fed, indulged in all the things that will show them off to best advantage (for this is in their masters' interest). Who shall read their hearts and say they are not so? Do they regret the past or fear the future? Or do they recognize neither, basking only in the warm sunshine of the present day?

"Now they stop marching. Pease introduces me to the dealer, a dark man but not ill-looking . . .

"Who is this girl with eyes large and black? The blood of the white and dark races is at enmity in her veins. The former predominates—about three-quarters white, says our dealer. Three-fourths blessed, a fraction accursed. She is under thy feet, white man. Image of thy Maker, Paleface.

Where is thy blush? Is she not your 'sister'? So she leans against a column apart from those awarded.

"She impresses me with sadness. The pensive expression of her finely formed mouth and the drooping eyes seem to ask for sympathy. The straight black hair is simply parted upon the forehead and covers the ear beautifully. It harmonizes with the rich, olive complexion—round youthful cheek. Where are the attributes of the race that claims her? Not here? The finely formed nose—delicate chin—came not from her mulatto mother.

"Now she looks up. Now her eyes before the rude gaze of those who are calculating her charms or serviceable qualities [illegible]. Silently they quail before this look they cannot meet. Oh! Is beauty so cheap? She is an excellent seamstress, makes ladies dresses, is 18 years of age, and from Virginia, says one man—value $1,000. And someone from the savannahs of Florida [illegible] meets in luxuriant Georgia for a like object.

"But here are two more girls, they look like sisters. Should one meet them in the north their color would never be suspected. Their master has dressed them like ladies. One seems about 18, the younger one I should say 13. For the [illegible] a high price is expected and will probably be realized for she is entirely her master's.

"And so we pass on strolling to the water's edge and seating ourselves upon a fallen tree produce our french fries. The city opposite must be beautiful when the spring comes and [illegible] in green. As it is, that stately tree of the south, the magnolia, with the holly palmetto and money, show green the seasons through."

Some thirty years after this journal entry, George painted *The Quadroon*, a picture widely exhibited and celebrated, now in the collection of the Metropolitan Museum. In it a young woman who is surely the "pensive," light-skinned mulatto he had seen at the Hamburg auction is kneeling at the edge of a cotton field, her cotton sack beside her. While other darker-skinned women are at work in the field behind her, she looks directly and seriously at the viewer, not making any pleading gesture, letting her situation speak for itself.

The Quadroon was far from the only work, or the only idea, that George took from the South. In 1856-7 he was in Montgomery for several months, and a different sort of inspiration occurred to him.

He had recently seen in New York the work of Edouard Frere who painted scenes of rural French life. The subjects reminded George of the Deerfield world he knew so well and gave him the idea of similarly depicting the rural South when he was not occupied with portraits. George wrote, "In the small pictures by Frere I find so much of my own feeling expressed that I feel as if I could hardly wait to put myself in the same class of subjects. These works are the expressions of what we call lowly or everyday life.

How much we pass by every day which only needs the interest and the hand to express it to prove pure gold."

As busy as he turned out to be with portraits, he could not attempt the series while he was, in fact, in the South, but he made a notebook of drawings of the kinds of scenes he intended to use. Some of the drawings are wide landscapes with slaves at work—ploughing, doing roadwork. Others have a surprising intimacy. Women are washing clothes or sitting by open hearths in the interiors of slave cabins, for example. The small-scale drawings are vivid and evocative.

Much later, in the early 1880s, George painted several southern scenes, none of them directly from any of his

drawings, which are among his strongest and most interesting pictures. At that time several critics labeled George's
paintings as Impressionist but several of the southern canvases are closer to Expressionism. *Negro Funeral,* in the collection of the Boston Museum of Fine Arts and *Hoeing
Tobacco* at the Worcester Art Museum, depict human beings
out of realistic proportion. The slaves stand and move in an
unnatural darkness under blazing skies.

The subject of *The Quadroon* was not to be the only
young woman George would paint with extraordinary
sympathy. In the same, late period he painted a number
white, young, New England women, some of them portraits, but most of them "ideal figures." He used models for
these "ideals," but by calling them such, or giving them fictional names, he removed any necessity to be literally accu-
rate or responsive to a patron's criticism.

In the fall of 1850, however, when George returned to
Brooklyn, these paintings and these changes in his vision
lay far ahead. He resumed his life among the "brethren,"
and he was again involved in family affairs.

Augustus was then serving his six-month sentence in the
Hampden jail, a sentence "most unjust," as George wrote to
Aaron, "considering the offence and the circumstances."
Augustus, in his humiliation, had tried to hide his situa-
tion from his family. Now that it had become known
George volunteered to send him money, as "he may need
winter clothes."

George wrote that he looked at the episode "as a philosopher in these matters." Augustus had not always behaved
properly and "perhaps a little punishment will be beneficial.
I think you may rely upon the intention of your sons who
are out of jail to stay out."

George returned to the South in late 1855, this time in the company of his friend and fellow portrait-painter Edwin Billings and Billings's sister. They settled in Montgomery, where Billings had spent several previous winters and thus had plenty of business and social contacts.

At first, the venture seemed idyllic. George wrote to Hatty that Montgomery was the "pleasantest sorthern city." There were "hedges of cherokee roses, wild orange trees, magnolia." And, "I find things in the business relation all that I expected." George had done six pictures in three weeks and had hopes of raising his volume to four or five a week.

His only note of unhappiness was in another letter. "I saw a scene today—negroes sold at auction together with horses and cattle. The poor children. No one to raise a voice for them, and God above us all."

George's affection for Billings, whom he would describe as one of the "best and dullest fellows in the world," would endure throughout their lives, but something "had not gone right" in Montgomery, and after only a month George took a riverboat down to Mobile.

The paddle-wheel steamers, of which there a considerable number on the Alabama River, made some fifty stops to pick up cotton along the four-hundred-mile route from Montgomery to Mobile. The larger boats would be carrying some two thousand bales on arrival at the seaport. George's boat put in at the former capital, Cohaba, where, he noted, his Uncle Joseph Negus was "resting on Alabama pine," but George did not go ashore to search for his grave.

Arrived in Mobile George wrote that "the people seem very fast and exceedingly mixed—French, Jews, creoles and negroes, all shades of color, and, lo, the poor Indian walks the streets, the last of his race." Twenty thousand inhabitants and a great place for business! George was delighted.

The night before the writing of a letter to Elijah a dance had taken place at George's hotel. There had been "a fine degree of beauty." Some of the women's toilettes had been "magnificent," and the dancing had been graceful. Many of the complexions of both men and women had been whitened by a floury substance, he noticed, but no matter her color, "a woman is a woman," he wrote.

George was determined to devote himself to work, not pleasure, and he was soon in a boardinghouse that cost him three dollars and fifty cents a week. He found clients quickly and began to send money north—including three hundred to William Ames, who had loaned money for Elijah's trip west.

George was expansive. He thought of New Orleans, only twelve hours away by boat, and of possibly traveling up the Mississippi on his eventual way home. "I am more successful and busier the longer I stay," he wrote to Hatty. Everyone was prospering, he thought. His Uncle Emery Fuller, of whom George would soon do a portrait, was "doing well in business in Havana."

During his five-month Mobile stay George did many portraits and he had also learned to tint daguerreotypes for considerable fees but, as in Augusta, there are no examples of his work or traces of him that I could find. With help at the Mobile Historical Society I quickly located the advertisements that Nathan Negus ran in 1823, but nothing on George.

He returned north in June directly to New York, noting in his journal that he weighed 189 pounds—that worried him. He visited William Ames, then continued to Deerfield for the summer. In November he was again in New York, and he saw there "finer collections of pictures than have ever been here before."

One show was from England. George's letters for the next several years would speak admiringly of the Pre-Raphaelites, whose label he detested but whose attempts to render "the ideal" in humans or in aspects of the natural world opened new possibilities in his mind.

Then George decided to go south once more with Billings—without Billings' sister this time. He wrote Hatty, "I know you will think it best for me when you know the conditions of things here. Nothing is doing in art."

As it turned out, commissions were not so plentiful in Montgomery either, but given George's enthusiasm for his Frere-inspired project, this was fortunate rather than infuriating. He made seventy-eight drawings on a cardboard-bound 5-by-10-inch pad. Besides scenes of plantation work and life there are portrait heads of *Grace*, full-figure drawings of a man, *Ellis*, and of a boy, *Our page, Harry*, slaves who kept house and did errands for George and Billings who were living in a brick-faced downtown commercial building near the Alabama River docks.

One drawing of a woman carrying a basket on her head shows a large house in the distance that is labeled *Briggins Plantation*, but it is not clear that this was the site of all the rural scenes.

George's access to slave life cannot have been usual for anyone apart from the families of plantation owners, but his letters provide no explanation for it. George wrote to Agnes Higginson, "We find here a fine field for studying negro character and his relations. There is with them always such free motion and unstudied attitude and their costume is so appropriate as to make them real prizes in an artistic way," the tone of which suggests that George stayed at a certain remove from his subjects.

On the other hand a man named Babbitt wrote to George from Montgomery nearly a year after George had returned to the North: "Mary Ann I learn is sold and her mother is dead. Folly is in New Orleans so I should see her." And George wrote a note to Billings, who was briefly absent from Montgomery, exclaiming, "Hetty has been sold and sent to New Orleans!"

George was discreet, but his feelings on the slavery question were clear. One evening in Montgomery he went to the statehouse, only a few blocks away from the river on a rise of ground, to hear General William Walker, the man who attempted to conquer Nicaragua and extend the slave system southward. George wrote of him, "The man has a half-insane manner, a quick anxious look as though he feared someone in the crowd. Such a jumble he made in the story of his exploits! 'The late affair in Casablanca,' etc. 'The reason of his interfering in Nicaragua.' It was a silly exhibition, quite incoherent." George "wanted to hang him."

Walker was followed on the podium by Senator Yancey, "the great leader of the Southern Fire-Eaters. He sustains a very bad cause in slavery."

There were at that time "two black slaves for every white person in Montgomery County," and the whites were "very sensitive on the slavery question," George wrote Elijah. George knew when to hold his tongue, however, and how to enjoy social life. "I have had some funny times at parties."

George intended to make paintings from his new drawings when he returned to New York, but because he made less money than he had hoped in Montgomery, he had an immediate need for portrait commissions. The increasingly bad health of both Elijah and Aaron made money still more imperative. The only southern painting from this time is *Negro Nurse and Child,* which is rather stiffly, perhaps hurriedly, rendered.

When George first wrote to Agnes Higginson he had not known in what role to see himself. Was he her mentor in art? Should he be like an uncle? She was eighteen then, and sixteen years younger than he. "Dear Miss Agnes," he wrote. "Why then should I not hurry to cultivate myself in correspondence with a fair friend who has so nobly come to my rescue"—from boredom, he meant.

His self-consciousness was perhaps amplified by his awareness of the eminence of her large family. The Higginsons were represented in virtually all the trades and professions in Boston, some very prosperously. Probably the best known of them today is Agnes's older first cousin, Thomas Wentworth Higginson, an educator, preacher, writer and poet, editor, and community leader who was to command the first battalion of freed-slave troops in the Civil War.

Higginson felt at the end of his life that he had run "second in everything." Emerson had outshone him as a preacher. Emily Dickinson, who he had "discovered" and published, had been a better poet. Bronson Alcott's theories on education had gotten all the attention. But Higginson had led—as he well knew and appreciated—one of the richest lives of his time.

George and Agnes met during his visits to Deerfield in the summer of 1858, and their letters afterward became more familiar. "Merry Christmas from Grizzled I," George wrote her from New York. But the thought of her still prompted him to make mentor-like pronouncements: "Nothing is better for one than to sometimes be a stranger that he may feel the kindness of others." Soon she became his equal, though, corresponding. She was, after all, a grown woman. She was teaching school in Boston.

Elijah died in January of 1859, and Aaron was then, George wrote, "almost helpless as a child." In the same month the only child of the Henry Kirke Browns died of scarlet fever.

George went back and forth between Deerfield and New York, oppressed and challenged by what he felt to be his obligation to run The Bars, pressure to finish the commissions he had undertaken, and wanting to comfort the Browns. No doubt Agnes's sympathy helped him. He wrote to her in March, "I see you plainly in what you write.

"I feel as though a thousand things were waiting for attention from me on tbe farm," he wrote. One of the twins, John, was studying agriculture but George, the eldest son, clearly had the responsibility. "You would be amused by my plans." He imagined lines of fruit trees and crops of "tobacco, indian corn and brown corn. I feel sometimes strangely separated from art in present occupations."

He continued to write deep thoughts to Agnes—it was simply his way of being in love, perhaps. "To feel the greatness of others is to be great ourselves. Even misplaced veneration is better than none. Our fortunes are the reaction to ourselves. We get what we have the power to attract."

In April Agnes brought his expansive musings up short. What must have been her angry letter is missing, but George responded, "You tell me we must not correspond more. What notion is this? Because we are not 'engaged,' and Society and money? What is this talk of not wishing to see me?"

Apparently, Agnes explained to him what had offended her and in late April he wrote, "Your letters made me at length feel that I have been really savage."

He apologized, his spirits quickly revived, and in May he was instructing her that "Thackeray is greater than Dickens." He had been told by someone that she was "losing her roses and growing thin in Boston," he wrote. He insisted, "I want to see you and judge for myself. Take exercise and laugh. Take good care of yourself and you will do much for me." He signed off the letter, "Good night my sweet friend." It was one o'clock in the morning, and George was sitting up with his dying father.

Aaron died June 30th. Agnes spent the summer in Deerfield with her parents, and she and George grew closer. Not long after her return to Boston in the fall to teach, George was presented with an unexpected and extraordinary opportunity.

A year before, George had been privy to a painful secret of William Ames's. Ames had written to him, "Bella has been away recovering. You will be the only one besides ourselves to know what has passed." The importance of secrecy suggests something scandalous, of course.

George had certainly been discreet, and this may well have had something to do with what Ames now proposed: that George accompany Ames's twenty-one-year-old son John on a six month grand tour of Europe to visit all the great places and works of art. Ames would cover nearly all the expense. John already spoke good French, which would help.

After some family discussion at The Bars, George felt free to seize the chance. He wrote to Agnes, "Here at home all are glad for me to go, and do not see why I should not." But he wrote that he was not greatly "elated." The trip would interfere with his plans at The Bars, and , "I feel very ignorant and awkward. I want to see living things, as well as pictures and antiquities. I wish I could divide it with you, whatever it might be." He told Agnes that she "must believe [the voyage] will be of great good for me and you, and I shall no more be gone than if I were in New York all this time."

Meanwhile, "I am given over to the demon of plowing and draining, hoping to come out of it some day and look upon a landscape I have helped form." He wrote, "You must know, beauty, I hold you to my heart."

George paid a farewell visit to Agnes in Boston and went from there to a farewell dinner in New York given by Ames and twenty-three friends on the eve of his departure December twenty-second. Before embarking George wrote Agnes, "Laugh all you can," and, distressedly, to Hatty, "I feel as if I were deserting you."

The ship sailed out into an Atlantic gale growing into a storm lasting a week, "only leaving us 300 miles off the Channel, full of seasickness and disgust," then calm. The ship made only ten miles a day for seven days.

George and John Ames stepped ashore at the Port of Torquay on the night of January 15th, and the following day was like "a June day with a blue humid sky." They saw Bristol, Bath, and the distant hills of Cardiff.

Arrived in London, George went straight to work. He made several visits to the National Gallery, and then to every other museum. He wrote Hatty that at the National he had seen all the fine paintings by Rembrandt, Titian, Correggio, Velasquez, Turner, and Rubens, and that he had found a particular virtue in each one. "You ask how I felt in such high company? I shall confess I grew with the occasion, and was not out of countenance in the least. It is only poor works that drive one to despair. There are none here. The great pictures have grown on me at each visit, and I have grown with them."

He began to pass judgements. George thought Gainsborough had learned a great deal from the Flemish masters, but that "he saw Nature through his own eyes, and with a kind heart."

He came to believe Hogarth was the greatest painter England had produced, but "perhaps the greatest landscapes ever painted" had been done by J. M. W. Turner. "Those of 1820 pleased me most. I cannot say this of all his works; those of the last years being of so exceeding vague art as to be the 'stuff that dreams are made of,' and not the most delightful dreams."

The Pre-Raphaelites were on George's mind. He had been hoping to be introduced to John Ruskin and was disappointed that Ruskin was away from London. He thought many of Holman Hunt's pictures were "absurdities" but admired the kind of realism Hunt achieved. He did meet Rossetti, and he had a good word for the works of Millais.

It was Paris, however, that changed George. He wrote, "I am able here to get the best possible idea of the powers of different painters." This advantage was minor as compared two insights that would remain fresh in his mind for the remainder of his life.

The first came after a visit to the Ecole des Beaux Arts. George wrote, "In this present high state of the arts one sees the extreme of refinement in the pictures of Meissonier, and of latitude in those of Delacroix. I mean as regards execution, the former so perfect in drawing and finish, and the latter so poor, yet both are famous. Most of the men who have distinguished themselves are not the result of the Academy, and are very different from each other. Can anything be done till one is free?"

A reverberating question, "Can anything be done till one is free?" In asking it (and finding the answer implicit in the question) George was focused on prescribed means and methods of accomplishing a "good" picture, a picture that would meet the contemporary standards of perspective, composition, likeness, and color. But it is truly a broader question—perhaps the deepest one—and I have tried to think of all the family artists in relation to it. In what ways has each one been free, or unfree?

The necessity of earning the next few meals has constricted the experimentalism of many, no doubt. Deference to their presumed "betters" inhibited others, and for several of the twentieth century criticism may have been too painful to be much risked. Still others were, I believe, hiding aspects of themselves, particularly their sexuality, and this cloaking inhibited their freedom of expression.

Secondly, after one of many visits to the Louvre George wrote, "What shall I say of this wonderful place? I will only say, and I am right, that these great men were children in all they did; the joy of doing what they loved governed all their method. They worked *all* ways but only to *express.*"

These two ideas—of the necessities of freedom and of

doing what one loved—were present in George's sensibility from then on, and they gave him a new confidence.

Thereafter, what George wrote in his journal and in his letters show him becoming more casual in his artistic judgements and more open to impressions of all kinds. Of the French he wrote, "Such a bustling, working, pleasure-seeking race as they are! Doing the most serious things without appearing to do so. One would think their whole duty was in theatre-going and filling cafés."

When he thought of all the art he had seen in Paris, he decided, "There are many very great pictures here, and many very poor ones, and both are sometimes by the same hand." At first the thought of saying anything critical of the great Raphael seemed impossibly audacious, but now he wrote that the Raphaels were "uneven," and that some paintings attributed to him probably "should not have his name."

Although he did not write much about them, George saw the new paintings of the Barbizon School—Jean Francois Millet, Theodore Rousseau, and others—and they refined his thinking on what might be done with rural scenes. Towards the end of his career George's work was often compared with theirs, not only because of their common subject matter but because the Barbizon painters had gotten away from trompe l'oeil realism and were using broad, Impressionistic brushwork. The more famous Impressionists, who were soon to follow the Barbizons, took much from them.

George and John then traveled south to Marseille and took a ship to Sicily, from which point they would go slowly northward on the trail of great art. In Syracuse they pondered the temple of the Greek goddess Pallas Athena,

which subsequently had become a Roman temple, an early
Christian church, and a Baroque cathedral without a stone
of its foundations having been replaced.

They looked at the spring where, myth had it, the nymph
Arethusa, in love with a mortal man who was at that moment near a similar spring in Greece, rejected the god
Alpheus's amorous advances and consequently she and her
lover were turned into water by Zeus. According to the
legend, their waters comingled underground although the
two springs were separated on the surface of the earth by
at least one hundred miles.

George sketched Taormina from a neighboring village,
believing, according to John's journal, that he might be
"totally devoured by fleas" while doing so, and the pair were
in Messina when news came that the people of Palermo
had revolted in Garibaldi's cause. The Americans thought
themselves lucky to be able to take ship for the mainland.

The winter had been harsh and there was still much snow
on the slopes of Vesuvius. After some time in Positano, Sorrento, and Naples, George wrote of the aristocratic and
peasant classes of the region: "One with much art and no
innocence, the other with no art and much indifference."

That the jaded upper classes should have surrounded
themselves with pious art was striking to him, and, too, the
knowledge of the chicanery these families had often practiced in obtaining the services of the artists whose work
they coveted.

After some time in Rome George wrote of its churches
that "even a heathen must be impressed with a feeling of
respect for the earnestness which has brought them into
being. I confess to *almost* reverence."

In another letter from Rome he wrote, "I don't think I could live here; the place seems all gone by; one can hardly work where so many seem idle. Paris and London and New York are real live places, people are making more of their short lives. One may come here and get his lesson, which reads a story of the shortness of life and how uncertain worldly splendor is in the great ruins of so many hundreds of years ago, and then he must hurry away, for he already feels life is too short to dream out."

George described Florence as "the most charming city for a stranger. The best pictures, or the greatest number of them, are here." Their good company made him feel "great." Poor works made him feel as though he were being sapped of strength to try again for excellence.

An exhibition at the Florence Academia produced these reflections: "I do not quite see how those brought up with these great things free to them can fail to do something themselves, but they do not seem inspired by them. A nation in its growth is great in art. I have hopes of America."

At this juncture George felt "tired of traveling" and wanted to settle down and paint, but each new visual wonder revived him. In Venice, although George wrote that "regarding saints, madonnas, and martyred ones generally, I am tired of them," he was still reflecting: "The greatest men in art are at times quite common, thereby linking me to them in a strong sympathy. The best things seem to me to be influenced by a *reasonableness* of purpose, which gives them the strength they have." Titian, more than any other artist, showed "independence of design and wonderful powers of imagination."

On they traveled, continually adding to George's museum of the mind. In Milan George judged that "Paul Veronese is not well represented here; he is great in Venice." And that "Giovanni Bellini is here, and always great."

By now George felt not only competent enough to criticize but a sort of obligation to do so: "The *Marriage of the Virgin* by Raphael is full of simple treatment and clearness and light, but the attitudes are affected, and the faces of the female attendants are unmeaning and Chinese-like."

By prearrangement, George and John met with fellow Brooklyn artist and friend, J. W. Skillman in Geneva, where Skillman was a guest of John Ruskin's. "In the evening took tea with Skillman and Ruskin. The latter was exceedingly kind, and put me quite at ease by his polite tact. His assertions in art were only such as any candid mind must admit, and his manner of speaking was elegant, simple, and clear."

Ruskin did, however, ask whether George had seen the Correggios at Parma, and when George said he had not, Ruskin made George feel that through his own incompetence he had made "an unpardonable omission" and had missed what should have been the highest point of his trip.

At this moment in Ruskin's long, odd life his attention was turning away from art toward social and political problems, but his aesthetics of "truthfulness to nature" as art's goal would become an increasingly accepted standard through the remainder of the century. It rejected exaggerations and extravagances, as in Baroque art. Ruskin had championed the early J. M. W. Turner and, in literature, William Wordsworth.

George and John continued north into Germany. In Nuremberg George made a sketch of Albert Dürer's house and wrote of "the walls within which he made so many good things in various ways. [Dürer] did his work manfully, only finally giving way and breathing his last before the continuous, small, but well-directed shots of a scolding wife, directed through an opening which consisted in a great fondness for her."

They stopped in Munich, Brussels, Antwerp, the Hague, and Amsterdam, and their journals became almost entirely records of art seen and appreciated. There were newly sophisticated insights into Rubens and Rembrandt, for example.

George could admire Velasquez now that so many of his works could be seen. He enthused over the early Flemish masters—and Rosa Bonheur—praising many technically, but always, too, considering their degree of expressed humanity. George seemed never to have a fatigued eye or a bout of envy or of meanness of spirit.

Because toward the end their journals are so concentrated on art, so meager in incident and anecdote, their relationship to one another becomes difficult to discern. Thus I was touched to read in a letter from 1869 that John Ames had named his firstborn son George Fuller Ames.

They sailed for New York on August 2, 1860, both of them ready to return to an America that would not look the same to them as it had seven months before. Not only had their ways of seeing been altered, America was—very suddenly it seemed—on the brink of Civil War and in a radically new mood. George became a farmer and a family man, and for years his artistic career was obscured.

In 1886, two years after George's death, William Dean Howells, by then a popular novelist and editor of *the*

Atlantic Monthly wrote "A Sketch of George Fuller's Life" for *George Fuller, His Life and Works, A Memorial Volume.* In it Howells describes George's return to the responsibilities of managing The Bars thusly: "Fuller's return to the farm at Deerfield, to take up the burden his father had laid down, was the poem of his life. Many men of genius have achieved fame and success in the teeth of hardship, privation, and alien circumstances, but not many have turned back from the opportunity won through all these, and simply, manfully, uncomplainingly, obeyed the call of duty. This is what Fuller did."

To understand "the poem of his life," as Howells meant it, it is necessary to know that starting in 1860, George showed almost no paintings during the next sixteen years; that in 1876 he took a number of his canvases to Boston and arranged for a gallery exhibition of them, and that the show established him in the eyes of the art critics and, very soon, the public as an artist of great, peculiarly American talent; and that, in the remaining eight years of his life, George's productivity was prodigious and his fame grew apace.

George's success was not confined to Boston, nor to any one group of art appreciators in those years. He showed again at the National Academy exhibitions, but he was also elected at its inaugural meeting to the Society of American Artists, a "Young Turk" opposed-to-the-Academy organization founded by such young artists as Augustus Saint-Gaudens and Thomas Dewing. George's prices soared and shortly after his death in 1884 his paintings of a single person or subject brought the highest prices ever paid for similar work by an American artist. It was in this atmosphere that Howells wrote his "Sketch."

But in 1860 George himself saw nothing poetic about his return to The Bars—nor did he ever. He had agreed to do it because there were no genuine alternatives. There was the support of Augustus, Hatty, and John and Francis to think of. The Bars was the family's only wealth and must be tended, and further, he hoped soon to marry and he had not been making enough money in New York to support a wife. He optimistically believed he could made such a success of the farm that he would be able to leave it in some sort of stewardship within five years and resume his life as a painter in Boston or New York.

George was not unhappy with this plan. He wrote Hatty from the customs house in New York shortly after his ship had landed that, "The pleasantest part of my travel will be in coming to our home and seeing you. I shall come to Old Deerfield Depot. I never like stopping at South Deerfield." The Bars lies about midway between the two towns.

Neither was George unhappy that he was not returning to New York. In November of 1860 he wrote to Agnes, who had gone to Boston to teach for the winter, "Why should I go to N.Y. to paint pug noses, even if I could get them to do? When I do go it is better that I have something to take with me."

In the "Sketch" Howells wrote that George "had taken the chance of losing all that he had ever hoped to gain in the world when he went back to Deerfield." This may have been true, but this was not as George saw it. He was hoping that the "something to take with me" would be paintings of the Edouard Frere/Barbizon School kind, whose subjects he knew to be at hand in Deerfield. "One must be fortunate in subject as well as treatment to make a public impression," he explained to Agnes.

Almost immediately after returning to Deerfield George wrote to Agnes's father asking permission to be engaged to his daughter, promising his "best effort to make her life a happiness." He wrote her mother less formally, and with charm:

"I must have your consent for your little girl.

"I want some kind words from you. I will not make an apology for being so old. I think Aggie is just as much to be blamed for being so young. I suppose she has some faults. I hope so. I will put mine with hers and perhaps if we work together we may keep them at bay. I will not fall into the error of assuming man and wife to be 'one,' if only for the reason that two are better and stronger. I shall try and not expect too much from another in any relationship.

"I can only thank you by asking this favor above all others, and holding it sacredly while I shall live."

Agnes's parents approved but insisted the engagement period last at least a year. George wrote jubilantly to Agnes, "I shall be so much improved by marriage that you will be every way charmed and contented."

Howells wrote that "George Fuller had found his account, even his account as a painter, in the act of self-renunciation." George was Howells's close friend during the last years of his life, but Howells's interpretation of George's return to Deerfield stems more from a wish to find a certain kind of hero than from George's real motives. In fact, George was glad to leave New York, supremely happy to be marrying Agnes, and more than willing, he was eager and enthusiastic in undertaking the responsibility of The Bars. He had ambitions for his new life and was willing to take risks to achieve them.

That winter of 1860-61 Agnes waited more than two

hours on a crowded Boston sidewalk to see a company of volunteers march off to war. Like many others, she was inspired by a pro-Union, Ralph Waldo Emerson speech, and she reported in a letter to George that every woman she knew was sewing uniforms.

Augustus pestered George to grow cotton at The Bars because it would be needed for uniforms. George let Agnes know that "A Company is to be raised in Deerfield. In what grade would you like me to serve?" But this was teasing. Nearly forty and the manager of a farm, George would be expected by no one to join what turned out to be a thirty-four-volunteers "Company."

Instead, George threw himself into the farm's redevelopment. He had often been critical of Aaron's management, particularly of his choice in crops, and George now set about preparing fields to grow a greater proportion of cash crops and some new ones. To do so would require going into debt, but the debtor's situation was not new to George. He had often borrowed.

As early as 1849, when George was twenty-seven, he had been "on bail" in a suit brought against him by a certain "Lorenzo" in Greenfield—for what, I cannot determine. In 1850, while George was painting in Augusta, a New York tailor, M. Bartram, was pursuing him through the courts. George never denied nor, in the end, failed on a debt, but attempting to satisfy creditors was a nearly continual part of his life.

Sometimes friends and relatives helped him. His older half-sister, Elizabeth, and her husband Asiel Abercrombie sent nineteen hundred dollars to George in 1866, promising more if needed, to cover an unnamed debt. 1n 1869 one Collis Andres called for speedy repayment of a two-hunded-dollar loan. In 1871 George paid five hundred against an outstanding balance but could not eradicate that debt, and was asked for interest on the balance the following year. In December of 1872 a bank demanded over one thousand dollars against what he owed. At about that time the Abercrombies assumed the mortgage on The Bars, but later, due to their own financial difficulties, they were forced to sell the mortgage, and this had wholly unexpected and extraordinary consequences in 1876.

However, in late 1860, and for most of 1861, George was principally involved in physical farm labor rather than financial manipulations. Augustus, the twins, and hired hands worked with him. When Agnes was in Deerfield she cheered him on, as did her letters from Boston.

Agnes had written to him in Europe, "God bless you, dear lover, and don't forget your baby," and the tone of her correspondence now retained that warmth. When they were apart toward the end of his life George would write Agnes every day. Together with his news, he might add this line or a variation of it: "If I had you on my knee I should not waste words upon you."

That winter of 1860-61 at The Bars George found that the north room pantry just off the kitchen made an excellent studio. It was warm enough and had a nice view and adequate northern light. This small room would be crucial to his life, but he would not have much time to use it during the early farm years.

As his marriage approached in the fall of 1861, George wrote to a cousin, "I am to be married in a week. I am married to death and have been so all summer."

Agnes and George were, in fact, married in Deerfield's "Old Church" just before noon on October 17th. Many parties had been held in their honor, and the local Glee Club had serenaded Agnes the night before. An arch of laurels had been constructed before the pulpit. According to a friend's, Lily Wright's, account, the bride wore "white tulle covered with lace." The sun had come out for the occasion and the "'I wills' were said with conviction."

The couple then departed for New York on a wedding trip, Hatty, exhausted, fell ill for a week, and Francis Fuller left Deerfield to enlist in the U.S. Navy, which would be his career. While the newlyweds were traveling George was dunned by a lawyer for having missed deadlines on expected interest payments.

Now that Agnes and George were together and living near their relatives fewer letters were written than at any time since before George had gone off to Illinois. William Ames wrote occasionally from New York, keeping George to some extent current on the art scene. Agnes corresponded with her parents when they were in Boston. But most of the smaller events and feelings of their lives went unrecorded. It is clear, however, that Agnes's transition to the life of a farm wife was not easy for her.

Agnes had trained to become a teacher at the Louis Agassiz School in Cambridge, a preeminent institution, and her family had taken her career seriously. Her Cousin James Jackson Higginson had written to Agnes in 1858, "Are you going this autumn to teach? Ah, Aggie, it is capital that you want or are willing to do this. All the talk in the world about women's rights will never accomplish as much as one woman showing her will and right to earn for herself, think for herself, in any hitherto forbidden direction. If more women would become physicians, merchants, artists, architects, gardeners, etc., this question of rights would settle itself."

Given this background and George's and others' "transcendentalist" encouragement of her to develop her full potential it is not surprising that early in her marriage Agnes's "emotional life was mercurial," as historian Laurel A. Spencer has written in a paper examining Agnes's evolution from feminist-independence to Victorian domesticity.

In September of 1862, Agnes went to Northampton for a visit and wrote to George, "I want to see you, but I do not wish to go back to life on the farm. Such a life as I could lead here [in Northampton] suits me a great deal better."

This crisis was somehow passed, and the births of Agnes's children, which were soon to begin, changed many things.

The Fullers' first child and son, George Spencer Fuller, was born in early 1863. About a year later, on a vacation trip to Boston, Agnes wrote that she had "less time to consider her dissatisfactions," but lamented, "I wish I had something to look forward to when I go back [to Deerfield]."

Robert Higginson Fuller was born in mid-1864, Henry Brown Fuller in late 1867, Agnes Gordon Fuller, known as "Violet," in 1873, and, finally, Arthur Negus Fuller in 1879, when George was fifty-seven and Agnes forty.

Some six months after the birth of Henry Brown Fuller, George wrote to Henry Kirke Brown, "The boy seems to be happy under the name of Henry Brown. He is one of the best of babies—a smile for anyone who notices him." George hoped his son would do the Brown name no dishonor.

Apparently the Browns had suggested that the Fuller family come to visit them at Newburgh (on the Hudson near New York City). George, declining, wrote that "a family of five is not moved easily, nor do they make their destination a paradise."

And perhaps that shut-inness, increased by each child, depressed Agnes. As late as 1871 she expressed discontent with her fate. "Oh, the chances I have lost," she wrote a friend. "Well, there are other worlds—I spent yesterday in reading my religious papers."

Laurel A. Spencer sees the birth of Violet as the important turning point in Agnes's mood and life. "[Violet's] need of care gave Agnes a renewed sense of purpose, which could only have served to improve the relationship between Agnes and George. Just as Agnes had been the Higginson family's 'Princess of Performance,' Violet became the Fullers' little Princess, doted upon and spoiled by her parents and relatives."

During the mid-1870s [Agnes] no longer wrote of her wasted ambitions and aspirations, or her conviction that she was meant for something better than life at The Bars. Agnes eventually wrote a friend, "I can look upon something accomplished in our four children. I only hope my life will be spared another fifteen years to see them well started in life."

When George Spencer Fuller, known always as Spencer, celebrated his twentieth birthday in 1883, a family friend wrote Agnes and George to congratulate them on "the noble bearing of Spencer, the wit of Robert, the beauty of Violet, and the poetic character of Henry Brown Fuller (HBF)." Arthur, age four, was too young, it seems, to be characterized.

The older children had the usual illnesses and routine

difficulties, but they all grew up "straight and strong." Spencer and HBF were over six feet tall—Arthur would grow to six-six, and Violet was certainly pretty. Robert's wit would soon be proven in the newspaper world, and Spencer's "noble bearing" was the exterior of a talented and vigorously responsible man.

William Ames wrote George his opinion that Spencer must certainly become an artist, and that perhaps HBF should, too. As it turned out, all five children would draw, paint, and exhibit their work, but only for HBF would it become a full-time profession. Violet's husband, Augustus Vincent Tack, was also a full-time and extraordinarily prolific and versatile artist.

When Howells was preparing to write his posthumous "Sketch," Agnes provided him with this view of George's life during the early years of their marriage:

"As soon as George came home from Europe he became absorbed in the business waiting for him and he entered into it with great ardor. There seemed to be no end to his activity of body and mind at that time, and, in fact, for years after. He was up early and late, and worked hard. Improving the land and making it produce more was fascinating to him. Even the last summer of his life, on coming up out of the meadow one day, where he had been overseeing some improvements, he said, 'This may lure me to my destruction, but there is nothing I enjoy so much.' He was very much attached to the family home, and to his mind no sacrifice was too great to be endured in order to keep it and free it from debt.

"He had no general interest in farming, like most farmers, and never identified himself with any farmers club or association." When they had married, "He said that he would stay here for about five years, and then affairs would be in running order, and he could leave them and take up his brush again. The fact is he never really laid it down, but carried on two occupations at once. He was much taken with the idea of having a studio here, away from the city, as he had seen some of the French painters do; so he at first painted in a room in the house, collecting all his things from New York and elsewhere, and afterwards converted an old chaise-house into a studio, where he could shut himself up on Sundays and a great deal of the time in winter."

The chaise-house studio to which Agnes referred is a building across Mill Road from The Bars that, later on, was "winterized" by HBF, then passed into the hands of Violet and Augustus Tack, and then to other, non-artist owners. It is a handsome house today, its origins as a chaise-house difficut to imagine.

Agnes continued: "George's subjects were his European sketches and small landscapes with figures, an occasional portrait of a relative or friend, often not finished, and his children in all stages of growth and development.

"George made a note to himself in 1862: 'Everything is pulsation, life, and movement,' which was perhaps the beginning of his new way of seeing.

"[George's] friend, Edwin Billings, would come in the summer, and they would make some sketches out of doors. [George] painted with only a very distant thought of exhibition or critic, and often did not seem to care to save what he did. Such lovely pictures were rubbed out and scraped off that his nearest friends became discouraged, and could not understand such perversity; but in his own mind he was only carrying out some idea plain to him, although hidden to us, and he would never explain. He never talked about what he was painting or was going to paint, but left us to our perceptions to see or not. Once or twice he sent unimportant pictures to exhibitions, but no notice was taken of them, and he began to think he would never claim any of the world's attention."

In fact, George went a number of times to New York during the 1860s and early 1870s, sometimes to market the cranberry crop, and he always attempted to catch up on what was being exhibited and by whom. Twice he showed paintings in the National Academy annual exhibitions—but Agnes is correct in saying that "little notice was taken of them." Nor was George favorably impressed by the work of others he saw in those years.

Agnes continued, "If it had not been for the appreciation and sympathy of his friends who came to see him occasionally he would have felt still more deserted. He was so buoyant and sanguine, however, and felt so much power in himself to compel everything to his own ends, that he never seemed disheartened about anything. His interest and enthusiasm in his work never failed."

According to "one of his sons" (so quoted in the *Memorial Volume*), George became in this period "emancipated from all traditions and set principles—the way to lay on color, the use of the brush, the way to use the knife. 'Color is the delicacy of gradation, of the proper relations of the masses. Use a large brush, and don't be afraid of color,' he would say.

"'Let whatever you do tell a story,' he sometimes said, and, more usually, he spoke of the 'idea' of a painting and the necessity that everything in the painting should be part of that idea."

Agnes wrote to Howells, "I once heard him ask an artist who said that he found it difficult to 'work into his picture,' 'Did you ever think of getting into your picture and working out?'"

The son again: "He kept his pictures in an unfinished state up to the last. When he painted at all he usually went over the whole canvas to keep it all together. Then he would let it dry thoroughly, putting it aside, perhaps, for some weeks. He used a great deal of color, and was fond of scraping it off to let the colors beneath show through, which gave a richness of texture. He was never confined to one picture, but always had several on hand. To avoid extremes, never to use pure colors, to keep simplicity and breadth, these are laws which all artists recognize, and which he felt deeply.

"He used materials with the greatest freedom, painting a great deal with the palette knife, and often rubbing the picture with his finger. He would sometimes mix color on the palette, and sometimes put them on his canvas pure, mixing them with the wrong end of the brush. This latter was a favorite practice of his, reducing one plane into harmony with another."

George's freedom in the use of materials may have been a benefit to his work, but by now it is clear that many of his paintings are the worse for it. He often painted on oil-cloth, a shiny-surfaced material usually used to cover kitchen tables. The shiny surface was inclined to crack as the artist's paint aged. Coal-based bitumen eventually causes discoloration when mixed with oil paints. Some of

George's paintings have lost all of their original quality because of its use, as have Albert Ryder's.

(In passing, paintings by both George and Ryder were at auction together in 1915. The Metropolitan bought a Ryder "marine piece" for $2,500, and the Frick family paid the highest price ever paid for an American painting sold at auction for George's *Romany Girl,* $10,500. In 1918 a joint show of George's and Ryder's paintings was presented at the Vose Gallery in Boston. They were coupled as "individualists," belonging to no school or movement.)

Another of the sons wrote to Howells that as an artist George "was impulsive, but his second thought was always temperate and cool. It was often disappointing to have him paint out a fortunate effect of color or pleasing expression, but he never hesitated to sacrifice these things when they interfered with the single idea of the picture. He preferred to remove the object of interest in his picture a degree into the atmosphere. He would, as he termed it, 'beat back the figure into the landscape.' He avoided going to extremes, for he said, 'If you go to the limit of your material you have spent your force.'"

Understandably, George was not a prolific painter during these years. According to the *Memorial Volume* he finished two paintings in 1862, one painting and two Italian sketches in 1863, three Italian sketches in 1864. In 1865 he made eight works worth recording but then his productivity fell again—four in 1866, two in 1867, one in 1868. Nothing is listed for 1869, then six for 1870, then production falls once more—one a year, two a year, until, in 1876, *nineteen!*

An extraordinary series of events had taken place. In Agnes's words, "The improvements on the farm went on, and were very successful; wonders were accomplished, and the production was greatly increased; but so, too, were the debts, until in 1875 he, with a great many other farmers who had devoted themselves to raising tobacco, failed, and was obliged to go into bankruptcy. The high prices that they had got for their crops fell, and they could not pay the money they had borrowed to put up barns, or even the interest.

"Then George turned to his art again. By a great effort he worked himself back into his old moods, feeling entirely uncertain what would be the result. He worked constantly in his studio during the winter of 1875–76, and by February he had about a dozen pictures ready to exhibit. He was inclined to take them to New York and try his fortune there, but some circumstances decided him to try Boston." (In fact, George had to appear before a bankruptcy court in Boston.)

"George took his pictures to Edwin Billings studio. Mr. Doll [a partner in the Doll & Richards Gallery] came to see them. [George] said afterwards that he had never passed through a more trying ordeal, though no one present suspected it—so much depended upon the success of his pictures at that time he of course felt anxious. Mr. Doll liked them, and put them on exhibition. They met with a warm reception, and there was a demand for all he could do. He was suddenly relieved from anxiety about supporting his family, and at the same time he found a public ready to understand and appreciate what he had been trying to express with his brush. He said he felt a cold chill run over him when he thought of the fifteen years he had spent on the farm."

Howells remembered George's first show at the Doll &

Richards Gallery thusly: "Even I could not go into that little gallery of Doll's, on Tremont Street, and find myself amid the delicate glow of the canvases with which he had hung it round, and not feel their exquisite, their authentic and singular charm. The pictures were the slowly ripened fruit of fifteen years, and they recorded not only the beloved faces of his own household, but the scarcely less beloved features of the Deerfield landscape and his happy memories of Italian travel.

"Their success was no *furore*—the *furore* is not the Boston way—but it was unmistakable; and from that time it meant full recognition and generous reward. Fuller came down from Deerfield that winter and opened a studio where he painted orders for portraits, and the ideal pictures which he loved better."

The paintings that George had brought were all in muted colors. There was no "beautification" of New England scenery. Many were impressionistic landscapes with human figures in the middle distance, several of these in the humid, golden light of New England summers—George was to be identified with that light. What was depicted, Howells and soon many others felt, was timeless America.

Like many other American intellectuals of the time, Howells was appalled by the brutalities being inflicted against both people and landscape by the rapid industrialization of America, and he believed these crimes were undermining the basic morality of the country. George's paintings, which seemed not to distort either the past or the present but instead to remind his viewers of forgotten truths, were thus exciting and moving, quiet though they were.

Howells wrote that "[George] seemed, indeed, to reach

his place at a single stride, and the recognition of his merit was complete at once."

While the turnaround in George's fortunes was certainly dramatic, Agnes's and Howells's memories make it seem too quick and complete. The Bars had been saved by the Abercrombies, who had managed to reassume its mortgage, but George would be years paying it down. When he rented a Boston studio he was, in fact, feeling considerable anxiety as to whether he could attract enough commissions to justify it. Agnes and the children remained in Deerfield, which George visited on the weekends.

While in Boston he wrote Agnes daily, loving letters. "I cannot express to you how much I love you." The endearments with which he signed off include "ever your lover" and "your old lover." Two of his letters were written on the Christmas Days of 1876 and 1877, when he keenly missed his family.

George never took his success for granted. As he had done in earlier days in other cities he paid strategic social calls where he hoped commissions might be found.

He spotted a Mrs. George Faulkner of Jamaica Plain—then a new suburban area south of Brookline where substantial houses were being built around a large pond, the grandest of them, including the Faulkners', looking west across the pond at the setting sun. George decided that she was the most important subject for a portait in the city, and that if he got her, and if his work were satisfactory he would have as many portrait commissions as he wanted. He angled for the commission for three years and was overjoyed to get it in 1880, and then very anxious that she and her family should like it.

It is clear that Mrs. Faulkner liked George. She brought violets from her greenhouse when she came to his studio to sit—George wrote Agnes that he wished he could send them on to her. Then the Faulkners, and everyone, liked the portrait and its effect was just as George had hoped. From then on there was a continual demand for his work, and he felt the freedom to tell his clients that he wanted to do "something of a portrait, and a good deal of a picture."

Today, Mrs. Faulkner's portrait hangs in the boardroom of Boston's Faulkner Hospital. I was very disappointed by it. George wanted so much to paint her I had come to think that Mrs. Faulkner must have been beautiful or must have had looks of some dramatic significance. Instead, Mrs. Faulkner looks proper, middle-aged, and plump. George's impulse had been not at all romantic, entirely political.

George was now called on to paint portraits of Cabots and Lorings and Marquands and Sohiers, and members of other families with long-established Boston names. When his subjects left the studio he turned to his own work, much of it the ideal pictures Howells wrote of.

In the 1880s, in the studio at 149A Tremont Street, George's imagination often returrned to the South. He painted *The Quadroon*, there, and *Turkey Pasture, Negro Funeral,* and *Hoeing Tobacco,* all of them among his most interesting works. His mind went back even further, to Illinois. *Moonrise on the Prairie,* is in the Phillips Collection in Washington, D.C.

Of more immediate effect on his reputation and life were the few historical New England scenes George painted at this time—*And She Was a Witch* and *Examination of Witnesses in a Trial for Witchcraft.* The former is a murky forest scene in which a young woman is watched by a number of distant, isolated people. Howells gave the picture its title.

These historicals reminded some critics of Nathaniel Hawthorne's stories, and the coupling of the painter's and the late writer's names created the feeling of an event, as though a conscious effort was being made to revive symbols of the puritan past.

These two paintings are far from George's most successful, but they undoubtedly added to his contemporary fame. It was declared that he and Hawthorne shared a "poetic" quality, and since Hawthorne had, to a large extent, created the dramas that had come to symbolize New England's early days, George's reputation profited.

The most frequent central figure in George's ideal paintings was a contemporary young woman, sometimes a specific person like *Ethel Reynolds Clarke* whose commissioned portait he had made into "a good deal of a picture," more often a portrait started from a model but given its character, its idea, by George, and named either for a fictional character—Hawthorne's *Priscilla Fauntleroy*, for example—or arbitrarily. Howells named *Winifred Dysart* after the picture was finished.

In these full scale pictures a woman in her late teens looks out directly at the viewer. She usually stands in a field, wearing what she might think of as her "best" clothes—her best is not elegant. The backgrounds of fields and hilly forests are rendered impressionistically, without exaggeration of any kind, but in one or more places they are vaguely threatening: the horizon line is a slope rather than calmly horizontal; dark clouds threaten to obscure the sun, or winds are bending far off trees; the shadows in a glade are so dark as to make impossible the certain recognition of objects or creatures suggested there.

The viewer senses rather than sees anything overtly menacing. The young women subjects seem to feel secure enough. But the idea comes across that they know something of what neither they nor we can see—that their environments and what lies ahead are not all blue skies and delight. The women seem to have paused a moment to show us who they are before going on into the hard part, the difficulties of life. They are not ignorant or overconfident. On their faces there is often a hint of a smile, but no more than a hint. They have faith in themselves perhaps simply because they must have.

The best of these paintings are unique and moving. *The Quadroon* fits interestingly in this sisterhood with *Fifteen, Miss Bradley*, and the others.

Agnes had felt certain of George's success as early as 1877, and in a letter she urged George, "Now that you have come to this point I hope you will seize the opportunity— forget that you want anything of the public but a chance to do your best, not in one work but in one hundred." In the same letter, in response to a cry of loneliness from George, she wrote sternly that "an artist with a studio should never feel lonely." And she added a funny note about herself: "I have been to church and envy those people who can sleep sitting up."

George was not yet ready to feel the freedom Agnes prescribed, but it was not long in coming. He quickly revived old Boston friendships. Howells paid a call at the studio, soon came again, and before long was introducing him to his friends, among them Samuel Clemens (Mark Twain),

whose career Howells was championing. George attended
Wendell Phillips's lectures and went to spiritualist seances,
which were then creating excitement. He became a founder
of the St. Botolph Club, which, like the Century Association in New York, was intended as a meeting place for artists
and intellectuals of all kinds together with business people
and professionals concerned with the arts. In short, George
was welcomed into the Boston Establishment.

Sister Hatty, who had become Mrs. Dammers not long
after George had returned to The Bars, was living in Brookline, and George saw her frequently until her painful death
in 1879. There was also a quantity of Higginson in-laws
and relatives of whom George became fond. It was the new
society, however, that affected his life.

The "Gilded Age" had arrived during George's farm
years, and now newly rich Americans were building mansions and buying art—most of it European art—to deco-
rate them. "Collectors" of art had come into being, and
there was a new breed of "patrons."

The first time George saw a Barbizon-like Corot hung
in a Boston salon he said, "I don't always know a bad picture when I see one, but I always know a good one." Not
long afterwards he met a collector who possessed three
Corots, and a few years later George wrote in a letter, "God
knows how many Corots there may be by now in Boston
and New York."

He went to see a Gainsborough in a Boston house and
visited a collection in another that included Tintoretto and
Millet. In that collection the only American painter represented was the Boston favorite, William Morris Hunt
who, incidentally, supported George and made his road

easier. Hunt had said to George shortly after they met, "I feel as if I had always known you." Many had similar feelings about George.

Of the house that contained the Hunt painting George wrote that it was "grand and overloaded." On the other hand, when he called on "Mr. Fairchild," Charles N. Fairchild, an investment banker who was a friend of Howells's, George thought that the house showed "what refined wealth can accomplish."

Some months later the Fairchilds commissioned George to do a portrait of Mrs. Fairchild's mother, which they duly applauded, and when George exhibited his painting of the mythical Arethusa in 1883, Lily (Mrs. Fairchild) wrote him, "I have never seen a picture that stirred me more profoundly than *Arethusa*! I wish crowns were in fashion—or that those dull people knew enough to harness themselves to your carriage when you go home at night. It is perfectly glorious. Accept my very deep reverence and homage." Poems by Lily in this exalted style were occasionally published in *The Atlantic Monthly* under an assumed name, C. A. Price (read caprice). Her husband Charles had not wanted her to sign her true name to her poems after their marriage, an indication of his sense of Victorian propriety.

The Fairchilds were friends with and patrons of John Singer Sargent, who painted portraits of a number of their family members over the years and often stayed as a guest with them. Charles confidentially commissioned Sargent to do a portrait of Robert Louis Stevenson, another Fairchild friend, as a surprise gift for Lily. When Sargent's famous and, at the time, scandalous portrait of *Madame X* was exhibited in Boston, George wrote that he "lost his heart" to her.

Arethusa and two other paintings done in his last years are evidence that George's imagination was stirred by the works of art arriving principally from Beaux-Arts France that glorified the new collectors by putting them in the company, in their own houses, of gods, demi-gods, and other mythological figures. For centuries artists had surrounded European aristocracy with such companions, together with saints and martyrs, and now the "Robber Barons" were being equally honored. Stanford White and other architects were combing Europe for ideas for pediments and cornices, entrance halls and ballrooms that would be proper settings for neoclassical sculpture and grand-scale paintings.

Compared to the vast majority of examples of this new decoration, George's depiction of Arethusa is modest in scale, brownish in tone, and dramatically flat. She seems neither to be cowering from the threat of Alpheus's rape nor looking forward to immersion in the spring's deadly waters. She is kneeling on a rock, naked but modestly positioned.

There are several reasons why Arethusa was not a good subject for George: he could draw well, but not especially the nude, with which he had done scant work; he had little sympathy with melodrama; and the dim, subtle tones he liked were scarcely Mediterranean. But there were others besides Lily Fairchild who called it his "masterpiece." Perhaps, in the social atmosphere of the time, his *Arethusa's* modesty helped.

As late as April of 1879 George was borrowing money. That year one E. D. Maynard loaned him nine hundred dollars, taking as security two paintings that were later to be considered among George's most valuable—*Turkey Pasture* and *Romany Girl*—and three more besides! But in the following three years George would finally repay all debts and regain sole title to The Bars.

By 1883 George was being paid higher prices than any American painter up to that time, yet his letters in these years of accumulating success do not show much change in his interests or reactions. That year, Agnes wrote him that his success had made his life "a fable," but George showed no interest in burnishing his history. His life was all in the present. He replied to Agnes, "I am delighted with myself, and with a wife such as yourself who would not be so?"

Earlier, in 1880, he had written Agnes, "I am yours till death." At age fifty-eight he had had, perhaps, an intimation. When she and the children were in Deerfield and he in Boston his letters were often concerned with their health: "Do not let the small boy near the horses' heels." "I cannot bear the idea of sickness at home."

He wrote, too, about his passing feelings, "I am all used up," and his day-to-day progress, "I am getting on well but more slowly than I would like." He reported his reviews, off-handedly liking the favorable ones, and mentioning those lukewarm or worse without comment. George reportedly said to a man who had disparaged his work in print, "I was a little hurt at first—but that is over. Everyone must see with his own eyes and speak quite honestly. I do not see and feel as you, but I will think it over. I must go on as I have been going."

The most frequent adverse criticism of George's paintings was that they were strongly felt but "inadequately seen." This seems sometimes a misunderstanding of what I see as his impressionism and expressionism, and sometimes a legitimate objection to a lack of rigor in his draughtsmanship.

George wrote often to Spencer, now nearly twenty, about the problems of the farm. It was assumed within the family that Spencer would inherit and run The Bars.

But to Agnes George wrote, "I want you to cultivate poetry. I am too practical." He encouraged her to collaborate with a friend on a novel—a project that was never finished. But George felt involved literarily in a new way: Howells came to the studio to read aloud a chapter of his new novel while George was painting, and they talked about a "painting scene" that Howells wished to write.

After several years it could be said that George "knew everyone." In New York he met the young painter, Frank Duveneck, and a "Miss Dixwell" who were "quite bohemian-like." "In what pleasant places does the lot of young and single artists fall!" George wrote.

A Winslow Homer exhibition in Boston thrilled George who declared they were the finest watercolors ever done. Younger painters called on him, as did collectors, and his time became harder to manage. Childe Hassam had a studio next door, and the African-American landscape painter Edward Bannister, "one of our best," became a friend.

In Deerfield Agnes began to feel like a shy country cousin. She wrote that she would not have known what to say to the dignitaries George had found himself among at a Fairchild dinner party.

Finally, in 1882, George felt secure enough to take a house, first in Belmont near the Howellses and Fairchilds, then in Brookline, and for the first time in five years the family was together, winter and summer. Their satisfaction would be brief.

Text continued on page 155

Joel Negus
NATHAN NEGUS
Petersham Historical Society

Self Portrait
NATHAN NEGUS
Memorial Hall Museum, Deerfield

Chilly McIntosh
NATHAN NEGUS
State Archives Museum, Montgomery, Alabama

Joseph Negus
NATHAN NEGUS
Petersham Historical Society

Portrait of a Lady Wearing a Red Pompom
AUGUSTUS FULLER
Springfield Art Museum

Fanny (Negus) Fuller and the twins
AUGUSTUS FULLER
Deerfield Academy

Portrait of Bronson Alcott
CAROLINE NEGUS HILDRETH
Orchard House, Concord, MA

Portrait of a Woman, probably Fanny Negus Fuller during her fatal illness
CAROLINE NEGUS HILDRETH
Private Collection

Self Portrait
GEORGE FULLER
National Portrait Gallery, Smithsonian Institute

Red Rock
GEORGE FULLER
Memorial Hall Museum, Deerfield

Negro Funeral
GEORGE FULLER
Museum of Fine Arts, Boston

Maidenhood, Miss Bradley
GEORGE FULLER
FINE ARTS MUSEUM, SAN FRANCISCO

The Quadroon
GEORGE FULLER
Metropolitan Museum

Hoeing Tobacco
GEORGE FULLER
Worcester Museum of Art

Self Portait
HENRY BROWN FULLER
Private Collection

In the Mirror
LUCIA FAIRCHILD FULLER
Private Collection

The Triumph of Truth Over Error
HENRY BROWN FULLER
Principia College, Elsah, Illinois

Portrait of Neil Fairchild
LUCIA FAIRCHILD FULLER
Memorial Hall Museum, Deerfield

Ebba Bohm
HENRY BROWN FULLER
Fine Arts Museums of San Francisco

'29
HENRY BROWN FULLER
Private Collection

Landscape-Winter
G. SPENCER FULLER
Memorial Hall Museum, Deerfield

Untitled Landscape
ROBERT FULLER
Memorial Hall Museum

Untitled Landscape
ARTHUR NEGUS FULLER
Memorial Hall Musem

Liberation
AUGUSTUS TACK
The Phillips Collection, Washington, D.C.

Portrait of Elizabeth Fuller
AUGUSTUS TACK
Memorial Hall Museum, Deerfield

Self Portrait
ELIZABETH FULLER, 1917
Memorial Hall Library, Deerfield

Photo of Chas and Jane Fuller
Photograph of Islip, Long Island Town Hall staircase in background, Jane's *Earthbound* to the right
Private Collection

Laundry Drying, Monhegan
ELIZABETH FULLER
Memorial Hall Museum, Deerfield

Western Landscape
ELIZABETH FULLER
Memorial Hall Museum, Deerfield

The Seventh Wave
ARTHUR FULLER
Private Collection

Portrait of a Girl (miniature)
ALICE FULLER GOODHUE
Private Collection

Almost There
BARBARA GOODHUE LEGLER
Memorial Hall Museum, Deerfield

Lotus Root
JILL FOX, 1991
Private Collection

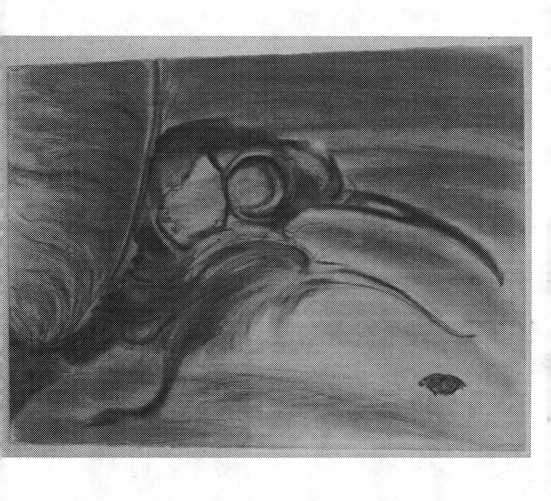

What Remains
JILL FOX
Private Collection

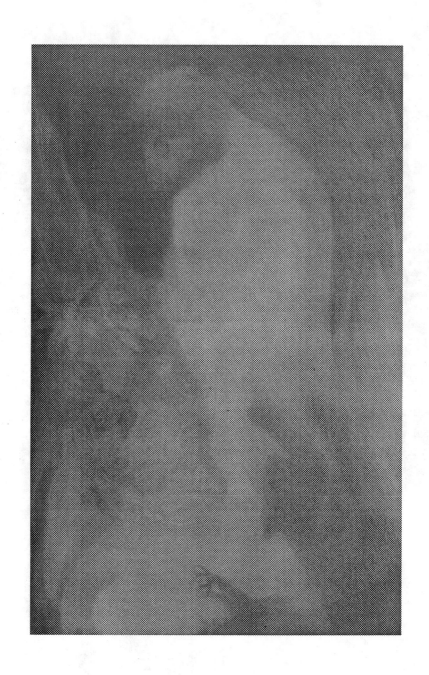

Woman Dreaming
JILL FOX
Private Collection

Hero
FULLER COWLES
Franconia Sculpture Park

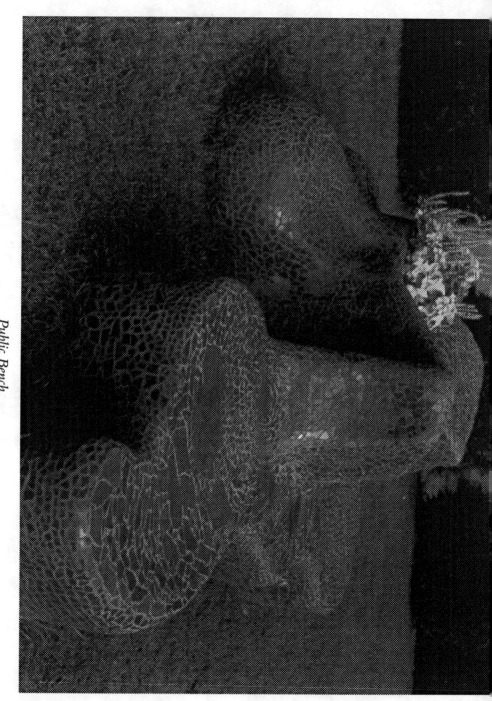

Public Bench
FULLER COWLES AND CONNEE MAYERON
Stillwater, MN Library

George suffered from Bright's disease, a kidney ailment. His heart stopped on March 21st, 1884, in Brookline. In the *Memorial Volume* Howells wrote: "He is present before me as I write: a tall figure, grown burly with years, and gray about the large, noble head, out of which look somewhat dimly the kindest eyes, while he slants his broad beard thoughtfully, and then with a quick turn of his chin goes on with his talk or his work. The last time I saw him he moved ponderingly over the Sunday-vacant pavement. That could not have been many weeks before his death and he now seems to me to have moved heavily, wearily, sadly, like a man nearing his end."

George's death was front page news in Boston newspapers. The headlines: *"The Leading Artist of America Passes Away." "Sudden Death of Boston's Greatest Artist."*

Among the subheads and in the obituary stories can be found the strongest homages their writers could think of: "He belongs to the men who will be greatly appreciated hereafter." He was "the colossal George Fuller," an artist "unique in being both poetic and American." It was "the most serious loss that American Art has ever sustained."

George's "endless experimentation" was admired. He had painted only "in order to say something, express his thought." For another writer his attempt had been only "to be himself, and to show himself as clearly as he could." And what a self it had been!

"No one, old or young, was a greater favorite with his fellow artists." He had been "above all tricks of the trade," and had "lived for his work, and it alone."

He was "ageless." In the introduction to the catalogue of the Memorial Exhibition, which was organized and hung only weeks after George's death, it was pointed out that George had been as old as the painters of the Hudson River School, but that while their work now looked dated, he had made "new art"until the end of his life. He was "of the present" and "among the youngest." He had been an "original artist" rather than a clever painter. He had been a "born seer and interpreter." His "life and work were insep- arable," and his living had been "a great work." "His life was gentle, and the elements so mixed in him that Nature might stand up and say to all the world, 'This was a man.'"

In short, George had been "the delight and glory of a nation." Those closest to him concurred. George's brother Frank wrote that George had been "a most lovable man with the physique of a giant and with the gentleness and purity of character of a woman."

And Howells again: "All the lovely, wise singlehearted- ness of the man went into his work; his soul expressed it- self there in all its richness and truth. One could not meet him without somehow being warmed and enlightened by his spirit."

In the Memorial Exhibit itself there were 179 items, many on loan from their owners, but many also for sale. Agnes was disappointed by the sales. She had children, still, to be edu- cated. Arthur was only five years old, and she was forty-five with, as it turned out, forty more years to live. But the show was by no means the end of George's career. Indeed, it could be said that it was the beginning of a greater career than anyone to that moment could have imagined.

The introduction to the Exhibit's catalogue did much to

make public and official the "fable" of George's life: that in 1860 George had "retired" to The Bars because he had been dissatisfied with his work, and that during those sixteen years he had worked "in seclusion from the public, selling only to friends." Eventually, those friends had insisted that he show his work again, and George had returned to the world with a "special and unique endowment, peculiar in kind and precious in quality."

The fable grew more fabulous. When a catalogue was written for George's 1915 exhibition it was said that George had painted during his years on the farm "only for his own comfort."

At the end of his life George's renown had become international. At an annual Paris Salon in the mid-1880s George's *Winifred Dysart* was declared by one critic to be *"le plus grand succes de l'annee."* Paris was then already preparing for the immense *Exposition Universelle* of 1889, for which Paris's Eiffel Tower was built to show off French engineering, and the *Grand* and *Petit Palais* were constructed to display French and international art.

The *Exposition* commemorated the centennial of the French Revolution, and its objective was to lay out an inventory of France's and the world's greatest accomplishments. Its spirit was the belief that humankind was perfectible, and that the disparate cultures of the world would eventually unify.

More than thirty-two million people came to see the 61,722 exhibits, of which 1,750 were from the U.S.—I am quoting these and other facts and opinions from *Paris 1889,* edited by Annette Blaugrund.

The display of American art was second in size only to France's. 336 paintings by 189 American artists were hung.

There were 16 sculptures by 11 sculptors, and drawings, engravings, and etchings.

About half of the American artists were then currently resident in Europe, and virtually all had been trained in Paris. To many Americans at home this exhibition proclaimed the coming-of-age of American art.

George's *The Quadroon* was the only painting by a deceased artist included in the American exhibition. "Fuller's inclusion in the *Exposition* is a measure of his importance within American art circles of the late 19th century," according to J.H., writng in *Paris 1889*.

The Quadroon reappeared four years later at Chicago's World's Columbian Exposition, whose enormous neoclassical "white city" undertook to outdo the French. At its opening more than half a million people came to the fairgrounds, between 100,000 and 150,000 of whom jammed into the Manufactures and Liberal Arts Building, where they were faced with 2,500 dignitaries on the speakers' platform and were entertained by a choir of 5,500 voices singing behind the Chicago Symphony Orchestra.

The Quadroon's presence there is seemingly denied by the Smithsonian Institution's 1993 book, *Revisiting the White City*, but the painting was singled out by a contemporary critic on the scene as the best work in the American art pavilion, which, like the Paris exhibit, presented work by virtually all the late nineteenth-century American artists known today: Sargent, Homer, Dewing, Hassam, etc.

Also hung in the pavilion was a portrait by Lucia Fairchild of her brother, Neil. Lucia, the second of Charles and Lily Fairchild's daughters, was also responsible for one of four large historical paintings that hung in the central hall of the Women's Building. Mary Cassat painted one of the others. Lucia was then twenty-three.

In Sadakichi Hartmann's *History of American Art,* published in 1902, the author asks the rhetorical question, Who was America's greatest painter? His answer: "If not George Fuller, who?" Not all art histories of the time claimed such a championship for George, but all put him in the first rank.

Museums of art were being constructed in cities across America in those years, and every one wanted a George Fuller—or more than one. Thus there are seven in the collection of the Boston Museum of Fine Arts, four in the Metropolitan, five in the Chicago Art Institute, two in the Los Angeles County Museum, two in the Fine Arts Museums of San Francisco, many in Washington in the National Gallery, the Museum of American Art, the Corcoran, and the Phillips Collection, and one in many other American cities—St. Louis, Portland, Oregon, etc.

In 1923, to celebrate the centennial of George's birth, the Metropolitan organized a retrospective exhibition, extensive and comprehensive in intent. George's son-in-law, Augustus Vincent Tack, then a highly respected portraitist, muralist, and pioneer abstractionist, wrote in that catalogue's introduction that George in his work had plumbed "the depths of human sympathy."

This was the zenith of George's career: a retrospective in the nation's greatest museum; recognition in some art histories as the country's greatest painter; and assessment by a fellow artist who had never met him that he had been able to express to its ultimate, "human sympathy."

The descent from this point was steep.

Although his paintings would continue to get high prices

for some years (an anonymous buyer, presumably a Rockefeller, bought *Miss Bradley* for $40,000 in 1928), the disillusioned eyes of the cultural arbiters of the 1920s and 1930s were inclined to see George's "human sympathy" as sentimentality, and New England scenes as quaint memories rather than significant ones. They noticed George's limitations in subject matter and draughtsmanship.

The curator of the Metropolitan's exhibition inadvertently magnified the critics' negative reactions by giving most prominence to works of George's very last years, when he did *Arethusa* and other mythologicals, and the New England historical scenes, which by the 1920s must certainly have looked like costume dramas. What had once seemed immutable in the farm scenes around Deerfield very likely looked like nostalgia, considering the rise of the great farms of the Midwest.

Written in the 1930s, Lewis Mumford's *The Brown Decades* treats George with respect but little enthusiasm. He is lumped with other respectable artists of the period. Another critic of the time mentioned George only to remark, "There is a name grown dim with time!"

In Russell Lynes's *The Art Makers of Nineteenth Century America,* published in 1970, George appears only as part of an anecdote about Thomas Ball. George had introduced Ball to a young woman of "glorious color in hair and flesh," Lynes wrote, and Ball's unrequited love for her and the fact that he could not bear to look at the portrait he had done of her led Ball to stop painting and take up his life's vocation, sculpture. There is not a word in the book about George's art.

Sometimes in the past few years it has been painful for

me to look at paintings by George dragged out of racks in the storage basements of museums. All of them needed cleaning but, worse, many have badly cracked, some beyond repair in my opinion. Whatever their condition, the paintings inspired by "Gilded Age" subject matter look rather silly. But my sharpest pains have been caused by the recognition that a canvas, tilted by a helpful curator so that it would best catch the light of a single overhead bulb, is a wonderful picture, and that the painting is nonetheless condemned to the dungeon or, worse, the *oubliette.*

One came out of its dungeon and was given prominent display not very long ago. In the spring of 1994 George's *Miss Bradley* was hung in the De Young Museum of the Fine Arts Museums of San Francisco as part of the exhibition of the John D. Rockefeller III and Blanchette Hooker Rockefeller Collection of American Art that had recently been given to the city. George was in very good company.

The evening of the opening I stood at a passageway between two of the exhibit's rooms looking to my right at the John Singer Sargent full-scale standing portrait of *Caroline, Marquise d'Espeuilles,* a beautiful woman whose dress shimmers and whose hair, eyes, and jewels flash—dramatic glamor. Painted in 1884, I think the portrait is one of Sargent's most effective.

In the room to my left hung the young woman of George's *Miss Bradley,* one of his ideals, painted in the same size and scale as *Caroline. Miss Bradley* is standing outdoors against one of George's vaguely disquieting rural backgrounds. She is wearing nice, maidenly, rather than glamorous clothes and she is regarding us with a complex of emotions: she wants to win us, she is wary of us; she is clearly malleable, she is determined; she wonders who she is and looks for an answer from us; she is proudly herself. All these things at once. I felt exhilirated.

In *Miss Bradley* there is no social commentary worth mentioning, no display of fashion or of wit or of great beauty either natural or created—all the things that are so strong in Sargent's portrait. But there is Tack's "depth of human sympathy." In a perfectly cared for, lit, and hung canvas, George's deep perception and his extraordinary ability to convey it, were unmistakably visible.

The fable of George's life became factually inaccurate over the years, but both his life and what we have of his good work are fabulous.

Chapter Five

GEORGE'S PROGENY:
SPENCER, ROBERT, VIOLET, and ARTHUR
and especially, HBF and his wife
LUCIA FAIRCHILD FULLER

All five of Agnes's children were delivered in her bedroom at The Bars, including the last one, Arthur, who arrived in May of 1879, when George's success was assured. Home-birthing was a customary aspect of rural life, and there was no reason to suppose Agnes would experience complications.

Three years later the entire family, excepting Spencer, became city people, living for the most part in the Brookline house and only paying visits to The Bars. For Agnes, the move constituted a kind of triumphant homecoming. She had been one of ten children, and her many Boston relatives now welcomed her, congratulating her on George's success, and some of them contributing to it by buying and promoting his work.

Robert entered the Boston Latin School and immediately did well. HBF, now twelve, was sent as a boarding student to St. Mark's School outside of Boston. In a few years

Violet would be sent to a finishing school in Greenfield, but she soon became a social Bostonian, anxious to be included in its events. Arthur grew up as a city boy and followed Robert to Harvard.

HBF's classmates at St. Mark's came entirely from wealthy families, but his years among them did not take him into the upper class. To the contrary, the record of his studies appeared to prove that only his artistic side merited encouragement. Rejecting the tenor of beliefs around him, he became not only a committed aesthete but a lifelong theoretical socialist.

This chapter gives more attention to HBF and Lucia than to his siblings for several reasons. While all the children produced impressive art, HBF was given the most serious training and encouragement, and produced the most original and "important" work. Secondly, he and Lucia moved into a social art world of a kind that had not existed before and was not shared by Spencer and Arthur, who remained rooted in Deerfield, or by Robert whose principal career was in journalism. Violet abandoned her own art when she married Augustus Vincent Tack. Their lives together and his art are recounted separately in Chapter Six. Thirdly, HBF's and Lucia's letters and papers have been kept—more than ten thousand of them—in a special collection at the Dartmouth College Library and are the richest sources of information on this generation.

Like his father, HBF was tall and strong, droll and good-looking. He was a talker and a voluminous reader and letter-writer. He was at least as inventive as George and as adventurous, but unlike George he suffered depressions and was often dependent on, rather than responsible for others.

He was exceptionally alive and attractive to people of many backgrounds.

All of the children felt both the glow and the shadow of George's astonishing rise and proclaimed greatness. Once HBF graduated from St. Mark's School and entered Boston's Cowles Art School, *everyone* told him that he had great talent and that a great deal was expected of him. Only in the last years of his life could he feel entirely free of the burden of these expectations.

Agnes's delight in having a daughter was apparent to all, most particularly to Violet herself, who became an adept manipulator of those around her. By the time she was in her teens her correspondence with her mother shows that Agnes was often begging for her daughter's understanding and affection, and apologizing for sleights Violet claimed to have suffered.

In those same years Violet made a strong ally of her brother Robert, nine years her senior, and she often used his morally-certain judgements as support in disputes with Agnes and other members of the family.

After Harvard, Robert had gone to work for a conservative newspaper and had adopted a full range of Victorian attitudes. An example: when Violet was eighteen she was infuriated by a young man who apparently promised to invite her to a social event but then did not and went instead with another girl. Violet wrote Robert about this who replied confirming to her that the young man had behaved "unspeakably," that his actions had been "beneath all civilized behavior," and that thus the young man could be dismissed from her mind "with happiness rather than regret."

With "Victorianism" in full flower Boston was a very different place than it had been when George and Thomas Ball had followed pretty girls to their residences to serenade them, and Emerson had found it natural to call a married woman, Caroline Negus Hildreth, "a superb woman." By the century's last decade the question of what was "proper" had replaced the large philosophical questions posed in Emerson's *"Self Reliance"* which considered the question of the individual's resemblance to and embodiment of God. Thoreau's belief in the necessity of "civil disobedience" by 1890 seemed an idea from another civilization.

As well as Robert, Violet had an ally in HBF during her teens. HBF's sentimental affection pleased and amused Violet but was of no real use to her since he was thought to be unreliably dreamy and artistic. She teased HBF mercilessly about his vulnerability to the charms of girls, writing to him once that he should "swear off all girls for a year." Then, however, when HBF broke off one flirtation, Violet wrote to him that another girl had been "glad to hear the news."

HBF and Violet began their correspondence in 1886, when he was at the Cowles Art School and Violet was at the Prospect Hill School in Greenfield. While Agnes was still writing to Violet as though she were a little girl ("My Dear Precious Child," "My Dear Little Daughter, I hear nothing from you"), HBF had adopted a mock-pompous tone of which Violet often made short work. They must have laughed a good deal over each other's letters.

He wrote, "I hope both you and Miss Willis will set a glowing example of strict decorum," which Violet rightly understood to mean that he was sweet on Miss Willis. She caught on to his interest in some others of her schoolmates as well—not a difficult task.

In the fall of 1887 HBF wrote Violet, "I like my drawing very much. I am in a class mostly composed of girls of all ages. I should either have been born a girl or a sultan, for my lot seems to be cast largely with the fair sex."

On the occasion of his twenty-first birthday that October he wrote, "I shall knit my brows more now, and often be somewhat preoccupied so that it shall be noticeable in company, sigh in conversation as though to relieve my mind of a burden—and in many other ways betray a sense of responsibility and importance. I am still, however, your obedient brother [HBF]."

Early in the new year of 1888 HBF wrote Violet he was "studying quite diligently for me. I go out very little and no more than I have to. Somebody has made a mistake. I am not at all gay. I like little Lucia Fairchild very much."

HBF had fallen in love, and eighteen-year-old fellow student Lucia, the Charles Fairchilds' daughter, had fallen even harder for him.

The Fairchild and Fuller families had had a considerable amount of contact since William Dean Howells's admiration of George had brought him into the group of artistic and intellectual friends that had formed around the Fairchilds' energy and bounty. In addition to this connection, Charles's most important friend and investment banking partner was Henry Lee Higginson, a cousin of Agnes's. This double connection between the families did not mean, however, that a match between Lucia and HBF would be easily approved, far from it.

Charles Fairchild had come from Milwaukee to Boston

to attend Harvard. His family had pioneered in Wisconsin, had prospered there, and Charles's older brother Lucious ("Bloody Shirt Fairchild") had become a general in the U.S. Army, and later, the elected governor of the state.

After Charles's Harvard graduation he used his own capital to form investment partnerships, and he did extremely well. He soon married Lily Nelson, the daughter of a Bostonian federal judge, and together they set out to create a family life of extraordinary luxury, cultural stimulation, and interesting friendships for themselves and their children. They produced seven children, of whom Lucia was next to oldest.

The primary Fairchild residence was at 191 Commonwealth Avenue, a large and handsome brownstone two blocks from the Public Garden. They had a house at Nahant on the shore north of the city and a summer "cottage" for longer stays at Newport, Rhode Island. For a number of years they also had a house at Belmont, a growing community in the direction of Concord that could easily be reached by trolley from the city.

Charles Fairchild bought up land on Belmont Hill which rises west of the rail station and commands a distant view of the Boston skyline and harbor. His aim was to induce "kindred spirits"—people he and Lily enjoyed and admired—to build houses there and create a lively, Fairchild-centered community. The Howellses, among others, built a "dream house" on land the Fairchilds provided and lived in it with pleasure until, like the Fairchilds' own children, theirs in adolescence became bored with the isolation of the suburbs.

The two Fairchild girls, Sally and Lucia, and the five boys

who were born after them seemed to have been endowed with everything nature and wealth could provide. They were all healthy, good-looking, lively, intelligent, and talented. They attended the best schools and did well in them. Some of the children's letters—and some of Lily's—suggest that Charles was somewhat distant and commanding as a father, and there is strong evidence of his priggishness, but no one depicted him as irrational or cruel. Presumably as in all Victorian households serious efforts were made to ensure that every family member and family occasion seemed perfectly realized, but as the children were growing up a few minor shadows can be seen.

When Lucia was in her late twenties she wrote an account of games played at Belmont by Sally and herself and Mildred Howells when they were, respectively, eight, seven, and five years old. Lucia wrote, "Sally was the goddess of my childhood, although I was infinitely more intimate with [Mildred]. Sally brought a grand severity into these games. This was hard for both [Mildred] and me. [Mildred] wept—never understanding that [to weep] was an unspeakable disgrace."

In the game Lucia uncritically describes, Sally and she were "teachers" and [Mildred] the pupil. The teachers would deliberately misinform Mildred about some common matter of fact and then would penalize her for giving them wrong answers during an "examination."

One day Mildred was wearing a new hat, and Sally and Lucia tore it as punishment for a wrong answer. Mildred cried, and, according to Lucia's account: "Sally and I were weak with laughter as [Mildred] made her way sobbing to her house, and we talked to one another very seriously about her shameless ways. What could we do to make her realize what a frightfully immoral thing it was to cry?"

This pattern of "play" apparently recurred often enough so that William Dean Howells wrote Lucia a cautionary poem and put it into her Christmas stocking when Lucia was ten. The poem begins by flattering Lucia: "Graceful as the pendant fuchsia/Is my charming Lucia."

But Howells then calls her "the wiliest of minxes ... this fierce and most unlovely maid" and says that Lucia "rails at [Mildred] and wilts and shrivels her up in despair, disregardful of her victim's sighs and squeaks." Howells writes that he is "just advising her to stop,/ Heed it! Else in vain a truce you/ shall implore, vile Lucia!"

This poem was saved and clean-copied by Lucia without apparent embarassment. Polly Howells Wertham, a great-great-grandaughter of William Dean Howells and a psychotherapist, interprets the "game" and the girls' injunction against crying as representing a kind of copying of male attitudes as the girls perceived them. I speculate that they may have been imitating treatment they had received from governesses or parents who wanted control and no complaints. A proper facade was required of the girls no matter what the provocation.

Mildred and Lucia remained lifelong friends, so the damage to their relationship cannot have been as serious as Howells seemed to think.

John Singer Sargent was glad to accept Charles Fairchild's commission to paint a portrait of Robert Louis Stevenson as a surprise for Lily. He and Stevenson were already friends, and Sargent had done his portrait once before.

When Sargent delivered the portrait to the Fairchilds he

was given a warm welcome and became a family friend, and from then on he was often a long-term guest when he was in Boston doing portrait commissions. Eventually he did portraits of both Lily and Charles, of Charles's brother, Lucious, of one of the Fairchild sons, Gordon, and more than one portrait of Sally, a favorite subject.

Lucia, who was an ambitious artist from an early age, idolized Sargent and made notes of his opinions—of everything he said during his first stay with the Fairchilds in 1890, and again the following year when he and the Fairchild family met in Paris.

So far as anyone knew or knows, Sargent never experienced a sexual life, and partly for that reason, perhaps, he was in social demand in the great houses of Europe and America as a charming but "safe" guest. What he said to the twenty-year-old Lucia characterizes him when off-guard, makes understandable his dinner-table popularity, and provides a snatch of the cultural dialogue of the time. Lucia's reverence and thirst for his thoughts is plain and touching.

Lucia wrote: "[Sargent] has said to me of [Augustus] Saint-Gaudens's work that nothing he does is quite complete in itself. Everything is an excellent study, a wonderful suggestion, but lacks that one great quality."

"[Novelist] George Eliot, he says, is 'quite inartistic.'

"He talked a good deal about the 'Tragic Muse,' which he admires greatly.

"He said it was fine how [Henry] James had kept his personality out of [his novels]. Hawthorne, he says, he has just been reading. He spoke of the *Blithedale Romances* as charming—Hawthorne doesn't seem to believe in it himself—the quaint, ironical way in which it is written suits him. He said, 'I must say I did not care for *The Scarlet Letter*.

It is so dreadfully morbid, and the whole thing seems so unnecessary. I fancy Hawthorne does better when he is not quite serious.' [Sargent] has a smoker's throat whch gives him an occasional queer half-cough, and he says hmm—ha—and draws long breaths, often leaving as much to be inferred as he actually says."

But Sargent said a good deal, some of which he would not have wanted repeated. He described one of his most important patrons, Isabella Stewart Gardner, as "looking like a lemon with a slit for a mouth," and spoke of another woman's appearance as being like a "boiled turbot."

Later in life Sargent was to declare that he had hated doing the portraits that made him famous, and Lucia may have been the first to know it. In 1890 Lucia wrote that Sargent had had "a very disagreeable time of it" painting a Mr. Peabody. "At breakfast he talks chiefly about going to Egypt where they mean to go for the winter. He is very nervous and tired, his hands twist and move all the time, and when he sits cross-legged he jiggles his feet. Then he went off to arrange with Mrs. Brooks who is to be taken out of turn [for a portrait] after all."

Despite his vinegary tongue, Sargent was always a diplomatic guest. When Sally Fairchild said one day that she "couldn't bear Dickens," Sargent said he was so glad to hear her say so, that he couldn't either, "but I should never have dared say so. I thought one was always set down as a bad character—something terrible—if one didn't like Dickens."

Sargent's light, sophisticated judgements extended to music—to everything, in fact. He played new, "serious" compositions on the piano with apparent ease, often disparaging the composer afterwards. Having been told an anecdote about a young woman ill-treated by her father Sargent laughingly "suggested state aid in teaching unfortunate children to rebel—a farm for vicious or neglectful or malignant parents, and so on."

Lucia wanted his seriously-held opinions and sometimes succeeded in getting them: "He thought [Thomas] Dewing and [Augustus] Saint-Gaudens fell into wanting something angelic, far away, and thin; the real, flesh and blood rustical thing (which of course was the point) not being good enough for them etc. He spoke of the Helleu picture of Mrs. Gardner's as very fine, one of the best pictures in Boston, and said, 'Did you notice in the hand the wonderful lilac fingernail? That's fine—that's what [Abbott] Thayer couldn't do, and to paint a dirty fingernail like that is better than any madonna's halo.'"

Sargent's admiration of Monet became very clear to Lucia and, in literature, his reverence for Balzac, whose enormous and enormously ambitious work Sargent seemed to know well. He was shocked that Lucia had not read the Holy Bible and instructed her to do so.

In 1891 Lucia, Sally, and Lily met Sargent in Paris, and later Lucia went to England to visit the painter Edward Abbey and his wife when Sargent was also a guest there.

On a tour of the Louvre Sargent seemed almost to own the place. Lucia wrote, "The *Venus de Milo* he wanted to have turned in another way with the light to strike full on her front—he said he had an idea it would suit her better—but the keeper would not let it be done. What he lingered over the longest was the *Winged Victory*—looking at it some time from both sides—which he says he always has to do."

Of Ingres, Sargent said, "'There's a man you probably detest now, but you must learn to see how fine he is.'" Lucia continued, "What surprises one in Sargent is his charm and gaiety and friendliness; one always thinks of him as far off and critical, and immensely great." This day he was at his friendly best.

He led her to an Ingres painting of a girl in white seated on a blue chair. "'See how the shawl is brought over?' said he, 'following the line there—splendid composition—I suppose you don't like the color. Well, it is rather crude. Still, it is rather fine now, like a bit of enamel.'"

They came to a room with a ceiling piece painted by Sargent's teacher and mentor, Carolus Duran, who was the most respected academic painter of the time. Sargent said he had done a good deal of work on the painting. "'A man [Duran] having a big thing to do like that gets tired of it—all his pupils I rather think had a hand in it. See that old man in armor? I did him. And the dark figure to the right, that's Carolus himself.'"

"[Sargent] spoke rather slightingly of the Gioconda. 'That's the one they have written volumes about? What does her smile mean? What is she thinking about? Her "unfathomable" eyes and all that ? I must say her expression doesn't strike me as particularly profound, does it you?'"

Lucia was avid for these pronouncements, so concentrated on her artistic education that the diary reflects no interest in fashion, amusements, or young men.

During her visit at the Abbeys' house in Fairford, England, Lucia got more of what she seemed to want most from Sargent: "I was painting out behind the barn," she wrote, "and he came over to criticize. 'Very green, those trees,' he said. 'You're under the impression that trees in England are green—whereas they aren't.' I asked him, 'What color do you see them?' They were two fat trees against the sky. He said, 'Oh, much blacker and duller, don't you know. Just a matter of technique. I'll show you a much easier way. Trees aren't ever green against the sky—they are gray—or purple or whatever along the edge. I've seen that so often in English pictures—yellow trees in the fall with patches of *green* sky—because blue and yellow make green—absurd. As a matter of fact it always makes the sky look pink, doesn't it? I don't know why it should, I'm sure—but it certainly is the fact. Haven't you ever noticed with willow twigs—after all their leaves have dropped off when they are quite orange, how very pink the sky looks through them?"

Lucia wrote, and partially erased, "He is so great."

Like many children of American wealth, Lucia perceived that money created freedom to buy whatever was wanted and to move about in the world at will, but it did not make its possessors spiritually free, necessarily, nor automatically happy. In fact, the effect on her parents seemed the opposite of liberating, deferential as they were to conventions. She thought Sargent and other artists with whom she studied saw things with "fresh," clear eyes.

Lucia was certainly aware of Sargent sexually. She noted that he and Abbey were "immensely fond of one another," and that Sargent treated Mrs. Abbey with strictest politeness most of the time. "He doesn't like her at all." But Sargent never gave Lucia a glance of romantic interest.

She learned something interesting, something "professional" from Abbey during her stay. "'It must be funny,' said

Abbey,' to look at a thing and intend to do it just as you see it. Now I never do, you know. I am all the time looking at everything sort of through a mist, seeing how I can use it— how I can change it into something I want.

"'I don't believe those old fellows ever used models. I think they just got up and painted from studies—and from the way they wanted things to look.'"

Sargent seemed never to have heard Abbey express these thoughts. "'Really!'" Sargent said and fell into an apparent reverie. "'Really!' he repeated, and nodded over it."

Abbey's thought is a world of attitude apart from Henry Kirke Brown's advice to George to "Seek the truth," both objectively and in his own feelings, and is a long way from Ruskin's objective of "truthfulness to nature." In this period the Impressionists were winning admiration for a new kind of visual "truth," but the Beaux Arts academics like Carolus Duran, who were the dominant teachers and standard setters, had long since adopted something like Abbey's method. The academic work was "realistic," object by object, but the objects were chosen and placed in such a way as to dramatize or sweeten the subject matter—or titillate the viewer.

A large proportion of the paintings that won Prix de Rome Prizes at Paris's *Ecole de Beaux Arts* in the 1890s used realistically rendered mythological or fanciful scenes for pornographic effect. One winner that stays in my mind shows three nubile witches, naked except for their distinguishing hats, seen from below as they take off in flight on their brooms.

Lucia stayed in Paris for part of the winter of 1891,

painting, but with whom I do not know. HBF was there, too, for an entire year, studying with Raphael Collin of the Academie Colarossi. The Colarossi, like the more famous Academie Julian, had come into being to meet the increasing demand for art training. Students at these academies were being prepared to take a *Beaux Arts* examination that, if passed, would result in the conferral of a certificate of professional competence, impressive, it was believed, world-wide.

HBF had first gone to Paris with Agnes, Violet, and Arthur to visit the *Exposition Universelle* of 1889 of which it was rightly said by the director of America's exhibition of art that "Never before in such variety and quantity have the productions of the arts and manufactures been brought together."

Despite two major military defeats—Napoleon's at Waterloo and the more recent Franco-Prussian War—and despite turbulent, sometimes bloody politics from first to last, France had had the most creative century of any nation ever. It led the world in many ways: in the health sciences with the invention of pasteurization, vaccination, and the sewer sytems that made possible the growth of modern cities; in engineering with high-speed railways and the world-changing construction of the Suez and Panama Canals (the Panama project bought up in mid-course and finished by the United States); and inventions such as the automobile and motion pictures. In a few years the French would very nearly beat the Wright brothers into the air. Small wonder that the French novelist Jules Verne was foreseeing still more extraordinary machines, like the submarine.

Add to these technical accomplishments French productivity and innovation in literature and the arts, and it is not surprising that the American painter William Merrit Chase declared that he would "rather go to Europe [meaning Paris] than to Heaven," and that Henry James would write that Paris was "the center of all life."

No doubt the Fullers were impressed by George's being honored at the *Exposition*, and no doubt a message came across to HBF that a majority of the painters on display had been trained in Paris and that he would do well to study there himself. The Americans shown in the American pavillion included Thomas Eakins, Winslow Homer, James MacNeill Whistler, George Inness, Sargent, and others still celebrated today.

In *Paris, 1889* Judith Hayward explains in the catalogue section why George was the single dead American artist included:

"In the years after his death in 1884, a romantic aura surrounded Fuller. In part this stemmed from the fact that he had died at the peak of his popularity, which followed years of obscurity while he lived in isolation. After his emergence in 1876, Fuller was welcomed by the young European-trained artists affiliated with the Society of American Artists. These artists saw parallels between Fuller's regionalism and that of Jean-Francois Millet. More important to them was their idea of him as an artist who did not merely transcribe surface appearances but rather delved into the souls of his subjects. Further, Fuller expressed the essence of his subjects in the smokey tones and hazy forms that became characteristic of the Tonalist aesthetic, to which many of these younger artists would subscribe. In short, for many European-trained artists attempting to reestablish their roots, Fuller was a father figure who, not insignificantly, was also an American." Another critic, Barbara Weinberg, described George's and the Barbizon painters' work as "tonal poetry" as opposed to the "bombastic prose" of the Hudson River School.

HBF's will to find an approach to painting which was both distinctive and his own must surely have been strengthened by the general enshrinement of George— the more impressive for taking place in a foreign land— and by the revered presence of Sargent in Lucia's mind. He needed to find new aesthetic values, and a way to express new feelings.

The general message of the *Exposition Universelle* was that world unity and peace were realistic goals. This apparent idealism cloaked but could not cover the facts of an era of ruthless aggression and bloody colonial wars.

In the 1890s, to take an extreme example, some nine to eleven million Congolese died as King Leopold of Belgium "tamed" the Congo, making that territory not a colony of Belgium and subject to that country's laws, but his own private preserve, subject simply to the discipline of his Belgian army. While official news agencies avoided reporting the horrifying human costs of such colonial expansion news of it was current.

Emotionally, HBF sided with the world's underdogs. He despised the obliviousness of the wealthy to the brutality of means employed in the accumulation of their wealth. This would make it difficult for HBF simply to accept the notion that artists, to make a living, must act as the wealthy's servants. But who else would pay the artists?

HBF's mentor, Raphael Collin, together with many other academic painters of the time, came to be known as *Artistes Pompiers*—"Firemen Artists" because of the nearly ubiquitous presence in their canvases of otherwise naked mythological figures who wore distinctive, identifying headgear. Mercury's winged helmet is an example.

The men of the fire department in Paris wore helmets that were equally identifying, and the phrase *Artistes Pompiers,* a derisive thrust by a forgotten critic, stuck in the public's mind. Over time the phrase became affectionate as new art—the *Fauves,* for example—confused and outraged viewers, and in 1908 Collin's work was part of a group gallery exhibition that proudly took the title, *"Artistes Pompiers."*

More important to HBF than Collin's technical instruction was a new movement in the arts that had been born in Paris by manifesto in 1886, *Le Symbolisme,* Symbolism. The manifesto, written by Jean Moreas, declared that all art movements of the past had fallen into "senile decrepitude." Through copying and imitating past works, all freshness in art had been lost.

Symbolism proposed an art of ideas, "primordial ideas," which would be illustrated or suggested by what literally appeared on the canvas (or in a poem or novel). Landscapes, human activities—none would ever be presented simply for themselves, but only as visible evidences of their *affinites esoteriques avec des Idees primordiales*—their expression of underlying fundamental ideas. Through this manifesto, HBF saw a possible way of his own.

In Paris in 1891 Lucia marveled at the painting of Degas, Renoir and Pissaro, among other painters who had *not* been included in the French exhibition at the *Exposition Universelle*. Quite likely HBF marveled at them with her, but he was developing symbolist skills. His first solo exhibition, in Boston in 1894, included portraits of two fictional women, Hester Prynne of *The Scarlet Letter* and "La Belle Dame sans Merci," symbolic figures both. His two best known paintings, executed years later, are still more clearly symbolist: *Illusions*, which hangs in the Renwick Museum of the Smithsonian Institution in Washington, and *The Triumph of Truth Over Error*, which hangs in the Student Union at Principia College in Elsah, Illinois.

HBF went to London in the summer of 1891, both to see the sights and to try to make decisions about his future. Apparently in reply to a suggestion from Violet he wrote her, "Why Deerfield? There is nothing there for me."

He then returned to Boston to live with Agnes, Violet, and Arthur in the Brookline house. During the next two years, which were dominated by his and Lucia's difficult love affair, he would paint the paintings of his first exhibition, and he would try to imagine how he could support a wife to the satisfaction of her father.

He considered the possibility of portrait-painting. He could not know, then, that Sargent would later say of his own career that "portraiture was worse than enforced collaboration; it was vanity's butter." And, "A portrait is a painting in which there is something a little bit wrong about the mouth," which was Sargent's way of sneering at the greedy image-improvements demanded by his patrons. HBF had a clear enough idea, however, of the incidents that would inspire Sargent to speak these words and he had no desire to experience their reenactments.

Early in George's career he had made a living doing portraits that simply and straightforwardly memorialized their
subjects. In George's last years it had been fashionable for
Bostonians to commission "something of a portrait" from
him. But by 1891 family memorials were more likely to be
done by photographers, and the painted portrait had become a luxury for which few were willing to pay, and from
which those who were willing were expecting flattery
rather than "a good deal of a picture"—although sometimes they got it from Sargent and a few others.

Later on, HBF apparently made several attempts to do a
commissioned portrait but family legend has it he never
finished one. Some of the portraits he did paint simply
because he wished to paint them are of great interest. *Ebba
Bohm* in the collection of the San Francisco Museum of
Fine Arts is one.

A painter's ethics and aesthetics were not as troubling to
HBF that winter as Charles Fairchild's disapproval of someone with "no money" courting his daughter—never mind
that the young man's father had been a friend. Agnes Fuller
also believed that a man owed his bride an income that
could be counted on.

Thus prodded from two sides, HBF dreamed up so many
means of making money that Lucia wrote to him, "You are
like a Balzac in your schemes of getting a fortune!" She
schemed a lot, too.

In August of 1892 Charles forbade Lucia to see HBF for
six months. Lucia wrote HBF that she felt she owed her
father her "obedience" on this issue but she and Charles
had struck a deal: she and HBF would not see one another,
but they could correspond.

A great many letters went back and forth. Lucia's letters from Newport were often decorated with delicate, small drawings above the "Dearest Harry," showing what she saw through the window or across the room—sailboats at their moorings in the harbor, or a couch strewn with books and clothes. "I have been thinking of you and to you all the time," she wrote.

There was a road on which she habitually took a walk at twilight, "sometimes with a moon in the sky—and with you beside me—if I could remember not to look around and find that you weren't there." One evening Lucia had a "terrifying hallucination" in which Endymion, the moon goddess, came to her and explained that she, Endymion, and HBF were one and that he "belonged to her."

"My Dearest King," she wrote in another letter. "Don't talk about your faults. Pretend you haven't got any like a Prince, which you are."

In a later letter: "Don't you think I know the difference, King, between you and me? You are a God—Jupiter or maybe sometimes Apollo and Kali and Botticelli and Marcus Aurelius and I am your humble servant." She had gone too far, though, even allowing for wild infatuation, and HBF doubted.

The money question assumed an unhappy importance when, in Newport, Lucia was stricken with an episode of a malady she had intermittently suffered since adolescence. No doctor had successfully diagnosed or treated it, and sometimes she was bedridden for weeks with headaches, painful vision, and loss of strength, and now it happened again with new force. In the Fairchild household she would be limitlessly cared for, but if she and HBF were alone together?

HBF then had a money-making idea about which he was enthused. He would buy up New England farm furniture at auctions, refinish the pieces himself in a New York shop and sell them directly to customers.

Lucia was doubtful. The current taste was for the gilded and ornate rather than the rustic. "Do you mean to live in your furniture shop?" she asked. "And paint your pictures there, as well? Write me details of your plan."

Lucia now had a plan of her own. "Harry darling, what do you suppose. I have thought out the most splendidly cheap way to live in New York." They would live in his studio, and she would share studio space with other women painters. "I will get two schools to teach and coach private architectural scholars two or three evenings a week and if I can I will get portraits to do. I can make breakfast, we can each get our lunch separately and go out for dinner. Don't you think that's a good idea? Goodnight dearest dearest dearest."

In the same letter she could not resist telling him that a letter had come from an Englishman "and it is a proposal, after all," by which she felt "humiliated." Also, an eligible young man, a "thing," had come to call. He had chosen to explain to her the engineering of the transatlantic telephone cable.

Lucia found it impossible to keep her word to her father. HBF had moved to New York to appraise their opportunities, and in late November Lucia came down from Boston, ostensibly to visit Mildred Howells. William Dean Howells had moved to New York to become editor of *Harper's Magazine.*

Lucia believed she and HBF had a rendezvous at the corner of Fifth Avenue and fifty-eighth Street, but some-

thing had been misunderstood and, after an hour, a police-
man told her to move along. Contact was made, however,
and confidence restored. In December, HBF came to Boston and they met in Agnes's house in Brookline.

The meeting had the unfortunate effect of involving
Agnes in the relationship, and Agnes would speak her mind.
She was in some respects "progressive." She was wary and
disdainful of the "aristocracy of wealth in this country." But
as regards manners she was certainly Victorian.

After HBF's return to New York Agnes wrote him, "Violet and I did not like the idea of your skirmishing around
in the dark with any young lady, no matter how charming.
I have a friendly feeling toward Lucia, but am not inclined
to recognize anything clandestine."

On the first of January in 1893 Lucia wrote to her
father: "Had a note from Harry saying he would be glad to
announce the engagement any time." Lucia to HBF: "I love
you entirely, forever, no matter what you do." By way of
news she thought that HBF would not approve of the "literal" painting she was working on.

In all likelihood this painting was the historical panel,
measuring approximately ten by ten feet, that Lucia painted
on commission for the Women's Building of the World's
Columbian Exposition due to open that summer in
Chicago. Her *Women of Plymouth* depicts sixteen early-settler
women engaged in the habitual tasks of that time—spin-
ning, weaving, fetching water, teaching, child-rearing, and
so on—all of them handsome women who looked a little
too neatly and cleanly dressed to be wholly credible as pio-
neers. The painting now hangs in the Grange Hall at Plainfield, New Hampshire, a village next to "Cornish."

It is likely that Lucia's commission and the inclusion of her portrait of her brother Neil in the American art pavilion at the Exhibition had been proposed by one or more of her influential teachers, Dennis Bunker of the Cowles School, or H. Siddons Mowbray or William Merrit Chase of the New York Arts Students League where she had studied in the late 1880s. Lucia had been only twenty-two years old when the portrait was chosen and the commission conferred, and she was probably the youngest artist to be shown in Chicago.

In mid-January Agnes wrote HBF: "I must go to the Fairchilds and show some cordiality. I hope you will not hear of any plans for marriage until you can support your wife in some fashion. I think, dear, you have been in haste to run into grave responsibilities. Don't lose manliness and independence."

Meanwhile Lucia was writing him every day hoping they could announce the engagement February first. Wouldn't he come for a visit? Her mother, Lily, wanted to know him better. "It will be terribly humiliating for me if you refuse. It is a great deal more dignified position for you to ignore the way my Father has behaved than to show your resentment. Don't be unyielding, please, this one time—really, I must see you."

HBF paid the visit in early February and Lucia wrote him afterwards, "You are the most noble person I know. I have been thinking of you all the time since you left and how immensely I love you."

Agnes, however, wrote him that she was suspicious of the Fairchilds' feelings about the marriage. And, "Don't imagine that any woman can make things go [economically] for it comes back upon the man, after all."

Violet attended a formal dinner at the Fairchilds', which seemed a sign of family unification, but Agnes wrote HBF March sixth that "it is a serious matter to become engaged to a young woman, and a still more serious one to break it off. It would be better to let the thing die a natural death." Clearly, HBF had told his mother that he wished to end the engagement.

On March fourteenth, Lucia, apparently unaware that any such changes in their relationship were being thought of, wrote him to say, "Father has met with some tremendous reverses in business." Charles was, she said, "Blue."

In fact, Charles believed himself to be a betrayed and ruined man, and the shock permanently changed him. His difficulties were part of the Bank Panic of 1893, which had disastrous effects across the nation.

In the same letter Lucia wrote that she was coming to see HBF "quite openly" in April, but only five days later there began an emotional, epistolary dance that, it might be said, lasted forever.

"If you really feel," Lucia wrote, "that you are essentially solitary and that you never could share your life with anyone, why then we must give up all thought of marrying. It is the kindest thing you could do to tell me and break it off now." But, she went on, "I love you, my darling, and belong to you at any time."

Lucia did go to New York in April and HBF made her the "happiest she had been all winter." Returned to Boston and reassured, she could write him about the great Russian novelists and to complain that "the sweetness of the Unfinished Symphony is suffocating."

Agnes wrote HBF in late April that "it is considered a wrong thing to do, to jilt a girl." In the same letter she disapproved of the editorial policy of the newspaper Robert was working for as "narrow and partisan—discouraging in these times of progressive, independent thought."

Small wonder, perhaps, that weeks later Agnes should write HBF, "Your notes have been so distracted, so sprawly and crazy-looking I fear for your sanity."

On May twelfth Lucia left Boston for Chicago, believing "there was a clear understanding" between herself and HBF. She was going to install her own and other works at the Columbian, which had been dedicated in October of 1892, four hundred years after Christopher Columbus's first voyage, and which now would open for the only summer of its existence.

An immense "city" had been built on the shore of Lake Michigan, and stretching inland around dredged lagoons and waterways. Gondolas with their gondoliers had been imported from Venice to offer the visitors transportation, and other boats from other epochs and cultures were afloat there for decoration.

The architectural style of the immense campus was Beaux Arts Greco-Roman. Columns and cornices, friezes and heroic-scale statuary dominated the exteriors of the major buildings, but instead of granite and alabaster for materials, the white-painted walls were made of plaster on lathes of something like chicken wire.

To rival the genius of the Eiffel Tower, however, the steel-framed Manufactures and Liberal Arts Building's ten-story-high ceiling was held up by a novel and complex system of interlocking arches rather than by posts. Thus interior views were unobstructed for the 100,000 or more people who attended the grand opening.

One of the most important objectives of the Columbian

was to strengthen the unification of the United States. Rapid expansion westward had stretched to thinness the feelings of historical and cultural identity the Civil War had reaffirmed among its victors—the South was still a very separate region. The "Wild West" looked exotic and lawless to easterners, and the East, particularly the New York banks and the federal government, was often seen as "the enemy" to westerners. Thus the "Pledge of Allegiance to the Flag" was composed especially for the Columbian. Its text was prominently published, and it was frequently recited.

Every U. S. state and territory was repesented by displays of its attractions. The many exhibitions from foreign counties were welcomed both to show that America need not "bow to anyone" in its technical skills and artistry, and also to show the superiority of American life to the ways of more "primitive peoples."

Thus European art as represented in the various national pavillions was not obsequiously applauded by the press, or by the visitors. An imported and reconstructed thatch-roofed village from Dahomey populated by lightly-clothed Africans, and a tepee encampment of Plains Indians were expected to demonstrate how much better "we" lived than they. One critic pointed out that, on the evidence, "our negroes" lived far better lives than their cousins in Africa and should be grateful to be here.

In the choosing of juries to select the art for the American exhibition there was a controversy over whether there was a "sex line in art." The first jury lists showed no women jurors on either the regional or the final jury. That was changed, but more cosmetically than importantly. In the end more than one thousand paintings were exhibited. One hundred thirty-nine of the painters were women.

In the Smithsonian's extensive recent catalogue, *Revisiting the White City*, 1893 appears to have been a strong moment in American art, some might think it the best. The painters who now are likely to represent the period on museum walls seem all to have been present—Sargent, Cassatt, Whistler, Homer, Eakins, Twachtman, Vedder, and so on, and many whose names have faded nonetheless showed interesting work. Among the sculptors were Frederick MacMonnies, Augustus Saint-Gaudens, Herbert Adams, and Thomas Ball.

For Lucia to have been included in such company at age twenty-three must surely have been a great satisfaction, and since she stayed on in Chicago into July to work on the installation of the galleries—few of which had been ready on opening day—she had the pleasure of firsthand reactions. Then a letter from HBF brought her down.

She wrote him back July fifth, saying she could not believe he meant what he had written. "Truly," she wrote, "has love never 'sustained' you. I cannot go on like this. It is too embittering."

Within a week she was somehow assuaged (HBF's letters have been lost) and wrote to him, "Life is too short and too serious for us idly to permit these misinterpretations." Not much later the entire eruption became her fault. She wrote that she hadn't realized until that month how "weak and hysterical" she was. "I am very sorry for the things I have done wrong, and to have behaved so without perception or nobility."

Lucia met HBF on her return to the East and afterwards wrote, "I am so glad after all that it happened. I think that we shall both of us be slower to doubt one another's affection another time." By mid-September the wedding was being planned.

Lucia was in Boston, HBF in New York. She wrote him that she agreed that only their two families should be invited to the wedding. Three days later she wrote that her father, however, was "conventional," and that he had decided he must visit the Fuller house "or people will think they [Lily and Charles] oppose the match."

Family pressure began to accumulate that the wedding be a "proper" one—Lucia wrote that the family had been "very hurt" by her and HBF's reclusive plans. Soon, she begged HBF to "do the thing" as her family wished.

The oldest of Lucia's brothers, Charles Junior, said to her, "You'll wait until after the Yale game, I suppose." Tickets for the Harvard-Yale game were offered Lucia and HBF as a recompense for any bad feelings created by the postponement.

Lucia now made a fateful pledge: in order to prove her seriousness and thus garner her family's approval, she vowed that she and HBF would accept no money from her parents during their lifetimes.

To prove his own seriousness, HBF came up with a splendidly romantic, economic plan: directly after their marriage he and Lucia would go to Deerfield to live in the studio-chaise-house George had built across the road from The Bars. HBF had already partially winterized it, and he would finish that work and then do repairs to the farm buildings as Spencer's employee. At the same time he would finish work on another project already started—the construction of a gypsy-style "caravan," a house on wheels that would be drawn by a team of horses.

His and Lucia's plan was to hitch up the horses once the weather turned warm and travel forth from Deerfield. They would move slowly from town to town, parking where the horses could be watered and fed and where, too, HBF's and

Lucia's talents, primarily as portrait painters, could be pub-
licized by the attention the caravan was sure to attract. They
would do whatever artistic work was offered them, then
move to another town. Their goal for the summer of 1894
was eventually to reach Cornish where an art colony was
coming into being around the presence of Augustus Saint-
Gaudens, who many thought to be America's finest sculptor.

In the mid-1880s an art-loving New York attorney, Charles
Beaman Junior, bought up a number of properties in Cornish—the decline in farming made them cheap. And in
1889 he had rented one of them, an abandoned post house
near his own summer place, to his friend Saint-Gaudens.

This building and its grounds were situated above the
Connecticut River and faced the beautiful Mt. Ascutney
on the river's Vermont side, and Saint-Gaudens, who had
grown up on the tough streets of New York, became excited and inspired by his new surroundings. He bought the
place from Beaman in 1891, renamed it "Aspet," and set
about constructing a fully equipped studio. Beaman was
soon finding and selling other properties at low cost to
other artists who wished to follow Saint-Gaudens's example, and HBF and Lucia hoped to find such a place for
themselves for the winter of 1894.

A year before his and Lucia's wedding in late 1893 Agnes
gave HBF somewhat more than two thousand dollars as his
share of a Higginson family inheritance. Perhaps that would
have amounted to fifty thousand dollars today. Shortly after
the wedding Agnes made HBF a loan, presumably to finish
work on the caravan. It was an omen of HBF's fiscal acumen.

As planned, Lucia and HBF moved into the Deerfield
studio after their wedding, and HBF went to work both for
Spencer and on the completion of the caravan. In March

HBF's exhibition opened in Boston, and some two weeks later Agnes sent him a report.

The reception of his work was respectful but not over-whelmingly favorable. "A Mr. Silsbee has written an enthu-siastic article," Agnes wrote. "Uncle Wentworth [Higgin-son] made the negative criticism that the people in the paintings 'looked like models,' but he does not know about paintings. We want very much to see your car [the caravan] which has got into the newspapers now."

No sales of HBF's paintings were reported.

Agnes concluded, "I have no doubt you will grow and improve as you go on. I am sure you will gain strength, courage."

In late May Lucia and HBF waved good-bye to the people at The Bars and set off northward in the caravan. They disappeared out of sight and went forward for miles and for days, but they did not get very far.

My mother, who became HBF's daughter-in-law, said that HBF had designed the caravan wrong, that the diam-eter of the wheels was so small the underside of the cabin scraped the roadbed at the crest of every rise of ground. Another Fuller-family explanation was that the caravan had been built too heavy, that too-solid framing, interior cabinet work, and the art equipment had made the rig impossible for a team of horses to pull over the sharp hills north of Deerfield that led into the Green Mountains. For whichever reason, perhaps both, the caravan was aban-doned well short of Cornish, and Lucia and HBF returned to The Bars. Three years later, Arthur Fuller went north with horses to bring the caravan back to the farm, but he did not succeed in doing so.

In the fall of 1894 HBF and Lucia, pregnant with her first child, Clara, went instead to New York and found an apartment in Greenwich Village. They had already sent "barrels of furniture" from The Bars to storage in Windsor, Vermont, across the river from Cornish, where they had rented a house for the following summer.

Agnes wrote them in December that she hoped Lucia would be "very careful not to overtax her strength," and, in January, that she knew HBF and Lucia had "good courage about the coming event, do not be frightened, remember what a common, everyday occurrence it is."

What Lucia or HBF may have accomplished artistically that winter is not clear, but she, browsing in an antique shop, found some miniature portraits that appealed to her, and this chance encounter would change their lives.

While for Nathan and Caroline Negus and Augustus Fuller miniatures were routine performances for any working painter, Lucia had to research their materials and technique. Miniatures had fallen out of favor in mid-century, and now Lucia with some other artists following her lead would revive their popularity. Her mastery of the genre was quick, and her success with it would become the family's main source of income for the next fourteen years.

Clara was born without difficulty on March seventeenth 1895. Two days later Agnes wrote predicting that the child would be "a new and original type, a young woman of immense strength, a famous bicyclist," perhaps. "Just think of it, Harry, she will inherit your car."

The Fullers did not, in fact, go to Cornish that summer. Instead they occupied a house offered to them by Abbott Thayer, the reigning talent of another, similar art colony at

Dublin, in southern New Hampshire. It is quite likely that Thayer did not own the house he assigned to them. He had a way of commandeering the resources of others for ends he thought justified. The furtherance of artistic objectives had all the prerogatives at Dublin, as it did at Cornish.

The town of Dublin lies on the shore of a lake and at the base of Mount Monadnock, whose peak reaches higher than any other in the immediate region. It had an important symbolism to Emerson and Thoreau, who could see its peak from Concord on clear days, and who had both climbed and camped on it.

Emerson's poem "Monadnock from Afar" reads in part:
"Well the planter knew how strongly
Works thy form on human thought
I muse what secret purpose had he
To draw all fancies to this spot."

Nobility of aim, aspiration to the highest were the "fancies" Monadnock inspired in the transcendentalists. They believed they were in the tradition of the Indians who named the mountain Monadnock, "Dwelling of the Great Spirit."

The transcendentalists had been followed there by visual artists who were seeking the fulfillment of their own lofty ideals. The painter Barry Faulkner wrote of Thayer and the Thayer family, "Monadnock was their totem, their fetish, the object of their adoration. They surrendered themselves to the sorcery of its primitive being."

The summer colony of intellectual and artistic Bostonians had begun to form in Dublin after the Civil War, Agnes' cousin Thomas Wentworth Higginson being one of the first and most faithful members. It remained small, select, and serious. Those not practicing an art continued in the study of the mountain's flora and fauna that Thoreau had initiated.

The Fuller's second child, my father Charles Fairchild Fuller ("Chas") was born in New York January eleventh 1897. By then Lucia's career as a fashionable painter of miniature portraits had caught on.

In other family news, Violet had come to New York to study at the Art Students League and met Augustus Vincent Tack who taught there and who painted a portrait at this time of Violet's aunt, George's half-sister, Lizzie Abercrombie. Arthur was playing football on the Harvard team and had been published in the *Harvard Lampoon*. And a Boston newspaper thought it newsworthy that Lucia's sister Sally had occupied a box at the performance of a play—Agnes sent the clipping.

Despite what Lucia remembered as her "idolizing" of Sally in childhood, there was a lifelong friction between them. From the first, letters to each other were formal in tone, and Sally's were often impatient-sounding or scolding. In this period she often described the Fairchild household as "quite desperate" about money, and she reminded Lucia a number of times of her pledge not to accept Fairchild money. Sally wrote, "If you had a husband who could support you. . . . Do not even think of asking for help at this time. . . . We cannot afford even the cheapest seats at Symphony this season." And she would sign herself off, "Faithfully yours, Sally Fairchild."

From this distance in time it is infuriating, touching, and saddening to read the letters of Lily Fairchild and the grown-up Fairchild children, which, in all the years that followed Charles's economic crash of 1893, are mainly and continually laments about money. It is true that they no longer had their "usual" seats at the Symphony, but they maintained a proper, expensive, Victorian front. They occasionally sold works of art but it was never suggested that they should abandon the most important symbols of their wealthiest days.

The family continued to live in the house on Commonwealth Avenue with a staff of servants. They kept the Newport "cottage," and both the houses were decorated with valuable art. The children were educated at the best schools, and Sally herself seemed to have limitless vistas before her.

Lord Bertrand Russell, the English mathematician and philospher, wrote in his *Autobiography* that Sally "was an aristocratic Bostonian of somewhat diminished fortunes, whom I first came to know in 1896 when we were staying in Boston. In the face she was not strikingly beautiful, but her movements were the most graceful that I have ever seen. Innumerable people fell in love with her. She used to say that you could always tell when an Englishman was going to propose because he began: 'The Governor's a rum sort of chap, but I think you'd get on with him.'"

Indeed, Sally had rejected a marriage proposal from one of Russell's own eccentric cousins.

Then, Russell wrote, "In the summer of 1899 she paid a long visit to Friday's Hill [Russell's estate, where he was living with his first wife] and I became very fond of her. I did not consider myself in love with her, and I never so much as kissed her hand, but as years went by I realized she had made a deep impression on me, and I remember as if it were yesterday our evening walks in the summer twilight while we were restrained by the strict code of those days from giving any expression to our feelings."

Sally never married. She was her mother's confidante and companion until Lily's death in 1924, shortly after which Sally wrote a pathetic letter to Lucia describing her own sudden realization that she had never to that moment had a life of her own. At the age of fourteen she had vowed to look after and please her mother so long as Lily should live, and in her fifties, Sally felt ill-equipped for any other life.

She was a formidable person, however, and she did recover. When I, age eleven, met her in Boston in the late 1930s she lived with a silent, uniformed Japanese manservant and two surly Pekinese dogs. Ten years later, when I was a student at Harvard, her servant and one of the dogs had disappeared, but Sally was cheerful.

One evening a man of perhaps forty-five was at her apartment when I arrived to call, then quickly left. Not long after his wife sued him for divorce, naming Sally, who was in her seventies, as his lover. When someone [not timid I] asked Sally how she felt about this she replied she felt just fine. "If that young woman can't hold her husband, that's her lookout."

By 1897 Cornish had become a kind of dream place for artists. The majority in the colony were either painters, sculptors, or architects of buildings and landscapes, but there were composers, novelists, and dramatists as well. Actors, producers, and editors—the famous Maxwell Perkins for one—would soon be added, and, in Cornish's declining years personalities of all sorts, including President Woodrow Wilson, came for summer stays. Today a few writers are Cornish's luminaries. Louise Erdrich and J.D. Salinger live there.

In its prime Cornish was described by one of its residents as a "state of mind" rather than a genuine place, and this had some basis in fact. It was not an incorporated town, and it did not have a post office. Its undefined acreage lay across the river by covered bridge from Windsor and south of the farming community of Plainfield, New Hampshire, a chartered town since 1761. One "member" of the colony—which was not a structured organization in any conventional sense, having no rules or bylaws, officers, elections, or other procedures—had printed on her stationery: "Post Office, Plainfield. Socially, Cornish."

There was no exhibition space at Cornish and no formal art instruction was ever offered. The artists had come to refresh themselves and to work on their own projects, rather than to carry on the customary business of art. That took place in the winter in New York. A direct rail line connected Cornish to the city.

There was ample space in Cornish for the artists to find privacy. When Charles Beaman had first come there he had created an icepond by damming "Blow-me-down Brook" with the objective of helping the dairy industry, but nothing could slow the decline of local agriculture. Beaman continued to buy up land, on which artists were welcome to choose sites. At his death, Beaman owned more than two thousand acres.

Saint-Gaudens and his painter-wife Augusta were then in full career. In his first Cornish years he was working on New York's monument to Admiral Farragut and the *Standing Lincoln* of Lincoln Park in Chicago.

Thomas Dewing who had been a friend of Saint-Gaudens's both during his Paris Beaux Arts years and in New York, was the first to follow his friend's lead, together with his photograher wife Maria. George de Forest Brush set up his studio soon after, and friends began attracting friends. It became something new in America, a rich and powerful artists' colony.

By 1905, perhaps the zenith year of Cornish's prestige and influence, some forty artistic families were in residence, either summers-only or, like the Fullers, "chickadees," so-named for the small birds that do not migrate but remain through the harsh and long New England winters.

Cornish's visual artists shared the French academic view that ideals of beauty were the objective. To generalize from their work, women were the most beautiful subjects for painting or sculpture, then children, men, and nature. A far-off mountain was beautiful and inspirational but nearby fields were not interesting in a natural state. They should be transformed into something more designed and artistically planted. The flower gardens of Cornish became famous and landscape architect Ellen Shipman and others became well known.

By the end of the 1890s the houses and gardens were becoming really grand as the fame and income of the artists grew. New arrivals were likely to be already rich.

In 1899 the best-selling American novelist Winston Churchill—no relation to the British prime minister who signed his books Winston S. Churchill to avoid confusion with the then better-known American—commissioned Cornish architect Charles Platt "to design a grand mansion in the Georgian tradition with a walled courtyard and a half-moon terrace facing Mt. Ascutney on a high bluff above the Connecticut." It would be named Harlakenden House and would contain "a great hall in the center of the house, a music room which occupied most of one wing, an isolated study for its master, and a separate wing for guests." Perhaps this was the grandest house, but it was far from alone in its aspirations.

No sooner had the Fullers moved into the modestly proportioned farmhouse they had bought on the north-south highway in Plainfield than it burned—not entirely, but enough of it was destroyed so that HBF could rebuild it into something "Italianate," with columns and a red-tiled roof. The house not only became handsome but a summer "community center," as Clara Fuller later described it, by virtue of a small swimming pool dug out where the front porch of the farmhouse had been and walled off for privacy from the road. The dirt from the pool's excavation provided fill under a two story studio with perfect, north light that HBF designed and built.

Agnes wrote HBF from Boston: "I am so glad you find yourself with pleasant, congenial people, that is really the most of life. Saint-Gaudens's monument here [the bas relief on the Boston Common of the African-American soldiers marching off to the Civil War] is so fine and full of feeling that it makes me love him." Agnes hoped the baby was "getting used to this sad and dreadful world." In the light of all of HBF's work of construction, she wondered if he could see his way "to do some painting."

Other full-time residents included the neighboring Maxfield ("Fred") Parrishes. Like HBF, Parrish had had a painter-father, although not one so renowned as George. The two families were relatively young and low in the Colony's pecking order, and both had to find unglamorous commissions to survive. Lucia traveled frequently to do her miniature portraits, and Parrish did illustrations for popular magazines, books, and advertising art. His paintings for full-page Mazda light bulb ads look both charming and ridiculous today—he depicted the most beautiful gods of Mt. Olympus working for the electric company.

The Parrishes and the Fullers thus had much in common, and they entertained one another and joined in projects. I possess a Parrish poster, about four by five feet, for a childrens' production of a play based on *Ivanhoe* by Sir Walter Scott. According to the meticulously lettered text Lucia made the costumes, HBF constructed the set, and Clara and Chas were actors in the production.

Two vintage Parrish heralds, one at either side, are holding up and displaying the text. They are wearing jewel-encrusted belts—designs in glittering stones glued to the poster's cardboard backing—an indication of the seriousness with which such projects were undertaken.

Adult *tableaux vivants* and masques were important features of the Colony's social life. There were no city-style events to go to so the members entertained themselves with pride in their originality and their serious execution of decorations and sets that only they, the members, would see.

The Dewings organized the first *tableaux vivants* in which members and local people were cast as figures in famous paintings by great Renaissance-or-later artists. Costumes were made to duplicate as nearly as possible those shown in the paintings, backgrounds were painted on large canvases, and the actors were posed with the required props in an effort at strict versimilitude. Adjustments in pose and costume were made over weeks of preparation, and then several *tableaux* would be unveiled in a single, grand social evening at one or another of the houses.

Parrish made a permanent theatrical set for the stage in the Plainfield town hall. He painted a number of "drops" and "flats" that had an interesting technical feature: by changing the intensity of the stage lights their colors could be made to change, rather than simply becoming lighter and darker.

While the Parrishes and Fullers were close friends there was a difference between them that the Fullers thought important. When my father told me as a child who Maxfield Parrish was he described Parrish as "an illustrator" while the Fullers were "fine artists." Once, when Parrish was asked what the difference was between a fine artist and a commercial artist he dryly replied, "About twenty-five thousand a year." Ironically, of all the artists whose names are associated with Cornish, Parrish's is probably the best known today.

There were a number of such distinctions to reckon with in the Colony, and there were lots of arguments. Thomas Dewing was reputed to have had the sharpest critical tongue, and he sometimes delivered harsh judgements in the form of a witty and feared "nugget," but in 1897 words failed him at an interesting moment. George de Forest Brush, who earlier had lived for several years among the Plains Indians, erected a tepee on Saint-Gaudens's land where it would be most visible to Colony members and plastered its walls with slogans in support of Henry George's "Single Tax" campaign for governor of New York. Dewing, incensed, burned the tepee down, and not long afterward the Brush family moved to Dublin in search of "peace."

One day, eight years later, Dewing said incredulously to another artist that he had just seen "men with tennis raquets" walking on the road near his house. Not long after, the Dewings moved away to more primitive Maine.

In different ways both the Dewing and the Brush families were eccentric and idealistic. Neither would send their children to ordinary schools, both for fear of "germs" and because they believed that the existing schools were suppressing and ruining the natural originality of their students. Both families were concerned with industrial toxins and wanted fresh air and water. And each had a distinctive and affecting vision of beauty.

Dewing was worldly. "Everything away from New York is just camping out," he said. Brush wanted to be above material wants and the worries of the marketplace. According to legend, Brush would put the money his paintings earned into a bowl on the family's mantelpiece, and every member of the household was told simply to take from it for whatever he or she needed.

A young sculptor named Frances Grimes came to Cornish in 1894 to be a summer assistant to sculptor Herbert Adams, and in 1901 she became a year-round assistant to Saint-Gaudens. In her brief memoir, "Reminiscences," she wrote that in the early Cornish years "everything else was subordinate" to artistic work. "It was the rule that no one ever paid a visit in the morning or before four o'clock in the afternon. This rule was broken when an artist was invited to see another's work for criticism or consultation, these were weighty visits, visits of state.

"The artists had parties and dinners planned days beforehand, and were always for eyes to look at more than affairs where friends met to talk. Palates were considered too (artists are usually interested in food and many of these young people were lately returned from Paris where they had learned the charm food can have even in inexpensive restaurants.)" The food, Grimes wrote, was reminiscent of French cuisine, and, later, some kitchens became Italian.

At the peak of Cornish's fame the newer arrivals, patrons rather than themselves artists, were eager to learn and imitate the ways of those who had attracted them to the place, and they began to present *tableaux vivants* at dinner parties in their own "philistine" homes. The custom of *tableaux vivants* then quickly died among the artists. "The word 'philistine,'" Grimes wrote, "was pronounced at Cornish as I have never heard it elsewhere."

According to Grimes, the most specific-to-Cornish entertainments were "the 'charades' They expressed the spirit of derision which was constantly woven with serious comment on art in the talk. No one has ever been able to describe these charades, as all depended on seeing the faces and gestures of the actors, and catching the improvised words as they came spontaneously, flashes of wit struck off at the moment, and not to be reproduced. The ideas were settled on beforehand, and the general scheme decided on, and sometimes the costumes—but what was said or done depended on what came into the actors' heads as they revelled in their idea, enlarged on it, and vied with each other in presenting it as absurdly as possible. Fred Parrish, Harry Fuller, and Charles Platt were the best at this game. I have never heard such laughter as I heard at these 'charades.' The audience was as carefully selected as the cast."

As for the domestic arrangements of the Cornishers,

Grimes wrote, "Most of the artists had one servant in the house and a man to take care of the horse and mow the lawn. The women did much of the gardening." Bicycles gradually replaced the horses.

"The women were all proud of their husbands' work, each household was more of a unit as presented to out-siders than households are now. Victorian standards were, even here, the rule when it came to what was considered presentable. Unconventional they were, but also in a way formal, with a chosen formality like that of their pictures."

Although money was a continuing and sometimes ser-ious concern in the Fuller family, and surely in others, it was a subject never spoken of to outsiders. Grimes remem-bered its mention only once, when Maria Dewing said that the Dewings couldn't possibly afford to keep a Dewing painting in the house.

In their own eyes the Cornish artists walked a narrow and elevated path. Beneath them on one side were the "Philistines," the patrons who sustained them by buying their work but who lacked culture and taste, and beneath them on the other were the "natives," the people of Wind-sor and Plainfield who sustained them by doing the neces-sary menial tasks and hard labor.

In *Choice White Pines and Good Land,* a History of Plain-field and Meridien, New Hampshire, written in the 1980s by fifty-six contributors in the region, this is what is said about the relationship between the artists and the "natives":

"'Little New York,' as the Colony was sometimes re-ferred to had a profound effect on the economy of the community. Local people, 'natives,' as they were called were hired as carpenters, chauffeurs, gardeners, and caretakers.

Women did housework, laundry, and cooking as well as waiting on tables for elaborate dinner parties. Colony people bought their vegetables, meat, and eggs, milk, and butter from local farmers. The 'natives' also earned a little extra income by opening their homes to boarders." And a few of them served as artists' models.

"The 'natives' were glad of the extra income, but at times resented the demands and snobbery. Social contacts between the townsfolk and the Colony were few and far between. The farmer was up at dawn and to bed early while the lifestyles of the artists drew them late into the night. The Victorian attitudes of the time also prevented employers from socializing with the hired help. Although one Cornish 'native' would muse, 'They wiped their feet on us a little,' the income from the Colony was too good to pass up."

Grimes wrote, "The Cornish children created a constant standard in our minds for all children. I still believe that there never were such lovely, interesting, well brought up children as these."

Likely enough, they were. Few groups of children have ever been so encouraged intellectually and artistically. They were taken very seriously and instructed and coached at the highest level of professional and artistic competence. A great many of the cultural elite of the time, from New York's Judge Learned Hand to Samuel Clemens to Ethel Barrymore, came to Cornish to contribute to the projects and entertainments—what could have been more propitious for the children's precocious development? But some of them, perhaps many, would pay prices for growing up in a small society so self-congratulatory that it found it natural to patronize or disdain virtually everyone else alive.

The Colony's hubris reached an extraordinary peak in the summer of 1905 when the celebration and Masque were organized to mark the twentieth anniversary of Saint-Gaudens's first visit to Cornish and the opening that day of his new and grand studio designed by Stanford White.

The form of the event was dreamed of and discussed for many months, and in February of 1905 HBF wrote to Lucia in New York that "a new idea" for it had been decided on.

The production was called "A Masque of Ours," subtitled, "The Gods and the Golden Bowl," and it was presented one summer afternoon at the western edge of a broad field below Aspet. The backdrop between the stage area and the high white pines of the bordering forest was a permanent Doric-columned temple dedicated to whatever gods or goddesses one chose.

No script of the masque has survived, and perhaps there never was one, although the play is credited on the program to Louis Evans Shipman, then a well-known playwright, and a prologue was written by dramatist Percy MacKaye. Music had been composed by Arthur Whiting and was performed by members of the Boston Symphony Orchestra.

If there were, in fact, only stage directions rather than a script to recite, it would seem a perfect symbol of the colony members' self-regard. Parts to be played included Venus, Jupiter, Priam, Apollo, Neptune, Juno, Ceres, Diana, and Minerva.

The spectators were certainly expected to laugh at the mock-heroic gestures, evident in photographs of the masque, and surely the language was mock-heroic too, but while the actors courted laughter they fundamentally believed that if anyone had a right to impersonate these gods, they did. After all, they were the artists who had brought these gods to America and established them here in the homes of the "robber barons."

The American neoclassicists, Cornish or other, had, in fact, claimed more immortal territory than even their European counterparts, using Asian, Native American, and Mayan deities as well as the Greco-Romans. Mainly, however, the interiors of the new mansions in America's industrial cities became Elysian fields. Goddesses now served as newel posts for the bannisters, lamps were held aloft by bronzes of Hermes, luscious nymphs reclined on the walls of more intimate quarters, and cupids might be shooting their arrows from many points.

Surely, *surely* the artists who were so often required to explain to their clients who Hermes was and what Leda was doing with the swan, were superior in culture to these ill-educated, American "aristocrats of wealth" whose fathers in many of the legendary histories had been horse thieves, and their mothers chambermaids and whores. "Philistines," they were, almost to a man and woman, the artists believed, ignorami who could be saved from public ridicule only by the tutelage that great artistry brought into their homes and the help the artists might give them in understanding it. They would have been poor lost children without such aid, and there were many who lacked the wit or time to comprehend the worth of what was being provided to them.

The concept of the masque was that the gods of Mt. Olympus heard rumors of the wonders of beauty being created at a community on earth called Cornish, wonders that might rival those of the palaces of Mt. Olympus itself. Zeus dispatched a party of deities to Cornish to investigate.

Who should better impersonate Pluto than the painter Kenyon Cox? Chronos was played by Charles Platt, Iris by Frances Grimes. Lucia was cast as Proserpina, HBF both as Apollo and as "a Countryman" (presumably a "native"), the only mortal in the show. The entire cast numbered thirty.

At the climax of the spectacle a "roman chariot," built by HBF and decorated by Lucia, fetched Saint-Gaudens from his spectator's seat. Brought onstage, he was proclaimed by the assembled gods to be the new Zeus! The chariot, drawn by "slaves," then transported him to his new studio, where he was suitably enthroned as the entire audience, which had formed a procession behind the chariot, applauded.

No honor was likely to top that one.

Frances Grimes wrote that at Cornish "there were quarrels and feuds between old friends, complicated relations sure to arise among people so sensitive and vulnerable. I heard of them later, and they explained many things." Most of these troubles no doubt had to do with the respect, or lack of it paid to the artists' talents and to their specific works, but . . . Did Thomas Dewing have an affair with Lucia, who was his model for two well-known oils and a delicate, silverpoint portrait (now lost)?

Susan Hobbs, in *The Art of Thomas Wilmer Dewing, Beauty Reconfigured,* states unequivocally that "sometime during the spring and summer of 1901 Dewing had begun an affair with thirty-year-old Lucia Fairchild Fuller. Estranged from her artist husband the attractive and magnetic Lucia supported herself and her two children by painting miniatures." One piece of evidence Hobbs quotes is an "anguished" letter from HBF to Lucia, written in January of 1901, in which he complained of the influence another man had over her. Hobbs believes the Dewings absented themselves from Cornish during the summer of 1902 because Maria Dewing insisted the affair be ended.

Did HBF have an affair with the actress Ethel Barrymore, who rented the Fuller house in the summer of 1906 and "coached" the children in a performance of Thackeray's *The Rose and the Ring?*

Among Lucia's papers there is a bitter little handwritten poem from around this time that ends "Harry loves another," and there is a splendidly absurd document, "In Defense of Miss Barrymore's Virtue," by HBF, pages and pages of mock—legal blather, typed—surely a sign of great import—and addressed to a Cornish-resident lawyer who had apparently been critical. HBF did a pencil and pastel portrait head of Ethel Barrymore in which she certainly looks beautiful.

In a place where Beauty was given such supreme importance can it be surprising that it was found in the flesh? Fred Parrish had a child with his model, who lived for many years in an apartment in his studio. Saint-Gaudens, too, had a child by another woman than his wife.

Liasons, feuds, and entertainments notwithstanding, the Fullers and other Cornishers worked hard. Lucia's miniatures won awards at several world fairs and expositions. In 1899 she cofounded the American Society of Miniature Painters. In 1903 she made a note that she had completed her 191st commissioned portrait, which would seem to leave no time for other painting—but some "recreational" painting exists.

There is a small-scale nude of Lucia's in the Smithsonian's Museum of American Art in which the subject is
the Fuller's model, Ebba Bohm, posed by the Cornish swimming pool. In this same period Lucia produced an affecting
portrait of herself at work, *In the Mirror.* She is behind her
easel, wearing eyeglasses, hair wisping out of its bun, regarding herself with sober intensity.

In 1905 both she and HBF were elected Associates of the
National Academy of Design.

HBF had had a second solo exhibition in Boston in 1899
that was no more commercially successful than the first,
although the critics were kinder. His *Illusions,* which now
hangs in the Renwick Gallery of the Smithsonian, was finished in 1902. In it daughter Clara, some six years old,
standing naked and in profile, is reaching upward for a
crystal ball deliberately held out of her reach by a mature
young woman who perhaps should be named "Experience." She is more naked than naked, her body visible
through a diaphonous drapery. The two figures are standing
on a formal "Italianate" terrace, and beyond them in the
background is the Connecticut River Valley, whose agriculture has been made neatly European and extraordinarily
fecund, and the grand but formidable Mt. Ascutney. Experience's expression is serious, a trifle sad. This is not a game
being played. The woman is protecting the girl from the
ruder facts of life and the painting says she is right to do so.

More clearly dramatic in its symbolism is *The Triumph of
Truth Over Error,* which HBF painted in 1905-6 and which
won the Carnegie Medal as the finest painting included in
the National Academy of Design exhibition of 1907.

HBF's award was somewhat clouded by a rumor in circulation after the exhibition's opening that the painting was the work of more than one artist, that HBF had help with it. The controversy was deemed important enough to be reported in the *New York Times*. HBF declared to the press that he was happy to say that he had asked several artist friends, Everett Shinn among them, to give him their criticism at several points during the work's execution, and he publicly thanked them for it.

The painting's idea came from a text by Christian Science Church founder Mary Baker Eddy. The central figure is "Truth," an ideal woman who resembles both "Marianne," symbol of France who, bare-breasted, leads the soldiers of the French Revolution with sword in hand, and "Columbia," white-clad and glowing, holding the torch of freedom aloft.

"Truth," wearing a brilliant white robe, bare-breasted and winged, is standing on a rock ledge, chin raised and arms held wide. In her left hand she is holding not a sword but a scythe (to "cut away the thickets of ignorance"). Her right hand is banishing "Error," a man standing behind her who is also winged but is grayish-green in color. He is shrinking back from the "blinding light of truth," holding a hand up before his eyes to protect them from "Truth's" glare.

One of Mary Baker Eddy's commandments, inscribed on the wall of the Mother Church in Boston, reads: "When Error confronts you, withhold not thy rebuke."

Blue skies are "Truth's" background in the painting, and dark storm clouds his. The figures are life-size, the entire canvas measuring $8^1/2$ by 11 feet. HBF certainly used Ebba Bohm as a model, but there is something perhaps of Ethel Barrymore in "Truth's" face as well.

The doctrine of Christian Science had come into the Fullers' lives because of Lucia's increasing disablity, and her search for relief from the illness that had intermittently attacked her since adolescence. Recently she had fallen sick in New York and had been bedridden for nearly two months in the Murray Hill Hotel. At another bad moment HBF had written to Agnes that he believed Lucia "would not be able to use her eyes this winter"—the disease particularly affected her vision.

Since medical doctors had been of no help, Lucia had become interested in Christian Science and HBF had also read the texts. To what extent either of them truly believed and practiced Christian Science I cannot say, but both seemingly wanted to be believers. Later, both consulted physicians without apparent feeling of conflict.

Triumph was exhibited in a number of American museums in the years that followed its unveiling. It was awarded the Silver Medal for Painting at San Francisco's Panama-Pacific Exposition of 1915, which prompted some further showings in the eastern states. HBF invented a reproduction process at that time, "mellowtint etching," in order to print cheap editions of the painting.

Triumph had gained semi-official status among Christian Scientists since Mary Baker Eddy had praised it in a 1907 issue of the *Christian Science Journal:* "This decorative and instructive picture by H. B. Fuller is the *coup de maitre* of art inspiring its object; it startlingly portrays the soul's sense of Truth's Omni-Science, All-Science, and the nonsense of Truth's unlikeness, error."

HBF would be selling copies of his reproduction until the last month of his life, most of them to Christian Scientists in whatever place he happened to be. One nicely framed copy hangs in the downstairs bathroom of the Mansion at Yaddo, a writers' and artists' retreat in Saratoga Springs, New York. The founders of Yaddo, the Trask family of Brooklyn, were avid collectors of neoclassical art.

For several years during the 1920s, *Triumph* hung at the San Francisco Art Institute. In 1929 it was bought for ten thousand dollars and given to Principia College, the sole Christian Science institution of higher learning, which was then being built on a bluff overlooking the Mississippi River at Elsah, Illinois. The handsome, brick and stone campus buildings were designed by Bernard Maybeck, and his overall campus plan called for *Triumph* to become "the central feature in the south end of the Great Hall, in an alcove particularly designed for it and especially lighted." The Great Depression prevented the Great Hall's being built. When I visited *Triumph* at Principia in 1989 the painting was hung in the main corridor of a post-Maybeck brick-and-glass student union building.

In *Truth* the drama is stagey and the colors hard to believe, but the longer I looked the more I admired the painting: the palpable fragility of "Truth," combined with her equally palpable courage and strength; the painting's idea that truth and error are in an everlasting dymanic relationship, and that this can be demonstrated in a sort of dancers' duet. Where could this action take place, after all, but in some extraterrestrial scene whose colors would be arbitrary?

Dated? Yes, certainly, and impossible for me—and I am sure, others—not to smile initially, but what a grandly ambitious work! How beautiful is Truth!

In terms of art history, *Triumph*'s most significant moment occurred at its first showing. In 1907 the young painter John Sloan went to the annual National Academy Exhibition and in his journal called the prize-winning *Triumph* "absurd." That such a mock-classical overdramatization should have the gall to speak of Truth! Sloan's reaction was so clouded by anger that he wrote that the painting was by George Fuller rather than by HBF.

Sloan's reaction was prophetic. Following the feelings of Winslow Homer, who went to Paris but "did no work there," and of Thomas Eakins, who had studied for two years with Gerome in Paris but who rejected most of what he had been offered, younger Americans were turning against the Paris-trained artists. Eakins particularly spoke out for making American art from American materials, insisting that only by doing so could America create an art that was distinctively its own. Filling up Fifth Avenue mansions with the deities of ancient Greece and Rome was sheer and disgusting Europe-worship!

By 1910 John Sloan's point of view was, "Socialism or nothing." He wondered if the "Independents" exhibition then being planned could accept the patronage of anyone wealthy without being tainted. He, George Luks, Robert Henri, George Bellows, and others were seeking common but significant American scenes to paint—the "truth," perhaps, as Henry Kirke Brown urged it on George—rather than metaphorical, constructed scenes. What they accomplished became known as "The Ashcan School."

Some of the feelings of these men were distilled in Robert Henri's *The Art Spirit,* a collection of his talks over many years to his students at the Art Students League. A sample of Henri's down-to-earth thoughts: "The mind is a tool. It is either clogged, bound, rusty, or it is a clear way to the soul. An artist should not be afraid to know." And, "There are mighty few people who think what they think they think."

The skepticism, the insistence on clarity of vision that Henri expressed, the absence of talk about ideals, mythology, and symbols would increasingly dominate the collective artistic mind. The disillusioning horrors of the First World War would put an end to all visions of Elysian fields, of Parnassus and Olympus as potential American resorts.

Many of the Cornish neoclassicists would continue to do work that met their own high standards for many years, but their prestige, the general interest in their aims and methods, swiftly waned.

To the end of her life Clara Fuller would speak and write of her Cornish childhood as a model for any child's education, training, and enjoyment. She wrote that among her companions "there was no sex emphasis difference between us—no saying that little girls shouldn't do this, and that little boys always did that. We all went barefoot and in hot weather wore nothing but shorts, and in swimming together we wore nothing at all. We wrestled and raced, played tennis and baseball—in fact I, as first baseman, was enrolled as a member of the YMCA so that I might continue to play with the team in its out of town games."

Clara wrote of the theatricals and other events that "Our house was the great gathering place, ours had the only swimming pool." When Lucia was at home she regularly read aloud to the children. "She was the one we adored that all the Cornish children loved.

"When we were very little we were taken care of by a nurse; as we grew older she was succeeded by governesses

who not only looked after us but who taught us our lessons every morning—writing, spelling, French etc. Though
we lived with him we didn't see much of [HBF] when we
were little. He spent his days in the studio and though we
posed for him from time to time he worked mostly from
his and [Lucia's] model who also—together with the nurse
and cook—lived with us."

There was "one drawback," Clara wrote, "which I only
became aware of years later; we never played with the country people whose ways were not our ways—this in spite of
[Lucia's] conscientious attempt to make us democratic. To
this day I am as embarassed and self-conscious with the less
educated as many people are with negroes."

A very long jump had been taken from a childhood at
The Bars. Her childhood may have been all Clara said, but
by 1905 when she was ten there were certainly strains in
the Fuller household. In January of that year Lucia wrote
to HBF, "You don't understand! You hurt me very much—
you haven't understood at all!" He had said "kind things"
to her in hopes of "personal results," and she rejected both
the things he said, and him. Her letter talks of "friendship"
and "consideration," seeming quite unmistakeably to be for-
bidding physical love.

A poem of Lucia's, undated, but certainly from around
this time:

"O Harry, Harry, let me cry
For I am deep distressed
And gladly gladly would I die
To know a moment's rest
You said you loved me long ago
And now it is not so."

Lucia was ill more frequently. In late 1905 Agnes sent some money to HBF to pay for a trip of his to New York to seek commissions. Lucia was recuperating at Cornish, and Agnes wrote, "All success is before you now, my dear, and you must give yourself a little more latitude and freedom for the sake of your well-being." While Lucia was at home it was "a good time for [HBF] to go."

One or the other of the adult Fullers had often been gone from the house, and now this condition became the usual. When she was well enough, there were many commissions for Lucia to fulfill. When HBF was at Cornish *Choice White Pines and Good Lands* states that he often suffered "deep depressions."

Although Agnes described Clara in 1905 as a "young Brunhilde," implying great health and strength, Clara suffered during her mother's absences and often wrote to her, distressed. "Mother, I miss you every minute." "Oh, Mother, I miss you awfully. I am dying for the 18th" (the date of Lucia's promised return). "Only two more days before you're here again." "I want to see you!" This note of deprivation persists through her childhood.

Doubtless, Lucia wished to be a loving parent, but not only were her illnesses, her need to make money, and her relationship to HBF distracting her, events in the Fairchild family became increasingly upsetting.

By 1905 the career of Lucia's oldest brother, Charles Junior, was a disaster. In principle he was the conservator of the family fortune and he had inherited seats on both the New York Stock Exchange and the Corn Exchange. But Charles's wife was now writing begging letters from a succession of small New England towns to her Fairchild in-laws, including Lucia, saying, for example, that she needed money to buy warm winter clothing for her children. Charles, meanwhile, wrote letters on the stationery of the best New York hotels, saying such things as that he was "staying alert for any opportunity that may present itself," but that he had no fixed address at present. Clearly he had just walked in off the street to avail himself of the hotel's free writing materials. In her letters his wife conceded that Charles "leans on alcohol."

Later on, a younger Fairchild brother, Blair, would write to Chas that Charles (for whom Chas had been named) was a "scourge" and should be entirely avoided. According to Blair, Charles "did away with over a million dollars of Maman's fortune," and had had no right to sell the seats on the Exchanges. Blair, said Charles, was "not normal, mentally, so not responsible."

Lily sold a number of the Fairchilds' paintings in those years, including Homers, Sargents, and a Gainsborough. She maintained the Newport "cottage," partly because her husband Charles had apparently sunk into senility there. In one of her letters she reported that he "talks bad," and that he tore up all business correspondence without reading it.

In 1906, the Fairchilds got a terrible shock.

Younger son Neil, whose cheerful liveliness had made him a family favorite, shot himself to death with a rifle in Manchuria, where he had been posted as a United States vice consul. His death occurred not long after his arrival there via the trans-Siberia railroad from which he had written happy letters.

The other Fairchild family members, deeply threatened by this tragedy when many things were going badly for them, refused to accept the idea that Neil's death was a suicide. Responding to their pressure, the Boston newspapers reported Neil's death as accidental.

It was indeed mysterious. Neil's superior in Mukden wrote to Lily that he was dumbfounded. No acquaintance of Neil's was able to offer an explanation. Obviously, however, it is next to impossible if not entirely so to kill oneself with a rifle shot to the head "accidentally."

All the Fairchilds must have wondered what seeds had been dormant during their seemingly idyllic earlier years to lead to such disastrous events. More were to come.

Son Gordon, who had a degree in law, gave up its practice to become a teacher at St. Paul's School for Boys at Concord, New Hampshire. In 1923, Sally and Lily, then in declining health, were living with Gordon when he was discovered in a sexual embrace with a student and was fired by the school. Some months later Gordon wrote a farewell note, dropped over the side of a ferryboat, and drowned.

Charles Junior took his own life in 1933.

Son Jack created little news or gossip. He married, but the union was childless.

Blair was a "dandy" as a young man—always well-dressed, talented in music, and sharp of tongue. He married a rich young woman with a disfigured leg, Edith Cushing of Boston, and they lived in Paris from early in the century until their deaths in the late 1920s.

Blair was the happiest of the Fairchild siblings. He became a composer whose works never achieved popularity, but were respected and performed in both Paris and New York. Family hearsay and the tenor of his correspondence make a strong case that he was homosexual.

Blair was financially dependent on Edith. Once, when a sibling appealed to him for funds, he replied, "I am on an allowance from Edith like everyone else." His spirit was alive, clever, generous, and he and Edith lived well in Paris and a summer house in St. Jean de Luz. Yet when he became a Roman Catholic in 1918, he described his new faith as a "solace" that had saved his life.

In my generation the only living descendants of the seven gifted and vigorous Fairchild children are Lucia's grandchildren—my two sisters and I and our cousin, Lucia Taylor Miller, and our children.

In the same period that Lucia wrote her bitter poem, HBF was writing poems, too—perhaps everyone at Cornish did. Two are addressed to Lucia. Their attempt to be appreciative and fond seems a bit willed rather than wholehearted. Two others are addressed to "Renee," and while their tone is playful rather than passionate, and they do not imply that she, whoever she was, and HBF were having an affair, the poems' existence suggests that he was not being altogether careful of Lucia's feelings.

During the summers of 1908 and 1909, Agnes wrote letters to HBF that assumed his entire family was happily at Cornish, but in 1909 HBF wrote Lucia to propose that they indeed become "friends and companions," protesting that he had "no criminal motive" in so suggesting. He continued, "You are, as always, right. You have had a complete idea, always.

"Whereas the pain I cause brings you nothing but pain, the pain you glory in causing me is immeasurably greater because it [illegible] the greater loss, the loss of value. I am myself degraded in your degradation, not because you affect me egotistically but because while I live with you I am zero. I enter your life inevitably because I include you, whereas you do not include me. I am no more a part of your psychological existence than a chair."

His letter ends, "You will have little more to suffer from me."

Late in 1909 Lucia traveled to Vienna to fulfill a portrait commission, perhaps her last. She and HBF would never live together again for any length of time, but, interestingly, separation did not mean that they had made lasting enemies of each other. To the contrary, no sooner were they apart than they began a supportive and loving correspondence that only death would terminate:

"Your sweet, kind letter means a great deal to me."

"Dearest, I think about you continually. I love you sharply."

In 1917, "Dear, beloved Lucia, I have been so distressed all day to think I could have hurt your feelings or depressed you about the war that I must write another line tonight."

Lucia consistently praised HBF's talent and prospects. "Above all it is your work that counts, Harry."

As early as 1908 Lucia's letters were written in a cramped and shaky hand. Undoubtedly, she could foresee the end of her ability to paint and the vision understandably frightened her. Not only must she sustain herself, she became determined to find the money to provide her children with the best educations to be had in America so that they could achieve financial security and never, *never* consider becoming artists themselves.

Her message to the children on this score was unquestionably very strong: careers in the fine arts were disastrously uncertain. Do not think of it! Both Clara and Chas were visually gifted, but neither of them questioned her judgement.

HBF returned to Deerfield and moved into Agnes's Main Street house with her and his brother Arthur. Lucia went to New York to work for an interior decorator.

Over the following years the Cornish house was rented out to a succession of artist-tenants, painter Ernest Lawson and sculptor Paul Manship among them. In the early 1920s the house was in such poor condition that its use was apparently given rent-free to abstract painter William Zorach on the condition that he effect repairs.

Although Lucia's hand was uncertain and her eyesight failing she succeeded as a decorator. Within a few years she would have her own firm. Her work made ends meet immediately, but it would not pay her children's tuitions. Scholarships were sought and, more importantly—because private school financial aid was rarer then than now—help from Lucia's richer friends and patrons. Clara was sent to New York's Brearley School and Chas to Groton.

Clara, age fifteen in 1910, wrote a letter to Lucia, briefly absent from New York, about Chas's being suspended from Groton for an unnamed sin against the rules: "I think it is just what he needs and it will be a good lesson to him. Mother, if he doesn't behave himself as a *scholarship boy* should when he goes back again, won't you let me stop school next year and learn some kind of trade such as bookbinding and with my would–have–been–school–money pay for [Chas's] school? You see I've got a pretty good education now, and it's much more essential for a boy to be well-educated than a girl."

I suspect this offer had more than a bit of grandstanding

in it and that Clara knew there was no possibility Lucia would entertain the idea.

Three years later, when Clara was about to enter Bryn Mawr and Chas's college entrance was two years away, Lucia appealed to Agnes for long-term support. Instead of funds, Agnes provided the advice that if there was not enough money the children should be apprenticed, Chas to an architectural firm, for that was the field he had already decided on, and Clara where she wished—perhaps to Lucia's own decorating company. The rejection permanently embittered Lucia toward Agnes.

Lily was equally unhelpful, she and Sally having embarked several years previously on a very long, round-the-world trip that included temporary residencies in California, the Philippines, and Japan. They left New England having decided not to have the senior Charles declared incompetent, for "it would kill him," but believing he was adequately cared for. Charles died during their absence. They returned to America in 1914 after the outbreak of World War I.

When Chas entered Harvard in 1915 his bills were being paid with four thousand dollars contributed by the J. P. Morgan family and one thousand from Edith Cushing Fairchild. He had turned out to be an almost-perfect *"scholarship boy,"* having been an excellent student at Groton, the quarterback of the football team, and captain of the baseball team from behind home plate. He was to have held the position of "Senior Prefect" during his final year, but at some point during the preceding summer he had smoked, and he confessed this to the legendary headmaster Endicott Peabody on his return to the school. His prefectship was withdrawn, but he was allowed to complete his senior year and continue to Harvard, where his war-shortened career resembled his Groton successes. He was elected treasurer of his class, played freshman baseball, and was elected to the A.D. Club. Something ominous, however, had appeared.

In 1916 Chas wrote Clara, "I broke my rule about drinking on a stag party last night, and I'm very sorry indeed that I did. I shan't again."

Chas became the one hundred and thirty-seventh man to have U.S. Navy pilot's wings pinned to his chest in 1918, and he was stationed near London and flying submarine patrols over the English Channel when he wrote to Clara that he was spending all his money on "cigarettes and whiskey."

By that time Clara had discovered something of great importance about herself—that she was bisexual.

Clara had entered Bryn Mawr on schedule in the fall of 1913, but a year and a half later she wrote to HBF from Madison, Wisconsin: "I am sure I made the wisest and safest decision in deciding to come out here. I couldn't have stayed at Bryn Mawr and any other Eastern College would have been almost as bad. Here I am much happier. It is nice knowing my Fairchild relatives. They have been very kind." She had been in Madison one week.

In later years Clara told others that she had left Bryn Mawr because it did not offer courses in journalism, which the University of Wisconsin did, but no letters of hers from that time give this as a reason. At Wisconsin she did take one course in journalism together with a number of standard undergraduate courses, but she never worked as a journalist.

Clara married a professor of English at the university, Warner Taylor, in 1918. According to their daughter, Lucia

Taylor Miller, Clara told Warner of her sexual preference before their marriage, and he accepted the idea. He also accepted the residence in his and Clara's house of his mother-in-law Lucia, for whom work of any kind had become impossible.

Lucia's illness had finally been diagnosed in 1914 as multiple sclerosis. It was a new diagnosis, and the label did not improve her condition since no treatment had been found. Lucia's left eye was totally blind by 1918 and the sight in her right eye, dim, and when Clara's invitation came to close her business and move to Madison Lucia did not resist. She was not yet fifty.

Lucia was uncomfortable and unhappy with her disabilities but her situation did have some pleasures. Clara loved her enormously. Affectionate letters arrived regularly from HBF that included a monthly check. (Since HBF sometimes wrote to others during this period that he lacked the money to buy paints, the source of Lucia's funds was probably most often Agnes's income although HBF did work as a cabinetmaker, a painter of ornamental screens, etc.) In the social circle Clara created in Madison Lucia was honored as an important artist. Like her brother, Blair, Lucia converted to Roman Catholicism.

And in 1923 something wholly unexpected and pleasant happened—a letter came from painter Edward Simmons, an "American Impressionist" who had shown his work regularly for some years with Childe Hassam and the others of "The Ten." Simmons had by then become an architect, at which he had also succeeded.

Simmons had been known to Lucia in 1891 as "Sunny" when, as he wrote, he had fallen in love with her. He had always been in love with her, he said, although, of course, he had lived another life. He had been married twice and was the father of three. But he was a widower now and living at the Lambs Club in New York.

Lucia wrote him back. I have not found the letters, but much that was in them can be deduced from Simmons's replies.

She sent him verses.

He wrote with greater eagerness and frankness. He was jocular and heady. He recounted a bawdy experience in a French hotel. In due time Simmons began to press for a meeting, if not in Madison, perhaps in Chicago?

It becomes clear from his letters that Lucia was putting him off but that she was reluctant to put an end to the correspondence. Lucia reported minor illnesses and family complications, but Simmons no doubt sensed that their meeting was not to be, for his letters come to an end.

Mildred Howells wrote Lucia in November of 1923 on the occasion of the death of a mutual friend. Mildred had spent part of the previous summer in Cornish, and, she recalled, "We used to ride past your house in Plainfield, and it seemed so sad and wrong not to have you there. A great many of the Cornish houses were empty, and the spirit of it all was a little sad."

How quickly the glory of Cornish had faded! And in this same year George's Metropolitan exhibition had brought an end to his eminent reputation. Artistically, the nineteenth century had truly ended.

Sally Fairchild wrote Lucia in January of 1924 from Concord that "Mama has died." Although Lily believed in "going right on," she, Sally, was "staying at home for a few days."

At Lily's funeral Sally placed Neil's postcard of the Temple of Heaven in Lily's hand, "as she had always asked," and "laid the little silk American flag she never moved without, even for a night."

Some weeks later Sally wrote, "Since I was 14 and had that sudden and complete realization that all I wanted in the world was to be with her and help her when I could, my whole inner life has been in reference to her." Sally had always slept in the room next to Lily's and had checked on her two or three times a night. "I loved her and love her as a dog does," Sally wrote.

Lucia herself died three months later. The tone of her obituaries was respectful. Her eminent teachers were listed, the medals won at international expositions, her National Academy membership, and so on, but despite Lucia's relative youth her career already seemed as passé as Cornish in Mildred's assessment.

Agnes died that May in Brookline.

New and changed lives began for Sally, and for Clara and Warner. HBF's life was already transformed because Agnes had financed his going to Paris in 1923 to revive his artistic spirit. Once he was established in a Montparnasse studio he was joined there by his niece, painter Elizabeth Fuller.

Elizabeth, born in 1896, was the daughter of the late Spencer Fuller and Mary Williams Field Fuller and grew up at The Bars. Spencer died young in 1911 but this did not hinder Elizabeth's talent being recognized and her being provided art training, notably at the Boston Museum School. Through a family connection she became a protegee of Abbott Thayer's and spent several summers at the

Dublin Colony. Now it was expected that HBF would oversee her education in the great art of Europe while renewing his own inspirations.

Elizabeth was twenty-eight in 1924, tall, slender, dark-haired and attractive. She and HBF became familiar and popular figures in the bars and cafés of the "Golden Age of Montparnasse," which had begun in 1919, it was said, when the Cafe Parnasse started hanging some of its patrons' paintings for sale. Other cafés and restaurants soon followed suit, and the entire quarter became an art bazaar. Artists from many countries flocked in, and Montparnasse quickly became "the crossroads of the world."

To American readers cafés like Le Dome, La Rotonde, La Coupole, and Le Select are mainly associated with the "Lost Generation" writers: Hemingway and Gertrude Stein, Malcolm Lowry, Kay Boyle, Ezra Pound, James Joyce and Djuna Barnes. But virtually every nation had a visual or literary artist there who was to become famous, at least in his or her own land.

There was Japan's Foujita, Holland's Van Dongen, Italy's Modigliani, Norway's Per Krogh, Russia's Diaghilev and Ilya Ehrenburg, Romania's Brancusi, Ireland's Samuel Beckett, Bulgaria's Pascin, Spain's Miro, and many more, and most could be seen in the cafés and at the Montparnasse parties, which became legendary—the Bal Negre, for example.

These foreign artists would not have been present if Montparnasse had not first become the center of French Bohemia. Jean Cocteau and surrealists with less familiar names but with greater presence then, like Robert Desnos and Andre Breton, were the organizers with their women friends of the theatrical and film events, as well as the social events, that became *the* events worldwide. The women artists of whatever nationality were more likely to be actresses and singers than painters or writers, although there were many of these. The French artists' model, Kiki, for example, played an important role as muse, center of attention, and social spark.

Indeed, *Kiki's Paris, Artists and Lovers 1900-1930,* by Billy Kluver and Julie Martin, has this to say: "At the heart of the Montparnasse phenomenon were the women. They broke with country, family, and convention and made as [Swiss-woman surrealist-artist] Meret Oppenheim said, 'a conscious decision to be free.' For each woman the freedom she sought was different: freedom to paint, to write, to live alone, to make love, to take a lover—or many lovers, or simply to be admired. All of this generated a highly charged atmosphere of self-perpetuating erotic and creative energy."

Among those women who had made such a conscious decision were the American photographer Lee Miller, sometime companion of Man Ray; art collector Peggy Guggenheim, who married the American surrealist Lawrence Vail and had a number of affairs with others, including Beckett and Max Ernst; Maria Lani, a beautiful actress from Prague who induced fifty-one Montparnasse painters, including Fernand Leger, Man Ray, and Chaim Soutine, to paint her portrait for the love of her. She then had an exhibition of these portraits, sold as many as would sell, and disappeared across the Atlantic to South America with the proceeds and the portraits that remained; Yvonne George, a Belgian actress who had found it impossible to work in serious French theater because of her Flemish accent and who had become a Music Hall star and a muse to several poets, including Robert Desnos. She and several other scene-makers were addicted to opium by 1925.

From England there was the wealthy and eccentric Nancy Cunard, and Lady Duff Twysden, the real-life heroine of Ernest Hemingway's novel, *The Sun Also Rises.* A few rebellious Frenchwomen, like Anna de Noailles, facilitated many of the then-scandalous projects.

HBF and Elizabeth lived in a building of comfortably proportioned studios at 6 Rue Val de Grace, a short and quiet street that ended before the courtyard of the graceful old hospital of the same name. Their building's rear windows faced north over a private garden with sizeable trees.

They had a three block walk to the Closerie de Lilas restaurant, nine blocks to the intersection of Boulevards Raspail and Montparnasse and the Golden Age landmark cafés Le Dome, Le Select, and La Rotonde, and a half a block more to the Dingo Bar, a famous serious-drinking place among the Anglo expatriates.

HBF and Elizabeth came to this new atmosphere already fully-formed as artists and neither pursued radical objectives, but the spectacle and feeling of liberation around them changed their lives.

The executor of Agnes's estate, her cousin, Frank Higginson, now wrote HBF that the estate would gladly reimburse him for any expenses Elizabeth's stay might incur. "What about yourself, dear Harry? Why should you ever leave Paris? Was ever a man more suited to its artistic atmosphere than you are? Your beautiful and lifelong devotion to your dear mother entitles you to whatever freedom you can enjoy for the rest of your life." And HBF's income from the estate would be worth more in Paris than in the U.S., Higginson pointed out.

It may well have seemed to HBF that while it had been Lucia, Lily, and Agnes who had died, it was he who had gone to heaven.

An important figure in this heaven was Lucia's brother, Blair Fairchild. He and HBF were friends, and Blair's stronger attachment was to Chas who had come to Paris in his Navy officer's uniform in 1918. Blair had then written emotionally to Lucia that Chas was "young in such a nice way," but also "mature in such nice ways." Chas had brought along a fellow aviator, Benny Lee, and when Lee was later killed in action Blair's letter to Lucia sounds truly heartbroken.

Blair's sentimental attachments were strong, and he treated his visiting relatives with kindness and generosity. In response, I am named for him and his "adopted nephews," violinist Samuel Dushkin and pianist Beveridge Webster, arranged memorial concerts of Blair's compositions after his death. The first of these was presented in Paris in 1934, with Nadia Boulanger and Igor Stravinsky participating, and the second in New York's Town Hall in 1938. During his lifetime Blair's music was performed at the Paris Opera, and his ballet, *Dame Libbelule,* was presented at the Metropolitan Opera.

After Chas's discharge from the Navy, which quickly followed the November, 1918, Armistice, he returned to Harvard, where many of the degree requirements were waived for returning servicemen. He graduated with his class of 1919 and went on to Columbia's School of Architecture where his informal Cornish education in neoclassic art and architecture, his quick intelligence, and his facility in drawing made him an outstanding student. In 1922 he married Jane White, a tall and striking young woman from a wealthy upstate New York family who had come to New York to study sculpture with Frances Grimes and, later, Paul Manship—familiar Cornish names.

Jane was not a rural innocent. She had graduated from the fashionable Miss Porter's School and had traveled the cities of the East Coast, but she had grown up in Syracuse, a provincial city, and perhaps the most significant aspect of her upbringing was the education—both literal and metaphorical—that her father had given her as a horse-woman. Chas, on the other hand, had grown up among all the American artists she most admired. She was dazzled by him, and he seemed very happy to have found her.

Two years after their marriage Jane, having inherited a "considerable" but "not really big" fortune from her mother, who had died young of cancer, sailed with Chas for Paris and a year's study of art and architecture. Jane was pregnant with her first child.

That winter of 1924-5 Jane spent much time in museums but did not attempt to sculpt. Chas traveled to some of the great sites—Chartres, for example—and everywhere sketched architectural features and details that interested him. Elizabeth drew and made watercolors on a number of long trips, some with one of her teachers at the Boston Museum School, Irwin Hoffman. HBF stayed in the Val de Grace studio, where he was starting a difficult relationship with his occasional model, Paulette. All of them found plenty of time to enjoy the pleasures of the "Golden Age."

Jane bore my sister Sage on May 5, 1925, in the American Hospital at Neuilly. HBF would do a drawing of her a few months later, and its quality endures. The family members came at once to visit, as did new friends, Paulette and Lady Duff Twysden among them.

Duff was then thirty-three, the daughter of a socially-ambitious, middle class English family. She had acquired the "Lady" from an aristocratic second husband from whom she was momentarily expecting a divorce. Duff had left him—and their young son—to go off with a younger, alcoholic, and professionless cousin, Pat Guthrie, who was at that moment in England entreating his parents for money. He and Duff had been living on family handouts, checking into the Ritz when they were flush, and cadging drinks and meals when they were broke.

In this month of May Ernest Hemingway wrote Sherwood Anderson that he and his wife Hadley were "as fond of each other as ever," but there is no doubt he was crazy about Duff. She had a style of her own. Her hair was cut as close as a man's but her face was made up to be inviting. She was tall and slender, dressed as a modest schoolgirl in loose sweaters and pleated skirts, and she could drink all evening without losing equilibrium or wit.

In her manner of speech Duff struck drolly stoic attitudes, which, two years later would resound in the dialogue of Lady Brett Ashley in *The Sun Also Rises.* Duff said such deadpan things as, "I have never been able to have anything I ever wanted." She said, "You can't hurt people. It's what we believe in in place of God."

Duff had many affairs, but she made it an absolute rule never to have an affair with a married man. For this reason Hadley Hemingway—and Jane Fuller—could like her. Hadley wrote affectionately of Duff, "When she laughed the whole of her went into that laughter." Jane corresponded fitfully with Duff for years after they last saw one another.

Hemingway, ardent and frustrated, told Duff he wanted

to be her adviser, her confidant, that he wanted to help her straighten out her life.

That same May another American writer, Harold Loeb, a first cousin of Peggy Guggenheim's and the founder and editor of the literary magazine, *Broom,* heard Duff's laugh and heard in it, according to his memoir, *The Way It Was,* a "combination of young joy and old awareness that gave her power." She had "an aloof power," Loeb wrote.

Loeb had left a marrage and sold his interest in a New York bookstore in 1921 and had come to Europe to publish *Broom* and to write. He felt passionately, together with Eakins, Sloan, and by now many others, that the "fine arts had so separated themselves from life and humanity," that a radical new direction must be taken.

Printing *Broom* first in Rome, then in Berlin, Loeb published many of the to-be-famous names of the 1920s during the magazine's two-year life: the poets e. e. cummings, Marianne Moore, and William Carlos Williams, for example, and reproductions of the work of Derain, Modigliani, and Matisse. Now the money to publish had been exhausted, and Loeb had come to Paris to work on a novel prior to his return to the serious world of New York.

Having heard Duff's laugh, Loeb managed an introduction and asked her to lunch, after which they made love in a friend's apartment. The next day they took a train to St. Jean de Luz.

En route Loeb said to her, according to his memoir, that "we"—a collective "we" of Americans his age—had thrown out "nearly everything we believed in. Not that we knew exactly what we were looking for."

Duff said, "You wanted to live more fully, to become what you really were."

Later, in a pension in St. Jean, she said, "It is like the first time we dream of, that first time that never is."

After a few days they moved to an inn in a Pyrenees village and, as Loeb records it, their time together was entirely idyllic. They philosophized.

Duff: "If someone is gone, there's no point being jealous. And if he's still yours, you have no reason to be jealous."

Loeb: "Perhaps, but jealousy isn't rational."

Duff: "There's love or there's nothing. When love is not, you drink or work or fornicate—it doesn't matter. There is nothing, nothing at all."

Duff had brought along a portfolio of her drawings. When Loeb admired them and urged her to work at her art she laughed and said, "I have nothing against work—for those who like it."

Reading between the lines of Loeb's memoir it seems that he had not thrown out quite everything he believed in. He was soon to return to New York, to the Loebs and the Kuhns and the Guggenheims and a lifetime of solid work, and the prospect of bringing along this extraordinary, hard-drinking Englishwoman began to chill his feet.

It seems clear that Duff, who earlier had suggested they take a ship for South America, felt the drop in his temperature. She reminded Loeb that Pat Guthrie was about to return to Paris and said she had better do so, too. On their last evening together Duff said, "May we always see each other as we do tonight."

But this was not to be, as readers of *The Sun Also Rises* may remember.

The Montparnasse expatriate excursion to the Festival of San Fermin, the annual bullfight festival at Pamplona, had been planned long in advance and promoted by

Hemingway, who had attended it twice before. Of the group, Loeb, being athletic and adventurous, was the one most likely to enjoy with Hemingway the morning runs before the bulls through the narrow streets of the small city, and getting through the pileup of people in the narrowing tunnel into the bull ring itself, and then the bullfights themselves in the afternoons. However, Loeb made a foolish, eventually humiliating mistake in not passing up his invitation. Perhaps he could not think of a way of explaining his backing out to Heminway, whose friendship and respect were of great importance to him.

Everyone in the party knew of Duff and Loeb's affair. Pat Guthrie, who was entirely without Loeb's and Hemingway's macho enthusiasms, was bitterly resentful of Loeb's presence and Hemingway burned with jealousy. Bill Smith and the Donald Ogden Stewarts and Hadley Hemingway tried to keep the peace.

Duff found a moment to tell Loeb "The spell is broken" but later the same day went off with him, and without the others, to an endless Spanish drinking party. The following morning Duff had a black eye and a bruised forehead, presumably administered by Pat, who asked Loeb if he could not see that he was not wanted here. "Why don't you just leave?" Pat asked.

As Loeb recounted it, his pride was then aroused. After all, he had as much right to be there as anyone. It seems probable that he did not want to lose face in Duff's eyes by meekly accepting Pat's suggestion.

That afternoon Hemingway challenged Loeb to a fight. The two men walked off to find a secluded spot, took off their jackets, and rolled up their sleeves, but Hemingway then said, "I don't want to fight you," and Loeb said, "I don't want to fight you, either."

Hemingway apologized to Loeb. From a knowledge of Hemingway's later work I imagine that at that moment he perceived that the troubles were all Duff's doing rather than Loeb's, and thus he, Hemingway, had been about to hurt the wrong party. The two men shook hands and returned to the others, but no one's emotions had been resolved. When the party's members all went their separate ways at the Festival's end the only comment on which they seemed to have agreement was that things "would never be the same."

Donald Ogden Stewart paid Duff and Pat's hotel bill so they could leave town. When *The Sun Also Rises* was published two years later, Duff's only comment was, "But I didn't have an affair with the matador. What a shame!"

Several weeks after the Pamplona trip Duff and Pat arrived in St. Jean de Luz, where HBF was living in a studio in a white-washed, tile-roofed building on one of the oldest of the port's streets, three short blocks from the town's center—the café-ringed Place Louis Quatorze, the cathedral in which Louis had married, and the docks of the fishing fleet. Chas and Jane were in Blair Fairchild's villa. Clara and Warner Taylor had been there in early August but had left. Elizabeth Fuller was expected in several weeks, and many familiar faces from Montparnasse were coming and going.

In late September Chas wrote to Clara and Warner back in Madison of what they had missed:

"The parties got worse." In the afternoons there were trips to visit a trained turtle dove, for example, "in an obscure bar out on the point. We went to Biarritz where Yvonne George invited [HBF] to live with her—really I suppose it was scandalous, but at the time it was quite entertaining.

"Of course, they were all delightful—eight or ten people all interested in the arts but with no axes to grind or appearances to keep up, but I began to be seriously frightened about [HBF's] health—the more he drank the more uncertain became his temper and judgement."

The group gathered every afternoon about five in HBF's studio and "he stayed up until the last shot was fired—usually about 6 a.m. Meanwhile, the group had dinner, went to the Casino on the promenade to gamble and dance, repaired to the Cafe Majestic near the bandstand in the Place Louis Quatorze to talk, and then went on to other bars or nightclubs. Chas thought it "a rare occurrence in all its childlike gayety. These others with their freedom and complete abandonment have so enchanted [HBF] . What he doesn't seem to realize is that they are all more or less egotists.

"For my own part," Chas continued, "I find that in the two weeks since I left St. Jean I have slept nearly twelve hours a day, and it's only now that I am beginning to get back to any kind of mental activity. What is [HBF]going through then?"

Chas suspected that [HBF] was going to "get Paulette to come down and perhaps spend the winter at Nice. Of course, I think he's just a plain fool to mix up with her again. He has already found out once that she worries him half insane, and now he expects that she will come back entirely sobered and industrious."

On September 29th HBF wrote Chas from St. Jean to say, "I am leaving here in a few days, as soon as our drunken nights are over and I can do anything at all by day." His letter continued on the 30th. "Another drunken night. Merrill did a movie in front of the Majestic. Pat, Duff, dog and myself. Then we went to the Pergola to take Pat and Duff dancing. Band in background, drinks. Then to Merrills to say goodbye to children. More drinks. To Pergola for dinner with Dickie, P., and Duff. Serious drinking begins. Lille turns up. Dickie becomes affectionate. Pat wanders continually. Gambles for ten minutes and wins—returns what I lent him. Gambles again, loses. Comes back and borrows again. P. & D. suddenly absorbent of cash—so it goes in our final round. I love them all more and more." But, "I become acrimonious and quarrelsome in my cups." And, "My drawing goes by the board to be continued in Paris sometime."

A surprise was in store. On October 11th Chas, having received a new letter from HBF, wrote Clara that "the one practical result of [HBF's stay in St. Jean de Luz] seems to be that Duff is serious in her offer to come and join him on the Riviera this winter, without Pat. The latter, while disturbed about it, seems to have left on friendly terms with [HBF]. Duff seems to have rather forced the thing and [HBF] says he hopes she won't come."

Chas wrote HBF, forthwith and vehemently, that he would be insane to accept Duff's offer, that life with her would be impossible, that he would never get any work done. Toward the end of October Chas and HBF met in Nice to discuss HBF's plans for the winter, and Duff's offer had been put aside.

"I can't get him to find out what he wants really to do," Chas wrote Clara from Nice. "He is more unbalanced than ever, and really I am in a sort of despair. He talks of wanting to get to work though he has little enthusiasm for anything at the moment."

HBF decided he did not like the Riviera and he and Chas took a ship for Algiers, but after a brief look, returned to Nice. Chas then rejoined Jane and Sage in Italy and they took ship for New York. HBF, as it turned out, returned to Paris.

HBF's letter of March 1926 is lost, unfortunately, but Jane relished describing it. HBF wrote that he had become increasingly worried about Paulette. She had been ill. Her mother was cruel to her.

Two days previously he had gone to the prefecture of police to explore the possibility of adopting Paulette, or of making her his ward in some way, but it seemed that French citizens attained their majority at sixteen and, in any case, his being a foreigner made impossible complications. "So I married the dear child this morning."

Snapshots of the newlyweds on their wedding trip to Algiers show HBF looking tall and pale. His hair is white and his eyes look solemnly at the camera while Paulette, the crown of whose bowl-cut dark hair reached the level of HBF's solar plexus, beams at his side.

HBF and Paulette arrived in New York in August of 1926, and they temporarily moved in with Jane and Chas at 1088 Park Avenue, then found an apartment in Greenwich Village. That November HBF wrote Frank Higginson requesting that all the stocks and bonds he owned be sold. "After consideration I find that there is no other way for me to do. It is a life and death matter," he wrote.

I find no evidence of a life and death matter. For whatever reason, the deserved-heaven that Higginson had imagined for HBF had not lasted long.

Paulette's mother fell gravely ill in 1928, and Paulette returned to France to look after her. Paulette had not managed to learn much English and had been lonely and unhappy in New York, and her leaving was a relief to HBF, who began to change his address restlessly.

He was sometimes in Deerfield where Arthur had remained, sometimes in Greenwich Village. He spent one winter at Martha's Vineyard with a young woman who was later to marry Chas's best friend, but after those months of stoking a wood stove and shivering he sought to go south every year when the leaves fell.

HBF came for protracted visits to Jane and Chas's house in Bedford Village, New York. I was born in 1927 and remember HBF during his visits in the early 1930s, his deep and loud voice, the shuffling of his slippers, and his frequent absorption in fixing things. A pretty, banjo-style clock hung in the front hall that confounded his efforts. Leaving the house, his visit ending, he would tell my mother, "I'll fix that next time, Jane."

During one lengthy stay he painted an ornamental standing screen depicting Jane and her two sisters as oriental princesses enjoying a succession of thousand-and-one-nights adventures, a pleasing and original work, but that he had time to do it makes it plain that his talents were not otherwise much in demand. He and Chas drank many highballs talking of things beyond my understanding.

Back in 1925, just before returning to New York, Chas had written HBF a letter that brought them much closer than they had ever been: "There are a thousand things between us—points of view, miles of ocean and all. But it doesn't matter. I repeat only that you as a person are the most precious human I know. Somehow you know, above all these fascists, above the noise of New York, you remain, 'The springs that pass and change and pass again.' You have a quality that I love—a quality you don't use to the fullest, but, whatever it is, it marks you as the highest that I know."

This letter began a franker and deeper dialogue. In a 1929 letter Chas wrote, "Your last letter was full of such deep questions that I have hesitated in answering, and have found that one finds out more about oneself in the pursuit of an answer than one finds out about the answer." Chas reflected on the news of a friend's divorce: "I suppose we *must* discharge our impulses—act on them—or we must absorb the poison of non-fulfillment." There, it seems to me, is a quintessential 1920s idea: the "poison of non-fulfillment!"

Chas wrote, "Just now I am still trying to formulate my ideas on life as a function, and to assimilate the experience of the last ten years. As far as I can see, looking back, they have been nothing but an attempt to recover—from what I don't know, partly the preconceived ideas of my youth, a little the war. I find that I have loaded myself with certain vices—a taste for drink, lechery, excess of various kinds—that no longer (if they ever did) seem wicked, but which eat up a great deal of time. Architecture has given me at last the assurance that I can do good work, and I am sure no other assurance can match [that] in its possibilities of self-development.

"All human relationships drive us into attitudes from which it is difficult to escape. All women want one thing from me—all clients—even artists fall into cliches humanly. You have kept your freshness—and I would like to save mine!"

There is no broad or coherent philosophy in HBF's letters but he had recovered from his St. Jean de Luz tailspin. He thought Aldous Huxley had correctly analyzed "the diseases of our souls" in *Point Counterpoint,* but, "What is the remedy?" he asked. He groused that if the federal government would only "turn on the spigot," that is, repeal the Volstead Act—the prohibition of alcohol—that the nation's economic problems would be solved. Mainly in his letters, however, there is an unwearying emotional liveliness as HBF reacts to everyone he meets whether old acquaintance or new, to every new idea and possibility of change in his own life and others.

And he was not forgetting.

In 1929 HBF painted an oil portrait, sketchy but complete and evocative, of an unnamed woman who does not look precisely like Duff, according to her photographs, but that surely reflects her spirit. The woman's brown hair is cropped very short, her lipstick is bright red, her eyes and cheekbones are emphasized, and she is wearing a short-sleeved kimono that is open before her small breasts. She is regarding the viewer directly, without a trace of coquettishness, challenge, or exhibitionism. She is not bored but grave, perhaps vaguely wounded. "Here I am," she seems to say. "Think what you like."

The painting is signed "HBF '29. It suggests nothing of the financial crash of that year, but seems to me to show much about the new woman of the era.

Pat had left Duff in the spring of 1927—his mother had at last got her way. Duff's son was with her that summer. Sometime in the following months she met and married an American painter, Clinton King.

In the fall of 1929 HBF wrote to Elizabeth suggesting she go out and "stay with Duff in Arizona"—Elizabeth hated the New England winters as he did. It is not clear whether or not Elizabeth went. In 1931 Chas wrote to HBF suggesting that he "go out and visit Duff in Arizona," but it is not certain that HBF would have found her if he had gone.

According to an article in the *San Antonio Light* of March 25, 1934, which announced the opening of an exhibition of Clinton King portraits and landscapes at the Witte Museum, King and his wife, "Lady Duff Twysden, English Caricaturist," had just returned from a three-year residence "on the west coast of Mexico." The article reports that "King was raised in Fort Worth where his family is socially prominent. His family sent him to Princeton but college life failed to interest him." He had studied with Robert Reid of Denver, spent some time in Provincetown, two years in Santa Fe, and had gone to Paris to study. The enthusiastic review of King's work mentions that one of his portraits was of Duff.

By the time of this exhibition HBF had found a way to live in the South. In 1932 he drove alone down the eastern seaboard searching for warm and congenial quarters. He proceeded slowly. He had a number of friends to visit along the way and his health required frequent rest. In a diner in a small Carolina town in which he had stopped for the night he met Susie, a very young, pale blonde who was waitressing. With her "parents' full blessing," as HBF stressed in letters both to Chas and Clara, Susie came along with him to be his aide in return for instruction in all the arts and crafts that HBF would practice.

The new couple's first stop was at the Desoto Hotel in Savannah, where HBF fell gravely ill. Recovering, he wrote to Chas, "My liver and gall bladder are practically cleaned out. I can sleep lying down again." However, several days later after tests, a specialist told him he had "hardening of the arteries." He was advised to "lift nothing, use stairs as little as possible. Whiskey limit is four drinks, coffee, one cup."

His health improved, but there was another problem. The doctor told him that he and Susie should not "take a cottage alone, but must have a respected third party to avoid scandal." That convinced HBF to continue south-ward, although he wrote, "My bootlegger advises always carrying a gun on the road in case of breakdown and passing ruffians."

Before leaving Savannah HBF received the news that he was the beneficiary of another Higginson family trust fund, this one certainly modest, of which he had been unaware.

From the Carling Hotel in Jacksonville, Florida, where they had paused for a look at the possibilities, HBF wrote Chas, "Know always Susie is the most perfect godsend I could have found at this time. Practical, exact, devoted in every way. Of all that anon, and much more." And in St. Augustine, the prospects looked even brighter. "They are getting up an art colony here. I have been received with open arms."

Soon Susie and HBF were in their own cottage. Happily settled, HBF thought expansively of others. To Chas, whose architectural practice was being cut into by the Depression, he wrote, "I feel sympathy for you caught in mid-career by the sins of the body politic—in the prime of life and power." He thought of his grandchildren: "You have not spoken of Blair, so I imagine he goes on with even tenor rejecting interruptions to thought. May he continue so. How I would like to see the children, now in their splendor. Sage must be a very titaness by now."

He was shocked by the news of the death of a Cornish playwright Louis Shipman, though he writes, "I finally had to differ with Louis over his barking-dogism. He was one that would bludgeon a lily before breakfast and be proud of it all day."

Susie planted a vegetable garden beside the cottage, and by the time they had onions from their garden HBF was thinking larger thoughts: "The only school of expression we have produced, the New England—Emerson, Emily Dickinson, Hawthorne, the Jameses—is carried on in [Robert] Frost. The element is terror—the consciousness of existence '. . . ghastly pale and full of fears, and lo she did depart.'"

In another letter, HBF asks Chas, "What gives you a sense of existence at all? Is it not a sense of wholeness, such as the lower animals have?"

And he had a grand, though not exactly new, idea.

True, the caravan he had built for Lucia and himself had failed them, but now, forty years later, there were automobiles and trailers that had been proved to be practical. He would use the trust money to buy a trailer to live in and a trailer chassis on which to build an ambulant studio. When all was ready, he and Susie would travel slowly thoughout the southern states exhibiting paintings, drawings, and photographs, and offering picture framing and cabinetwork. In the towns and smaller cities where they hoped to go no one would have seen the equal of their skills. "The road will be a success financially and every way," HBF wrote.

Lawyers were still holding the trust's assets and, HBF thought, diminishing them. He constructed some "modernish" furniture to sell and then thought to ask Jane if she would advance some money against the inheritance. When she did so HBF wrote her, "There is a book by angels writ where all thy deeds reside."

HBF ordered a chassis from the factory and built the studio on it, sheathing the exterior with copper, a task that took him longer than he had estimated. Elizabeth Fuller then drove down from the North and hitched her car to it, and she and HBF and Susie drove the two rigs along the shores of the Gulf to New Orleans, where they installed themselves in the Dixie Tourist Court, a trailer park situated a short distance back from the banks of the Mississippi in an industrial section of the city. Today, high, fenced-off levees make the river invisible from the site, but then it must have had charm.

HBF wrote Clara, "We stay here till the end of June, when we plan to go to the region of Biloxi." It would not be cooler there, but they might "find a market for [our] wares in the summer colony." He was having some teeth pulled by a New Orleans dentist and was in no hurry to depart.

He had been having trouble with a painting he had been working on for some time, and he found an explanation for Clara, "I must take myself with more good humor. I find the Masters I like most do not ask too much of themselves, nor their medium, nor subject matter, but work on friendly lines with all three. I am not on friendly enough terms with it all. Handled right, the work would do itself—has done itself so far as it has gone. The composition refuses to change any more now than it refused to change continually for weeks." Of what he should do in future he wrote, "It is like what horsemen do when lost, give rein to the animal to find its own way home."

HBF had at last become free, in the sense of his father's "Can one do anything till one is free?" He had struggled with the burdens of symbolic idea, perfection of composition, and tonal novelty in all of the work he had thought to be important. While his best work—always—was work over which he could relax.

There had been a flurry of excitement at the Dixie Tourist Court one day when it became evident that the famous bank robbers Bonnie and Clyde Barrow had been residents until a few days before they were gunned down. The manager had gone to register the Barrows' license plate number, as required by law, and the Barrows had abruptly departed. Their newspaper photographs clearly identified them to their Dixie Court neighbors.

In telling the story HBF thought Chas should know that "Mr. Early, Manager, is a balancer by trade. He puts a broom between two chairs, a chair on the broom, sits on the chair so balanced for any length of time. He has done this on the ledges of high buildings all his life."

HBF sold the last of his reproductions of *The Triumph of Truth Over Error* to a local Christian Scientist, having arranged for Susie to make frames for them. Susie had "taken hold of wood working" and was "very happy in the work."

Clara, Warner, and their daughter Lucia were soon to go to Monhegan Island for the summer, driving cross-country from Madison as was their custom. HBF wrote Clara, "You may go by way of Cornish and see Jane and Chas who are there for the summer. Do say howdy to Arthur and Constance going through Deerfield. Much love again—and from Susie."

Indeed Jane and Chas and their children Sage, myself, and newly-born Jill were in the Cornish house when HBF died of heart failure.

It is one of the most vivid memories of my childhood— the mystery of the news of HBF's death, the heavy darkness of Chas's reaction, and the arrival perhaps a week later, of the two trailer rigs. One was driven by a woman who left very shortly, the other by Susie, who stayed with us for some days.

Susie wore sleeveless blouses and shorts and was so delicate-looking and beautiful that it seemed incredible to me she had been able to drive such a huge and cumbersome rig across the country. Her deep-South accent was so thick and unfamiliar that she seemed to have come from some faraway, geography-book land.

One day she said she would like to talk to me and we sat down by the pool. She asked me, "Did you love your granddaddy?"

Aged seven, never having thought about it, I said, "Yes."

"Did you know him much?"

I told her about his visits to Bedford.

She said, "He loved you. He thought about you a lot."

I was stunned.

She said, "He was a great man, your granddaddy, you ought to know that." She told me about his skills and the things that he knew and how much he had taught her.

Susie said, "He was the wisest and the kindest man in all the world. You should be real proud he was your granddaddy."

She left the next day although I proposed she stay on with us. She said, "I have to go and do the things your grandaddy taught me how to do."

Four years later I came upon Chas one day, sitting alone and preoccupied. The weather was hot and he was holding a handkerchief to mop his face. I asked if something were wrong.

"A woman friend of mine died," he said. "Not someone you know." She had died in Mexico, he told me, and her death had not surprised him for "she had lived very hard." It was what had happened after her death that was upsetting him.

Chas said that the woman's husband had invited her former lovers—a number of them—to be pallbearers at the funeral. They all got drunk together before the ceremony, and perhaps Duff would have liked that. But when the bearers had to carry the coffin out of the church they were so drunk they dropped it on the steps of the church and the coffin had broken open and her body had rolled down into the street. Chas shuddered and shook his head to dismiss the picture from his mind.

In fact, Lady Duff Twysden, who had led a seemingly blameless life as Clinton King's wife, died on June 27, 1938, in Santa Fe, New Mexico. She died of tuberculosis, having been treated for the disease at Santa Fe's St. Vincent Hospital and then released to die at home. Her body was immediately cremated.

According to A. E. Hotchner and others, the story of Duff's terrible funeral was entirely the invention of Ernest

Hemingway, who put the disparaging-to-all-parties tale into barroom circulation. Hemingway at last avenged the frustration Duff had caused him.

Clara, reminiscing, wrote of her mother Lucia that when she returned to Cornish from her trips to fulfill portrait commissions she would often say with relief that now she could do a "real picture." In this category, surely, are the *In the Mirror* self-portrait and the nude of Ebba Bohm by the Cornish swimming pool, *Pres d'une Claire Fontaine*, now in the collection of the Smithsonian's Museum of American Art. Her best work, like HBF's, was produced when she was free of theory or clients' expectations.

The work for which Lucia and HBF were celebrated in their lifetimes was produced in an epoch of human self-approval and optimism which was never wholly genuine or deeply believed, and their "official' work is dated by it. In the Cornish masque the gods envy the Cornish artists! Not really. Never, really. And the catastrophe of World War I brought such pretensions to an end.

The lives of Lucia and HBF and the "real pictures" that they made are contemporary and vital.

Chapter Six

SPENCER, ROBERT, and ARTHUR FULLER
VIOLET and AUGUSTUS TACK

When George made his fateful trip to Boston in 1876 to see the bankruptcy judge and to arrange the exhibition that so radically changed the family's fortunes, he took with him among his dozen paintings a just-finished "ideal head" of a thirteen-year-old boy who was, in fact, Spencer.

The portrait, which is in the collection of the Metropolitan, had been painted that winter in the cramped studio off The Bars' kitchen—or perhaps in the kitchen itself. George was in a hurry to finish enough work for a gallery show and would have used any space warm enough to work in.

The painting shows a boy at that pubescent moment when his muscles become visible and his nose and ears and lips seem too large for his face. His eyes are puffy, as though he could not get quite enough sleep. The picture conveys a sense of the irresistible strength of the organic changes breaking through the boy's body, confusing his mind and reforming his soul.

254

Overall, Spencer was undoubtedly made happy by the changes that were happening to him. Like many of the eldest among rural children he wanted to be adult and responsible, and when his parents took a house in Boston several years later he argued that he was old and wise enough to manage the farm. He did not immediately prevail on the management issue, but he remained on the farm, and by George's death in 1884 he was firmly in charge.

In 1889 Spencer married Mary Williams Field, daughter of an old Deerfield family—"old" meant of longer residence than the Fullers—and the couple settled down to a life of family, farming, and art.

Although Spencer was never sent to a formal art school he became an able painter of the Deerfield, and later other, landscapes. He worked steadily at it, painting mainly during the months of winter's frozen ground, and he had a modest, continuing success.

The dark tonalism of his canvases, the low, heavy clouds and the misty, sometimes golden air he depicted are strongly reminiscent of George's landscapes, and the resemblances likely account in part for Spencer's success, but also for his not being given more serious notice. His art was not shown outside of Deerfield until after his death.

Spencer's younger brothers and sister all followed his lead in becoming visual artists. That George's talent had finally been highly paid and made him a friend to the cultural elite of the nation was surely a strong example for his children to attempt to follow. Also, the demonstration that both George's pictures and his conversation provided—that there was more to be seen than one automatically saw—was like an initiation into an inspiring family secret.

The new generation tended to "see" in George's manner rather than in ways uniquely their own—an irony, considering George's belief in the neccessity of aesthetic freedom, but one surely to be expected. No other examples of visual "depth" were before their eyes. They did not paint entirely alike, of course, but only HBF cast off all feeling of resemblance, and to do so he had to adopt an intellectual standard not truly his own.

In 1906 Spencer and Mary and all four of their children—George, Elizabeth, Katharine, and Alfred—made a trip to Monhegan Island some fifteen miles off the coast of Maine. The often fogbound, isolated, rock and forest island was attracting a very small but growing colony of summering New York artists.

One of the first of these was Rockwell Kent, who had come to Monhegan in 1904, worked as a fisherman and a carpenter, and built himself a one-room house. Over the years Kent would draw, paint, and make woodcuts of the island and its people, and would become best known as an illustrator, for which he developed a distinctive and dramatic style.

The child of a wealthy New York family, Kent had reacted against its conservatism and self-satisfaction. His sympathies would always be with the working man and woman, or the downtrodden, and in the island's hard-pressed but proudly independent fisher-families he found people who aroused his fervent admiration.

In the late 1940s, when Kent was among America's best-known artists, he became famous in another way—by declaring to the U.S. Congress's Un-American Activities Committee that he had, indeed, been a member of the Communist Party. He refused to tell the Committee the names of other party members and challenged the Committee to put him in jail for his refusal to do so—which the Committee did not do.

In the winter of 1907, after having become acquainted with the Fullers on Monhegan, Kent paid a visit to The Bars and he wrote of it in his autobiography *It's Me O Lord*. In the house "there were four Fuller children from eight-year-old Alfred through Elizabeth and Katherine to the oldest, tall, sixteen-year-old George; there were their mother and their artist-father, burly, bearded, genial Spencer Fuller; there were in all of them and all about them in the house the childrens' famous artist grandfather, George Fuller, and the generations of his forebears; and there was in all and everything—in the people of that household, in their perhaps two-century-old homestead, in Old Deerfield as next day I saw it, and the landscape's far-extending snow-covered fields and distant spires—New England. And at the Fullers I was at its heart."

The very "heart" of New England! The residents of The Bars of previous generations had seen themselves as people working a farm near a small town with a history of which to be proud, but they had not seen themselves as being at the heart, or at the center of anything. They had all either dreamed of leaving to seek greater worlds, or had, in fact, gone. Of George's eleven brothers and sisters (by his own mother, Fanny, and by Aaron Fuller's first wife) only deaf harness-maker Aaron Junior, Elijah, and Augustus had remained at Deerfield to their deaths, and the latter two would not have chosen to do so but were forced homeward by their illnesses, tuberculosis and alcoholism. Other brothers died in Montana, Ohio, Pennsylvania, and Maryland, and George himself in Boston. His sisters died mainly in Massachusetts but none in Deerfield.

But by 1907 a myth had grown—and George unwittingly had helped it grow—that there was something uniquely valuable, something to be revered in the New England "heritage." To Kent and many others the heart of New England symbolized certain values and a way of life that was specific to the place and important to conserve.

Whether or not Kent expressed these thoughts to the Fullers, they were aware of and caught up in that myth and would become more so.

George's *Girl Driving Turkeys* and *A Gatherer of Simples* and other rural scenes had fostered the idea of an unchanging New England landscape and unchanging customs. In appearance the Pocumtuck Valley through which the Deerfield River flows was indeed cultivated in 1907 much as it had been in George's youth and is today, but the vast majority of New England farms had been or were being abandoned for the more fertile Midwest.

The hilly and rocky land of the Northeast is now almost entirely covered with second-growth forest. One often stumbles over the remains of stone walls when walking through these woods. And there is another change that is startling in relation to the conception of New England immutability—most of the farmland of the Pocumtuck Valley is worked today by Polish families who immigrated to America in the twentieth century, some from Poland after the Second World War. So neither the region's population nor the population's work has been unchanging, but the appearance of Deerfield and its valley, both in 1907 and now, would make it seem so.

When Mary married Spencer she brought some family

capital with her, and Agnes helped, too, by dividing the proceeds of posthumous sales of George's work among their children. Life at The Bars was not as confining as it had once been.

In the summer of 1907 Mary had a house built at one of Monhegan's loveliest locations, on a shelf of rock that overlooked the narrow northern passage into the island's cramped harbor. Two islets, High Duck and Smutty Nose, which protected the harbor from northerly storms, lay in the channel just below the house, and to the south was the harbor scene of the ferry dock and the fishing dories riding at moorings or pulled up into the rocky coves. Together with the gray-weathered sheds and houses and the rocky paths, these Monhegan features have appeared in literally countless paintings. Among many others, three generations of Wyeth family painters have painted Monhegan scenes.

In design the Monhegan Fuller house was much like a scaled down version of The Bars, a conventional New England box with a gambrel roof into which some dormers were later built to improve the second-story rooms. Among the small and rudimentary houses lived in by the resident Monheganites, the house must have seemed grand.

Later on, Mary Fuller also converted a Williams-family house on Deerfield's Albany Road into an art studio and gallery. Albany Road is perpendicular to Deerfield's Main Street and passes now through the extensive grounds of Deerfield Academy, past the oldest of the cemeteries, and down to the flood plain toward distant Albany, New York.

Unhappily for Spencer and the members of his family, he had little time to use and enjoy these important additions to their life. Spencer died of heart failure in 1911 at the age of forty-eight.

Both the Monhegan house and the Albany Road studio remained in the family and were rented out for many years. Monhegan's most illustrious tenant was George Bellows, who painted a harbor scene from its terrace in 1915 that hangs in the Rochester Museum of Art. He used the living room as his studio and had the habit of cleaning his brushes on the bricks of the fireplace, so splattering them with paint that the fireplace bricks were painted-over white after his departure.

Together with a few places on Maine's mainland, Monhegan remained one of the last sites where artists could truthfully paint the "timeless" New England of myth. Monhegan's lobstermen continue to put out their pots as they have for scores of years, and the colors of the rocks and evergreens, of sea and sky, protected as they are from any industrial effluvia, are as pristine as can be found.

The island is so small that the need for motor vehicles has not been felt, thus conventional streets and roads have not been built. A garbage truck and a fire engine are the island's only motorized transportation, and they lurch along rock paths when needed.

Many of Andrew Wyeth's best-known paintings were done at Port Clyde, from which the Monhegan ferry sails. The weathered houses and barns, the rusted and worn farm and fishing equipment, and the plain, spare furniture that Wyeth made familiar were as present in Port Clyde as on Monhegan, where Andrew's son Jamie now has a house.

Interestingly, however, the people Andrew Wyeth painted were not the rugged fishermen and straight-backed young women that Winslow Homer made famous, but rather the inbred, poverty-stricken members of the families who did not seek wider worlds but clung to what they had. Retardation, alcoholism, and a variety of disabilities were their fate. The enormous popularity of Wyeth's depictions of them makes a strong but mysterious suggestion about their enthusiasts.

Like Spencer himself, his oldest son George, then eighteen, assumed the responsibility of the farm upon his father's death, but unlike his father and grandfather he would not practice an art. He was a graduate of the University of Massachusetts, served as a Navy officer in the First World War, and was a member of the Massachusetts legislature in the 1940s. He died in 1950 never having married.

Robert Fuller was born only one year and a half after Spencer but the family's move to Boston gave Robert a very different upbringing and career. He was enrolled in the Boston Latin School, famous for its academic rigor, and he continued to Harvard where he was member of the class of 1888.

In family photographs taken in the mid-1890s Robert appears to be relatively short and stocky next to his brothers, but this does not mean that he was small. Spencer and HBF were over six feet tall, and Arthur was six feet six. Balding Robert looks both vigorous and intense—not at all overshadowed. It was said that he was "more a Higginson than a Fuller" and indeed his career was literary rather than in painting—although now it is plain that he was a lively and accomplished painter as well.

Agnes disapproved of Robert's first newspaper as "being out of step with the times." Robert soon changed jobs but his conservatism did not. He worked for the greatest number of years on the *Albany Union* and later wrote a column for children for the *New York Tribune* under the byline Acton Archer. He published a biography of Diamond Jim Brady and a boy's adventure novel entitled, *The Golden Hope, A Story of the time of Alexander the Great.* Robert also served as press secretary to Charles Evans Hughes when Hughes was governor of New York State.

At thirty-one Robert married a woman six years older than he, Bessie Adams Claggett, his third-cousin. Both were great grandchildren of Azariah and Mercy Bemis Fuller, the parents of Aaron. Robert and Bessie had two daughters of whom one, Alice Fuller Goodhue, would be a painter.

Robert's conservatism is apparent in his writing, both in letters and his published work. He was morally certain and sometimes severe and his loyalties were often passionate. In gratitude for his unfailing support his sister Violet named her only son Robert Fuller Tack.

Robert was forty-one in 1905 when he published *The Golden Hope,* which appeared on the same Macmillan list as Jack London's *The Sea Wolf.* In *Hope,* a trio of young Athenian men, fast friends in the manner of the then extremely popular *Three Musketeers* by Alexandre Dumas, take leave of their families and their normal duties in Athens to join the Macedonian Alexander's army in his campaign to conquer Persia.

Prejudices widely held in 1905, which seem also to be Robert's, jump out of the text: "Agile as monkeys, the slave girls darted about pelting each other with blossoms and uttering peals of shrill laughter." One of the trio grabs a slave girl and kisses her, and although the girl runs away to the slave quarters no criticism of the Athenian is implied. It's just good fun.

The trio attend a debate held in the Athens theater as to whether a treaty of peace between Athens and Macedonia should be respected or broached. Demosthenes is presented as an orator who is convincing in every word he speaks, but who reaches no conclusion, no point on which the Athenians can simply vote yes or no. The trio—and Robert—are contemptuous of this willingness to see both sides of an argument.

More anti-intellectualism is apparent in the portrait drawn of the philosopher Aristotle, who is also present in the theater and had once been Alexander's tutor.

Aristotle is asked his opinion of a rumor that Alexander has been killed in battle.

"'I do not know,' lisped Aristotle. 'It is his habit always to expose himself in battle.'" Aristotle is asked if he believes Alexander can make himself "master of Hellas."

"'Only the Gods can answer that,' Aristotle replied. 'It is safe to say that what human ambition can accomplish, he will do. He was my pupil, and there are those who maintain that he knows more than his master!'

"'You hear that?'" one of the trio cries. "'Here is a boy who begins by conquering his instructor. Where will he end?'"

Making Aristotle look small is not a tack many writers would take, but it is a tack consistent with the glorification of "manly" virtues in the book. Foolish risks and needless sacrifices are applauded if taken in support of a chum.

Alexander himself is presented as an aloof, brilliant young loner who arrives at military decisions with swift intuition. The only important business of his life, as the book presents it, is in his relationships to other men—whether allies or enemies. Similarly, the importance of the relationships between the trio of Athenians transcends all others.

The Athenian fiancee of one of the trio says to her betrothed, "'Thou art strong and I am but a weak girl. Whatever may come I shall always be thankful that thou didst love me. I am thine—heart and mind, body and spirit, here and in the hereafter—forever.'" But he is not, of course, hers. His greater loyalty is to the trio and to Alexander, and shortly after his beloved has spoken these words he leaves her and is gone for years.

Was Robert aware of Alexander's homosexuality, which is now generally acknowledged? On other points he had certainly done his research.

Robert painted as an avocation. Some of his landscapes were included in group shows, and one in an annual National Academy of Design exhibition. His earlier canvases much resemble George's landscapes, but later ones seem distinctly his own. He painted with broad and confident strokes and used bright colors, departing entirely from muted tonalism. A bright red flower is bright red in these paintings, not "harmonized" with the other vegetation.

Robert's granddaughter, the painter Barbara Goodhue Legler, who has several paintings by both George and Robert in her house in Orchard Park, New York, says of Robert's work, "They could have been painted now, while George's could not."

The Golden Hope, on the other hand, could not have been written at any time later than 1914. It would have been mocked in the 1920s. If it is true, as I also believe, that Robert's paintings "could have been painted now," there is a seeming paradox. Writing was his profession, a profession at which he was successful, while for him painting had the status of a hobby.

Was it because he could paint without regard for what buyers were expecting or critics might approve that the canvases look as fresh as they do? While unspoken agendas seem to control the motivations and morality of *The Golden Hope,* the paintings were done without apparent cerebration.

Robert Henri told his students at the Art Students League that they could not possibly get rid of their individuality or originality no matter how hard they might try, that the task for them, and everyone, was to uncover their originality, buried as it might be under strictures about what was good or beautiful or likely to be bought. In a letter to a student, Henri wrote, "What I would say to you is that you should see that it is the voice that comes from within you that speaks in your work—not an expected or controlled voice, not an outside 'educated' voice." Robert's writing was, in this sense, an 'educated' voice, his painting voice was not.

Robert died at sixty-three in 1927 in New York.

It is difficult to imagine that Agnes, over forty, and George could have looked forward to the birth of Arthur in 1879 with unqualified joy. Indeed the letters exchanged between George in Boston and Agnes at The Bars waiting for the delivery show mutual worry and efforts to reassure one another. But Agnes was immediately charmed by Arthur, "my sweet boy," and doted on him.

Arthur grew up a Bostonian and by the time he entered Harvard he was of exceptional size. At six-six and two hundred and forty pounds he was a natural for the football team on which he played all four of his college years. He was also on the staff of the *Harvard Lampoon.* Celebrating after a winning football game Arthur was arrested on a charge of vandalism for tearing down a sign, and this relatively harmless prank was taken seriously by his family, who had to bail him out of jail.

After college Arthur remained with Agnes, both in Boston and Deerfield. He looked after her property and interests, and he began to paint the Deerfield landscape.

For several periods in these years Arthur was a student at New York's Art Students League. His brushwork became progressively freer, and in some of his later canvases bright colors seem more the expression of idea and feeling than of the reality of what was before his eyes. These are pleasing pictures.

When Arthur was forty-one in 1920 he married Constance Trowbridge, a woman of some means and delicate health. Arthur and Constance inherited Agnes's house on Main Street when Agnes died four years later. They spent their winters there and in summer they owned and managed an inn on the "Mohawk Trail," the highway that runs east-west over the Berkshires between Greenfield and Williamstown.

Chas and I stopped in Deerfield on our way to Cornish in the summer of 1934, the summer in which HBF later died. We paid a visit to The Bars where I met my Great Aunt Mary, Spencer's widow, and her son, laconic handsome George. The strong and heavy smell of the tobacco barns he showed us is still real to me.

Aunt Mary gave us iced tea in the parlor of The Bars, which was the most exotic house I had ever visited. A hand pump was used to draw water from the well just outside the kitchen door. Every room was crammed with dark furniture, most of which had been in use for more than one hundred years. The walls were thick with ill-lit family paintings. I was accustomed, instead, to new houses, new furnishings and art on the walls.

That evening Elizabeth Fuller came to see us at the inn where Chas and I spent the night. I have a clear mental picture of her, tall and slender, wearing a light, flowery summer dress. She had come from a rehearsal of the Pioneer Valley Symphony Orchestra, based in Greenfield, in which she played one of the violins.

She and Chas chatted in the dim evening light, leaning against the railing of the inn's verandah, and I was quickly excluded from their conversation as they reminisced about the Paris of nine years before, Duff, and HBF in St. Jean de Luz and since. My father was suddenly in a world entirely unknown to me.

As vivid as anything during that visit was our meeting the following morning with Great Uncle Arthur—the largest man I had ever met. His hand when I shook it seemed twice the size of other men's, and his trousers, held up and away from his body by broad suspenders, were like a barrel around him. He seemed amused by my staring and his voice boomed.

What he and Chas had in common was Harvard and, more specifically, Harvard sports. They agreed there didn't seem much hope for that fall's football "squad."

For a period in the 1930s Arthur was president of the Art Students League's Board of Directors. He died in 1945, leaving no children. Not long after his death, Elizabeth arranged a memorial exhibition of his paintings at the Deerfield Artists Association.

Like Spencer's, most of Arthur's landscapes are gently moody. Some suggest mysteries under the forest canopy— agreeable rather than threatening ones. Many have the familiar fields of the floodplain in the foregrounds, but Arthur had a brighter view of the world than his father or his brothers, and his pictures are his, not copies or imitations.

Spencer's, Robert's, and Arthur's work reminds the viewer of George's and the indebtedness in subject and tone is easy to recognize, but George made people central to his pictures while his sons did not. George's landscapes reverberate as psychology, while his sons' must speak directly and only rarely is there a compelling voice.

When as a child I asked Chas who my Great Aunt Violet's husband was he replied, "A portrait painter. Very successful." His dismissive tone reflected several things: his feeling that Augustus Tack's apparently unequivocal membership in the Establishment, symbolized by the many board room portraits Tack had painted, were unseemly for a true artist; a family dislike of Violet that Chas shared because of her superior airs and cutting tongue, which affected feelings about her loyal husband; and, very likely in Chas's case, an uneasiness with Tack's spirituality. Tack was a practicing Roman Catholic all his life and he expressed religious feeling frankly and made art from it.

Chas's tone was unwarranted, I believe, although in Tack's lifetime many artists and critics sounded similar notes about him. Tack was, in fact, an exceptionally versatile and able artist, and if he failed, finally, to achieve a place among the most revered in American art it was not because he aimed low—for those board room portraits. At his best his aim was very high.

Tack sought, in the words of Duncan Phillips, founder of Washington's Phillips Collection and Tack's greatest supporter, to find "a new way to make the painter's raw materials serve the uses and ends of the spirit." In his abstract paintings Tack attempted to suggest an underlying order in the universe by depicting, in his own words, "the poetic world of spirit fringing on the world of facts."

Art historian Russell Lynes aptly called Tack "an eccentric conformist." While he was financially among the best rewarded painters of his time, he paid heavy prices, I believe, both for his conformity and for his eccentricity; his fellow social-conservatives rejected his abstract work; his fellow bohemian artists demeaned him for his well-paid, skillful, but not strikingly original murals and portraits. No one celebrated the whole Tack.

Tack, born in 1870 in Pittsburgh, was the second of fourteen children of a well-off Catholic family that moved to New York when Tack was thirteen. He was educated in Jesuit schools and received his Bachelor's degree from St. Francis Xavier College. He became a student at the Art Students League in 1890. H. Siddons Mowbray, Kenyon Cox, and particularly John Twachtman were his teachers, and Tack was most affected by the aesthetic movment, which rejected the Ruskinian idea of art as being in itself a moral expression and declared that art's purpose was to create beauty. Tack's mentor became, and remained, John La Farge.

Tack took extended painting and art-study trips to Europe in 1890, '93, and '95. Although Violet was sometimes a student at the League in the '90s, she and Tack did not make significant contact until 1897 in Deerfield, where Tack had joined a small colony of younger artists attracted there by the legacy of George Fuller's work.

Tack had been an admirer of George's from his first exposure to the paintings, especially to George's "spiritual" side. George's best pictures, whether portraits or people in landscapes, asserted something deeper than his subjects' personalities.

Thus there was every reason for Tack to be interested in meeting George's daughter. He and Violet had much to talk about, and they soon were taking walks, riding horseback through the valley, and painting together.

After a trip to Boston in 1897 Tack wrote to Violet, "I am back again at the studio [in New York] all fired with enthusiasm having seen such fine pictures in Boston. The finest of all was [George Fuller's] *Winifred Dysart.* It is the purest picture I have ever seen. I think I shall never forget Duveneck's wife [the subject of another George Fuller portrait] also. Do you know how much you have to do with both of these masterpieces? I felt my love for you in them both."

That same year Tack painted a self-portrait to be given to his parents that shows, in Leslie Furth's words, Tack's "gentle, tentative character." He painted himself in shirtsleeves but wearing a starched white collar, bow tie, and his eyeglasses. Another self-portrait, done many years later near the end of his life, shows a man whose face has remained virtually unchanged but whose hair has gone white. He is wearing an only slightly less stiff-looking shirt, a necktie, the eyeglasses, and a three-piece suit. In fifty years Tack had not gained or lost a pound.

Augustus and Violet married in June of 1900 and began a life wholly given to the professional practice of art. While I believe Tack's character was indeed "gentle," I find nothing tentative in it. There is no hint in his history of there ever having been a doubt in his mind that he was and should be a painter. He made and continued to make sensible decisions to perfect his skills and to advance his career.

Tack's work had first been shown in a number of group exhibitions and he had had his first solo New York exhibition in 1896. Now he had married a woman who was the opposite of a "shrinking Violet" and who knew the workings of the art world as well as anyone. In fact, he had married a full-time manager—for Violet soon ceased to paint.

During their courtship Tack had written to Violet, "I can imagine no life so full of possible beauty as an artist's. It means the highest comprehension of life—the deepest faith in religion, and is the happiest existence." Tack would keep this faith, and Violet would pursue and count the pennies, often finding that more of them were needed.

Violet bore two children, Agnes in 1901 and Robert three years later. In 1908 the family was dealt a hard surprise when Violet was diagnosed with tuberculosis. No medication had been found for the disease and, like many others of that era, she went to a sanitarium at Saranac Lake in New York's Adirondack Mountains to recuperate. She stayed there, almost without vacation, for five years.

Tack worked extremely hard. He kept a studio in Boston—he had one gallery exhibition there during those years. He maintained a studio in New York, a city he had come to detest but where the majority of his commissions were obtained. And he had a studio in Greenfield, where he was happiest because his children were living with their grandmother, Agnes, in Deerfield.

Necessity and Tack's ease and familiarity in the conventional and monied world combined to increase his production of portraits and marketable landscapes, but Tack was seeking at the same time to go beyond what he and his contemporaries had done and were doing. He was interested in Seurat's "pointillism," a technique he mastered and used. The objectives of the symbolists got his attention and approval, and he admired the semi–abstractions of Maurice Prendergast. In 1914 Tack defended the cubistic abstractions of Pablo Picasso to a perplexed Duncan Phillips.

During the years of Violet's illness and of the outbreak and slaughter of the World War, Tack's religious feelings found their way onto canvas as they had not before. He painted a series of biblical paintings—*Madonna of the Everlasting Hills, The Voice Crying in the Wilderness,* and others, and painted the beautiful mural of New Testament scenes behind the altar of South Deerfield's modest Roman Catholic Church.

These were figurative but not "realistic" works. Tack wrote that he was seeking an art that would "eventually be able to exert a great power over the mind and the emotions without any resort to literary associations." In other words, an art that would produce religious feeling without reminding the viewer of the literal events of the life of Jesus or Mary, or of any other historical religious figure.

Such thoughts won over Duncan Phillips, a man of Tack's age and background who possessed a fortune he was eager to spend on the acquisition and promotion of art that aroused his passionate approval. Phillips published an article on Tack in *International Studio* in 1916, after which the two men became close friends. They thought alike in many ways and even bore a physical resemblance to one another. A portrait Tack made of Phillips at this time much resembles his early self-portrait both in features and in the pose and attitude.

Phillips initially consulted Tack on the design of the Phillips Gallery in Washington, and subsequently Tack became a director of its corporation. Phillips remained Tack's committed supporter throughout his life, often attempting to sell his work to other collectors and museums. After Tack's death in 1949, Phillips continued to buy up what remained in the studio of his work in order to provide Violet with an income.

"Without any resort to literary associations" meant, of course, that the resulting painting would be abstract, and by the early 1920s Tack was developing an approach to abstraction that was very much his own. He did not begin with the premise of cubism, which virtually all other abstractionists then did. Instead, rather than attempting to paint simultaneously the several sides of an object or person, Tack worked from his own photographs or drawings of the natural world. He would limn the outlines of the photographed boulders, let us say, in a canyon, and the shapes of the distant mountain peaks and the clouds above—many of the original scenes were of the dry and rocky West. He would then flatly color the various shapes, but not with colors that matched their colors in nature. Instead he used color to express and affect mood. The upward thrust of the peaks was emphasized.

Some of these paintings are entirely without depth. Color

borders color without gradation. Thus the "canyon" is un-recognizable unless one has seen the original photograph or an early version of the painting. These works have re-minded many of the later works of Clifford Still, who may well have studied them.

In Tack's first attempts to make abstracts he had not used landscape but attempted to abstract from familiar, often-represented biblical events, wanting and hoping to arouse religious feeling through subliminal recognition of these familiar symbols. *The Crowd*, for example, painted in 1921, is a panoramic scene of Christ's crucifixion. *Magi's Journey* bears an explicit title, but both paintings are confusing rather than inspiring. So much is made obscure by rapidly shifting color planes that the intended "great power over the mind and emotions" is not achieved. Viewing these two pictures is instead an exercise in guesswork and puzzle-solving.

The later abstracts, most of them commissioned by Phil-lips for the Gallery's Music Room, are much the stronger for having been based on landscape. Some of them, *Ecstasy,* for example, and *Liberation,* seem to me masterpieces of evocation. These paintings do have depth, but in wholly unfamiliar territories.

The Music Room works were accomplished in the last years of the 1920s and early '30s, and when they were completed Tack returned to the mural and portrait work that usually sustained him. Only in the early '40s did he make a few more abstracts.

In 1924 the Tacks inherited from Agnes the studio across Mill Road from The Bars, and they later bought a second house in the nearby township of Conway. The Conway house was several hundred feet above the level of the Pocumtuck Valley and thus somewhat cooler in summer.

Also in 1924 Tack leased an extraordinary studio situated at the roof level of New York's Grand Central Station. Reached by an elevator near the station's Vanderbilt Avenue entrance, the studio's single room was perhaps three stories high from floor to skylight, with a half-floor balcony midway. Tack kept this studio until the end of his life, although he was often absent for long periods fulfilling important commissions. He painted the historical murals at the state capitol of Nebraska, and the murals in the capitol of the province of Manitoba, Winnipeg. When there was time, he and Violet and the children took vacations in Carmel, California, and other scenic places.

By the 1940s Tack's reputation as a portrait painter was such that he was commissioned to portray General George Marshall and the other members of the Joint Chiefs of Staff, and President Harry Truman. When Tack died, a group portrait of Truman and his cabinet was left unfinished.

Duncan Phillips wrote regretfully in 1933 that "if Tack had been painting his unique maps of color for the last twenty years he would now be reaping the reward in universal acclaim for having invented a new decorative language. His other researches of earlier years have not been so successful, and his conservative portraits and traditional mural paintings have made him a limited reputation as an eclectic painter rather than as one of America's most original painters."

Not long after he published this evaluation, Phillips wrote Tack that the plans for the expansion of the Phillips Gallery would have to be changed. The Depression had made it impossible to go forward with the construction and, due to the restrictions of currently available space, Tack's abstracts would not be permanently and exclusively installed in the Music Room. Sweetening this message, Phillips pointed out that showing the abstracts in the company of such other "modernists" as Van Gogh, Rouault, and Cezanne should help establish Tack as an equal among them.

Tack apparently accepted this turn of events as unavoidable, but three years later, when Phillips went further toward vitiating his and Tack's original vision by suggesting that he might make trades or sales of some of the paintings, writing to Tack, resignedly, that "the whole plan [of the Music Room] was a beautiful dream," Tack responded strongly:

"I am not happy in the idea of breaking up the decorative scheme of the really heroic abstractions," he wrote. "I consider the conception my magnum opus. It may never be carried further, but it is complete. It is in a sense cosmic—a poem on Life itself."

Leslie Furth writes of these paintings that "Tack drew on a dictum of St. Ignatius of Loyola—art as an aid to meditation—to explain his own painting. The titles seem generally to correspond to St. Ignatius's belief in the phases of spiritual development leading to ecstasy and the union with God." It is hardly surprising, then, that Tack did not want the series broken up and dispersed.

Both of Violet's and Tack's children died young, one of illness, the other in a car wreck. Tack simply went on working. While it is clear that Violet was the controlling partner in the marriage, there is no evidence Tack ever resented this or the economic demands she put upon him.

Tack's life and career make me think of Spinoza's conclusion that all events in all lives are controlled by God, but that man is "free" when he accepts and loves the fate God has dealt him.

Tack loved to work, loved to do the work that came to hand, and when, as rarely happened, the work allowed him to depict the spiritual, he loved it more. But he did not suppose he was owed more opportunities to do it than he was given.

Like George's, Tack's work had a life after his death and then, apparently, an ending. In 1993 the Phillips Gallery's major summer exhibition was a Tack retrospective. The paintings were selected from the seventy-nine Tacks then in the Phillips's permanent collection, and while they represented Tack's entire career and the various kinds of pictures he painted, the emphasis was on the abstracts. It was as though Duncan Phillips was, from far beyond the grave, making another attempt to establish Tack as a major figure in American art history.

After the exhibition's run at the Phillips it traveled to several other museums, and it did attract notice, but the notices were not what Phillips would surely have hoped. Roberta Smith wrote in the *New York Times* that the exhibition "fills in Tack's career and may present the best possible case for his achievement, but it never makes him seem like much more than a curiosity, a relic whose work only intermittently comes to life."

Smith's article is headlined, "Early Blueprints for Abstract Expressionism," a period she says she believes to be "American painting's finest hour," but rather than celebrating Tack as an innovator and forerunner, she finds that his work rarely satisfies and that much of it seems forced.

Hers should not be the final word. Gallery-goers continue to react with surprise and pleasure to the Music Room paintings, whether or not they know anything of Tack. But the print reactions to the exhibition make it unlikely Tack's position will rise in the American pantheon.

In July, 1944, five years before his death, Tack included in a letter to Phillips a quote from a Japanese artist, Hokusai, who wrote at the age of ninety-five, "If the fates will only give me five more years I may do something."

Tack did not "do something" exceptional in his remaining years. So far as I know, neither did Hokusai. But the spirit of the statement reflects what Tack wanted to express in his "Poem on Life" series. In possessing such a spirit Tack was—despite the tragedies of his childrens' deaths, the disappointments of his career, and what must have been a difficult life at home—a blessed man.

While his religious faith, his early education, and his relationship to John La Farge were certainly important in blessing him, the spirit that he perceived in George Fuller's paintings also played an important part. It was an attraction so strong, after all, that Tack had come to live in Deerfield to better feel its sources.

The ideas of the impossibility of doing anything before one is free, of starting within a picture and painting one's way out, the description of the arts as "soul-absorbing"—these Fuller-family heirlooms had become Tack's significant heritage quite as much as they were George's childrens', perhaps more so. And, dedicated craftsman that he was, Tack, like Joel Negus, might have said that whatever came from his hand was a work of art.

Chapter Seven

THE GLAMOR OF ART:
CLARA FULLER TAYLOR
and WARNER TAYLOR
CHAS and JANE FULLER
ALFRED FULLER, ALICE FULLER GOODHUE
and ELIZABETH FAIRCHILD

Lucia Fairchild Fuller's message to her children that they must not become artists was never challenged by them. I imagine that her anxieties were overwhelmingly impressive to them.

One source of anxiety of which the children were constantly aware growing up was HBF's inability to bring in sufficient income to support the family. While Lucia worked as hard as her health would permit, HBF dreamed of "great" pictures, and experimented, and changed his mind. He had done some good things, but this was not a career! If only he could have made up his mind to accomdate himself to the wishes of those who might have helped him!

But while Clara and Chas were told to prepare themselves for lives outside the fine arts, the entire atmosphere of Cornish, and surely of every casual remark spoken by their parents or visitors to the house told them that the only thing of any real worth in the world was art of the highest order. HBF might not succeed in creating it, but at least he was trying—as was Lucia whenever she could take time off from making money.

Thus the children's upbringing had shown them what was of value and what was not (the values of the "philistines"), and they had, at the same time, been commanded to pursue only things of lesser value, objectives beneath their talents. Training and encouragement from some of America's most successful artists had convinced them—quite rightly—of their own talents, and now they were told they must have more mundane careers, which meant second-rate lives.

If I go into their histories, which did not produce art, it is because their dilemna seems unusual and because their outcomes were tragic. Through HBF, Clara and Chas were in the fifth generation of Negus-Fuller artists, and their mother was also an artist. Was a genetic imperative being denied? Or was the implicit mediocrity—from a Cornish point of view—of what they were encouraged to become enough to make shambles of their lives?

When Clara left Bryn Mawr and matriculated at the University of Wisconsin she soon found that her acquaintanceships with many of the greats of American art hastened and ensured her acceptance in Madison's society. My guess is that her bisexuality was understood by many—including Warner—as an artist's eccentricity, and that it added to Clara's glamor. She was already eye-catching, bright-eyed and square-shouldered, with a brilliant, broad smile.

Clara's connection to the art world was emphasized by Lucia's coming to live with the Taylors in 1918. Lucia embodied past artistic glories.

Francis Steegmuller, who later became well-known for biographical and interpretive works, especially on Gustave Flaubert, published a novel in 1930 entitled *The Musicale,* which is a *roman a clef* on the lives of Clara and Warner and their Madison friends. The novel's action takes place during an evening piano recital at the Taylor home—Steegmuller, of course, changed all the names.

Steegmuller's Warner is presented as a brutally witty, socially perverse, and unfriendly Professor of English. He and his attractive and suffering wife are living in the town of Fox River, the "Athens of the Middle West." Half of the guests that evening are pining for Europe or New England, to which some are lucky enough to be able to repair each summer.

Many of the hostess's mother's paintings are hung in the house, and one of the guests, a successful teacher but a disappointed man, muses, "Had she been a great painter? No, but a famous one, an 'important' one and a fashionable one in her day (the last generation had thought her fine; her pre-Raphaelite heads and very Greekish sylvan pictures were never mentioned, except to be scorned, in books on paintings published now). One heard she had a daughter somewhere; here he was in the daughter's drawing room, and [she] was content to live sociably and provincially and talk with pride (occasionally) of her mother, surrounding herself meanwhile with people who were more or less intelligent, pleasant, and quiet."

Several of the men guests at the recital are impressed with the hostess's attractiveness, but none imagine an affair with her, although they universally dislike her husband. Is this because her aura of inherited glory has put her above their reach?

At the novel's end, after the host has made a minor but disagreeable scene, the hostess makes up her mind to leave the marriage, but, "Of course, I have been as decided as this in other years, she thought."

Clara did not leave the marriage. In 1928 she bore a daughter, Lucia, and as this Lucia grew up Clara told her of the perfections of her Cornish childhood, creating a picture of an infinitely gifted society concerned exclusively with the making of "fine art" and the extraordinary education of its children.

Since Cornish as a colony had vanished, together with the power of the Beaux Arts ideals that inspired it, nothing resembling it would be seen again. Clara and Warner's lives and, eventually, young Lucia's would in their own minds remain always second-rate in comparison to the half-remembered, half-imagined Cornish.

In *The Musicale* a woman who comes in to serve and clean up at the party notices with disapproval the many bottles of gin shelved in the pantry. In the Taylor household alcohol was an important factor that became the dominant one.

Clara never worked as a journalist or at any other job that might have provided independence and satisfaction in accomplishment. Warner became the artist of the family as a photographer. During the Taylors' summers on Monhegan where they built a house, he photographed the sights that had drawn so many artists there—the artifacts of the fishermen's lives, the barns, the rudimentary tools, and the fog-shrouded land and seascapes. According to daughter Lucia, Warner spoke only of his technical rather than his aesthetic problems as a photographer, but many of his pictures are artistically strong, unsentimentally evocative of the spare means of living of the islanders and thus of their lives and character.

Warner may have gotten from Clara exactly what he wanted—insight into the creation of art, acceptance among artists and identification with them—while in return Clara neither received nor created anything fundamentally substantial on which to live and develop herself.

Many besides Warner wanted identification with artists in the first decades of the century. Now it is a commonplace, but then it had novelty.

The arts had acquired two sorts of glamor. Firstly, the acquisition of the great art of the past had become the ultimate symbol of bourgeois wealth. Paradoxically, the new art of the twentieth century symbolized the ideological attack on bourgeois ideas and power. The deliberate and often brutal nonsense of Dada, the vision-twisting of cubism, and, in America, the "Ashcan School" of painting all declared that the bourgeois structure of power and its choices of imagery were bankrupt of virtue, that that art had lost humanity and interest of any sort.

Thus there came into being a new stereotype of the artist—the artist as radical hero. First a small, then a large number of people, disillusioned by the horrors to which the nineteenth century had led, wanted to identify with that hero, a new slayer of dragons.

In the year of Jane White Fuller's birth, 1897, it would have been quite unthinkable that a young woman "of family" should marry an artist. Like the musicians who played in the grand houses of those years, artists, except in rare cases, came in through the service entrance to do their work. Patrons were not shy about telling the musician or the portrait or decorative painter what was wanted and what not, or in telling the artist his results were unsatisfactory. Prices were agreed on in advance and money withheld if the patron was not pleased.

By the 1920s this order of precedence had not been entirely reversed but was much changed. Adventurous young women of wealthy backgrounds, perceiving that while money had liberated people in many ways it had, at the same time, created a stultifying, defensive, self-protective, and insulated upper class in which they were expected to play pawn-like roles in games of family betterment, were increasingly having affairs with and making romantic marriages with artists. Jane's second cousin, Kay Sage, the surrealist painter, married the better-known surrealist, Yves Tanguy, for example. These relationships resembled in their clarity of ambition—and the greater wealth on the female side—the earlier marriages of rich young American women to titled Europeans of which Henry James and Edith Wharton had written. But the milieux in which the new couples lived were very different, and the anger they shared was against the bourgeoisie rather than in celebration of both aristocratic and bourgeois comforts.

At the time of Jane and Chas's marriage in 1922 they seemed mainly to have shared aesthetic tastes and beliefs. Indeed, in the '20s and early '30s they accomplished much work together, Jane making sculptures for the cornices and gardens for a number of the houses that Chas designed.

At some unfixable point, however, Chas's heart went over to the avant garde and the radical artist, and once it had he no longer much believed in what he was doing as an architect. He had an outstanding facility for designing the sort of structures he was offered to do, and he wished, certainly, to make a place for himself in the 1920s sun, but at bottom he was more interested in what Picasso and Man Ray were doing than he was in the design of the neoclassical banks and the neocolonial city halls that were rising around the country. Construction itself did not interest him. Engineering was done "by the engineers," as he would say. He never out of curiosity learned to drive nails or use a saw.

While Paris had provided George Fuller with important revelations in 1860, and thirty-one years later had given HBF a means, symbolism, to break away from his artistic heritage, the effect on Jane and Chas in 1924-5 was not in aesthetics but in how they saw themselves. When they returned to New York they felt they had found "their contemporaries," as both would say, the people with whom they would identify.

The poet Archibald MacLeish and his wife, Ada, had become friends, and to a lesser extent they had got to know Gerald and Sarah Murphy, but mainly the left bank expatriates they had bonded with were less known. Chas often spoke of an American who made a living handicapping horses running at the Paris racetracks, and sometimes of an Englishwoman, a former showgirl, who disappeared one day from the Dingo Bar and was never seen or heard of again.

The freedom in all sorts of choices these expatriates and the Fullers experienced had their dangers, but the shared, tangy taste of them would remain irresistible on their palates.

Many opportunities seemed to have been waiting for Chas in New York. His Groton and Harvard friends had married and were building houses for themselves, and then a wider circle of acquaintances wanted his services. His greatest opportunity would come from within Jane's family.

Jane's two younger sisters, Marian and Babs, had by now married, and not only were the sisters close friends, the husbands were friends of Chas's. One, Tim Coward, had spent part of his childhood at Cornish, and the other, Douglas Burden, had followed Chas by several years at both Groton and Harvard. "At a café table in Arles," Jane said, she and Chas had conceived of the idea of jointly buying a piece of property within commuting distance of New York with her two sisters and their husbands, and building houses for each family on it, all designed by Chas.

There were a number of Cornish-like features to this scheme. As the Fuller swimming pool had been "communal" at Cornish, so would there be one centrally placed pool and one tennis court. At Cornish certain responsibilities had devolved on certain people—the Dewings were in charge of the *tableaux vivants,* Parrish of stage sets, and so on. At Crowfields, the one-hundred-thirty acre failing farm the three couples bought near Bedford Village, New York, similar responsibilities were assigned. Sister Babs was in charge of theatricals, Tim of competitive games, Douglas of all things pertaining to nature (there were two stands of forest on the property in which he made trails and erected a tepee), Sister Marian of the arts of painting and singing, and Chas and Jane of the plant—the three new houses and two leftover houses and a barn from the property's farm. All would take part in joint houseparties, which required further assignments.

Several important things distinguished Crowfields from Cornish. One was that the three couples were not much concerned about expense, at least initially. There was talk about creating lots on which other artists might build houses, but this was not realized. Perhaps most striking of the differences was the three sisters' belief in planning parenthoods, something not easily accomplished thirty years before.

I, Jane's second child, have first cousins almost exactly my age, Wendy Burden Morgan and the late Jennifer Gregg Coward Sims, and my younger sister, Jill Fuller Fox, has cousins her age, Douglas Burden Junior, and the late Sue Coward Marquand. Our mothers thought that being pregnant together would have advantages, and that we children would gain from having playmates within the family.

A young architect would have had difficulty finding a better chance than Crowfields to display his talents, and Chas responded with three memorable houses, each in a different adapted style. The Fullers' was Georgian with a mansard roof, the Cowards' French Provincial, red tile on top, and the Burdens' was a slate-roofed, native stone "cottage" that grew to be the largest of the three. The houses were so sited on the hilly terrain that they were entirely out of sight of one another.

The Burden house was not completed until 1932, and it was built to plan, but the stock market crash of 1929 did eliminate some features of the original scheme. A hillside amphitheater was never built, for example. Crowfields was completed just as the market for new housing dried up.

Relative to many other architects, Chas had some choice jobs in the 1930s. He designed the town hall of Islip, Long Island, a science building for the Choate School—both of them neocolonial—and in 1937 he won a competition to design the first jointly-financed federal, New York State, and New York City housing project, the Harlem River Houses at 153rd Street and the Harlem River.

The Houses are extraordinary to see today. While the Harlem that surrounds them is a desolation of boarded-up, unreclaimable buildings and rubble-strewn empty lots, the one and a half blocks of Houses are in excellent condition, their walls without graffitti, their sidewalks and interior courtyards swept clean. It seems that a large proportion of the tenants have been resident for many years and have seriously cared for the buildings and grounds.

The thinking that went into the Houses design must be partly responsible for their success. The four-story brick-clad buildings are without elevators, flat-roofed, and with unadorned facades. There is nothing grand about them.

The low-rise ensures that there will not be overcrowding, however, and the large interior courts are pleasantly shaded by high trees and contain benches and children's playgrounds. In the largest yard are two sculptures by Paul Manship, one of a muscular, African-American man stripped to the waist, the other of an African-American woman with a small child at her knee. Both adults are standing proudly straight.

The choice of Manship to make these sculptures was not Chas's. He had wanted someone "more contemporary," he told me. But although the depiction of African-American ideals as lower-class manual laborers may seem patronizing today, the figures project strength and dignity. It is surely significant that they have stood where they were placed more than sixty years ago without being damaged.

On a wall by one of the entries to the larger courtyard there is a bronze plaque commemorating the names of those who brought the Houses into being: President Franklin D. Roosevelt, Secretary of the Interior Harold Ickes, New York Governor Robert Wagner, Mayor of New York Fiorello LaGuardia, Commissioner of Parks Robert Moses, Housing Authority Director Lang Post, and Architect Charles Fuller.

Chas's life had become chaotic by the mid-1930s. As his drinking increased his automobiles were frequently dented, trains were missed, connections and phone calls not made. He and Jane took a number of "vacations" from one another, Chas sometimes writing painfully contrite letters to her.

He went twice to a kind of alcoholic recovery program, a "farm" in Rhode Island where the objective was to teach the patient moderate drinking rather than abstinence, but Chas could not control his drinking for long.

Chas had many love affairs during these years, some with Jane's knowledge and even collaboration. At least two of his paramours became weekend guests at our house, one with her husband, and both of these women became friends of Jane's—friendships that lasted many years beyond the womens' relationships with Chas. With Chas's encouragement Jane had at least one affair of her own.

Chas was psychoanalysed in this period but, whatever the merits of the analysis, his behavior did not change.

In August of 1937 Jane told Chas of her decision to divorce. When she returned from Reno Chas moved into a small apartment in New York. Within a year Marian and Babs decided to divorce as well. The sisters would all get fresh starts, and there would soon be three new resident men at Crowfields, but the Cornish aspects of the place came to an end. The men were of different personalities and interests, and no doubt the sisters had lost some faith in what had seemed a utopian idea.

The Choate School science building was Chas's last important job as a design architect. He kept office space, but had little work though the last years of the 1930s. In addition to new women partners he experimented with at least one homosexual affair. The "poison of non-fulfillment" that he had feared in 1929 had been avoided, but nicotine and alcohol and purposelessness diminished and depressed him.

In 1940 he took a job with the Federal Housing Authority and moved to Washington D.C., but resigned his job shortly after war was declared in December 1941. He wanted to be—and was certain that he would be—recommissioned a Lieutenant in the U. S. Navy, and he was profoundly shocked by the Navy's refusal to do so. He then tried the U. S. Army with the same result.

I believe that he felt deeply shamed by these refusals and the evidence of his physical deterioration. He returned to the Rhode Island "farm" and after some weeks of total sobriety shipped out as an ordinary seaman in the Merchant Marine.

During the following two years he sailed on a number of high-risk Atlantic convoy voyages, then seriously injured a hand in a shipboard accident. He was on disability pay in New York when he met and subsequently married Anne Jones Thacher, a fashion editor at *Town and Country* magazine.

During the few sober years that followed it seemed that Chas had found a new life and a much happier one. In 1945 he enrolled as a graduate student in city planning at MIT and received his masters degree in 1947. That led to a job as a project architect with the New York State Housing Authority, and in 1952, under the federal program that became AID, to a position as city planning advisor to the recently created independent government of Indonesia.

But he had begun to drink again—without restraint once he reached Djakarta. Nonetheless, he was sent temporarily from Djakarta to advise on an urban project in a Mideastern country. The U. S. ambassador to that country gave a dinner party on Chas's arrival to introduce him to the dignataries with whom he would work. Chas got drunk and—apropos of what he could not remember—he declared to the table, "I hate America!"

That broke up the dinner party and ended his government employment.

He spent his six remaining years in New York and Stonington, Connecticut where he and Anne had bought a house in the late 1940s. They bought, refurbished, and sold several Stonington houses in the 1950s, the most interesting transformation being that of a deconsecrated Methodist church on Main Street into a dwelling.

Something I heard him say in those years both shocked me and seemed enlightening. He was drinking one day with a painter, longtime friend Louis Bouche. "Fuck *taste!*" Chas said. "Isn't that right, Louis? Fuck *taste!*"

Bouche agreed, as it was perhaps logical that he would. An original artist whose aim is to produce something both unfamiliar and "true" must suppose that his or her work may look strange to some, particularly to those concerned with "good taste." But good taste was precisely what Chas possessed as an architectural heritage from his Cornish childhood. His acceding to Lucia's command that he not be an artist had confined his working life to "good taste," and now he openly despised it.

Would his feelings have been different if he had set out be an original artist? Perhaps he would have been more bitterly disappointed, but I do not believe that in his own eyes his work and life would have been reduced to trivia. I do not believe he would have announced that he hated America, which surely can be interpreted as, I hate myself.

Chas suffered from emphysema. In 1960 he was hospitalized to dry out, and died there of a heart attack.

Jane's best years as a sculptor were the years of her partnership with Chas. Believing in the Beaux Arts aesthetic as she did, sculpture combined with architecture offered her her best opportunities.

The neck and head and gilded horn of a unicorn that jutted from the cornice of the Fuller house at Crowfields, a bull's head with a laurel streamer draped over its horns that fitted into a similar cornice at Syosset, Long Island—these and several other of her pieces are both bold and in harmony with the overall design of the houses. They "distinguished" these houses—that was a word and an idea Jane liked.

Her work after her divorce from Chas consisted mainly of stylized birds and other animals, work that was smaller in scale and rarely site-specific. Many collectors were charmed by these pieces, and they sold well at her several exhibitions at the British-American Gallery in New York. One sculpture of a greatly enlarged moth with folded wings is in the collection of the Whitney Museum.

On commission, she did a number of lifesize animal sculptures for collector Paul Mellon's garden and for other outdoor settings.

Critics were respectful of the pleasing qualities of Jane's exhibited work. Jane would place a sign, "Please Touch" at the entrance to her exhibitions and the rounded shapes and interesting materials, much of it stone in later years, did invite handling. But the critics were unexcited, sometimes a trifle condescending. She had followed Paul Manship into a "smoothing-out," as she put it, of the forms of animals, but only in a few pieces—particularly in the enlargements—did she seem to go beyond him.

Sometime around 1950 Jane read and was appalled by Rachel Carson's book *The Silent Spring* which revealed for the first time the ruinous effects that DDT and other chemicals were having on the world's wildlife, particularly on its birds, but the book's message did not affect the art Jane was then producing. I do not believe she ever considered depicting dying birds or eggs broken because thinned by chemicals—her training required ideals rather than grim realities. What could the effect be on her art, then, of the knowledge that thousands of species were going extinct largely as a result of human efforts to grow bigger tomatoes? What did this mean about human idealism?

Jane's output diminished over the years, which seemed understandable since her marriage to publisher Cass Canfield required her to travel and to entertain. Nonetheless, I was shocked and pained—far more than I would have guessed beforehand—when, in her early sixties, she told me she had decided to make no more sculptures. She said she did not feel she had sufficient energy to continue, and that there were other things she wished to do. In truth, there were not other things she was truly eager to do, and her energy was sporadically, at least, strong. Perhaps what Carson had exposed had invaded Jane's Platonic imagination without her recognizing it, and had made the creation of ideal figures increasingly irrelevant, thus harder to accomplish.

Jane lived into her late eighties. Her Beaux Arts standards never wavered in judging the work of others, indeed, the years seemed to reinforce them. Exhibitions of contemporary art often caused her genuine, vocalized anger and distress.

The talents of Spencer and Mary's eldest child, Katharine, born in 1891, were encouraged in childhood by her parents, and in her late teens she was sent to the Boston Museum School. After graduation she became a teacher of painting at Boston's Miss Sacker's School, an arts and crafts institution. She taught there, producing little work of her own that has survived, until 1927. Then, at the age of thirty-six she returned to Deerfield to marry Richard Arms.

The Arms family was among Deerfield's oldest, and had been close with the Fullers at least since a previous Richard Arms had gone with George Fuller to Illinois to work on the railroad survey. Katharine moved into the old Arms house on Main Street, and soon became involved in Deerfield Industries which was reviving colonial crafts such as crewel work and needlepoint and selling the products to the visitors who were coming to Old Deerfield in increasing numbers. Artisans, most of them local housewives, produced a widening range of artifacts including hooked rugs and kitchenware. Deerfield Industries was the precursor of the Deerfield Craft Fairs, which still are popular. The New England myth lives on in the demand for these artifacts.

Undoubtedly Katharine's choice of craft over fine art was economically motivated. She continued to teach painting when the opportunity arose, and found other work as well. She had married a "difficult" man.

Richard Arms had been a Navy pharmacist's mate during the World War, and he had afterwards entered Harvard's Medical School, but he was dismissed from it. Troubles at least partially due to alcohol continued throughout his life. He was involved in a number of business ventures, among them a partnership in a "pioneer" gasoline station that continues to operate near the south entrance from the state highway to Deerfield's Main Street.

Mary, Katharine's mother, was not an admirer of Richard's. In a letter written in 1932 to Elizabeth who was then in Oracle, Arizona, Mary refers to Richard as "the lion," "an erratic boy," and "a handful," and says that Katharine "needs a visit away from him." By that time, however, Katharine's first child, Richard Junior, was four years old, and the household was as hard to get away from as perhaps it was to keep together.

Katharine's second child, Mary, was born in 1933. Eventually this Mary would inherit The Bars from Elizabeth who inherited it from Mary, Spencer's widow.

The elder Richard Arms died in 1956, suffering from ulcers. Katharine survived him by nearly thirty years. She continued to live in the Arms house into which her son, Richard and his wife Joan, moved and raised their children. Katharine's involvement in the crafts movement continued until her death.

Augustus Tack's portrait of Katharine's sister, Elizabeth, which hangs in Deerfield's Memorial Hall Museum, shows a pensive-looking girl of perhaps ten with exceptionally wide-set eyes and blonde curls, most of them obscured by a bulky winter coat. HBF also made a portrait of her as a girl, and these two uncles nourished her ambitions as an artist and gave her a stout confidence in herself.

Elizabeth would "speak her mind," as her niece and heir, Mary Arms Marsh, has said. Elizabeth sat and stood straight, chin up, and she spoke well, tartly or not, but she was surprisingly diffident or silent about her own art.

During the summers of the years 1910–1920 Elizabeth was often at Monhegan Island staying in the house that Mary and Spencer had built. It seems likely that arrangements had been made for her to stay with the renters of this house as part of their agreement with Mary. Rockwell Kent opened the Monhegan Summer School of Art in 1910, and he and George Bellows are often mentioned in Elizabeth's letters to her mother, although it is not clear that she was a regular student at the school. Monhegan affected her deeply, however, and her earliest preserved paintings were done there.

In a 1916 letter, written in her characteristic telegraphic style, Elizabeth wrote that "it is not Monhegan itself that appeals it is just the way the quaint life is set off by the beautiful background." She writes of Spencer's landscapes that "never [are] humans connected" to them, but that she believes "to be genuine it has to be loved, does it not? I believe I will do my best after something I love, no matter it perhaps has had the misfortune to be the sea or fishermen." The word "misfortune" apparently had to do with Mary's feelings that Elizabeth should not be associating with the Monhegan "locals." Elizabeth wrote, "I think I like people who don't know enough to be cynics. I love love love this place & the life."

Elizabeth was sent to the Boston Museum School in 1915 and during her several stays in the Dublin Colony she was treated as one of the most promising students, accompanying Abbot Thayer on nature walks, and posing for him when asked. His portrait of Elizabeth as a handsome, seemingly preoccupied and perhaps troubled young woman, is among his most interesting.

In the summer of 1920 Thayer's wife wrote to Mary Fuller, "Mr. Thayer has nothing but praise for [Elizabeth's] work. It is so good to have her here." Thayer had qualified Elizabeth to his wife as "a superb draughtsman, and most delicate colorist." He had lamented that "It's too bad she's not a man," and Thayer had said directly to Elizabeth, according to his wife's letter, that "he was sorry she was a woman."

How deeply this condemnation of her chances as an artist because of her gender affected Elizabeth it is impossible to know. The issue itself is puzzling.

In the library of The Bars was a collection of Caroline Negus Hildreth's drawings, and it seems probable that Elizabeth knew something of Caroline's successes among the transcendentalists and in New York and Italy. Elizabeth could even have read Caroline's letters. Another woman artist who was much closer to Elizabeth, her aunt, Lucia Fairchild Fuller, had had exciting recognition and commercial success during Elizabeth's childhood. While Victorian niceties had prevented Lucia from doing art school life studies in the same room with male students, nothing had prevented her work being included in the Columbian Exposition or her election as associate of the National Academy of Design. Lucia's example made it clear that a woman's art was not necessarily condemned either to obscurity or to the status of a hobby.

Still, in 1920, seven years after the famous women's

march for universal suffrage and on the eve of the constitutional amendment's passage that conferred the women's right to vote, Elizabeth was being told her future was stunted because of her sex.

On the face of it one could think she might have laughed—as some of the women then moving to Montparnasse surely would have—but it is also possible she read into Thayer's remarks a dismissal, at the highest level and in the most diplomatic terms, of her talents. She may have believed he was using her gender to let her down more easily. On the other hand, Thayer asked her to stay beyond the residencies of other students—surely she must have understood that as an affirmation of his enthusiasm for her work.

Family lore has it that Elizabeth was in love with one of her Museum School teachers, Ercole Cartoto, and her letters mention him often enough to make it doubtless the two were close. The legend continues that Mary disapproved of this relationship and required of Elizabeth that it be broken off. No other serious suitor of Elizabeth's can be found in her letters, although she had a long and close friendship with fellow Museum School student, Irwin Hoffman.

After joining HBF in Paris in 1924 Elizabeth remained in Europe for three years. She at first shared HBF's Val de Grace studio, then moved to share a studio with another artist, Helen Pratt. In 1925 she made a number of trips with Irwin Hoffman who had won a travel fellowship, and her letters, then and later, show that she sketched and painted in Italy, the south of France, and Spain, as well as in St. Jean de Luz and Paris.

Elizabeth sometimes wrote crisply when describing who and what she saw—Spanish men have "no necks," she observed, for example—but she was often caring about Chas and Jane and others whom her Deerfield correspondents would know. She consistently worried about HBF's health. Her clear sympathies helped her make many friends.

Neither firsthand viewing of the classic European masterpieces nor exposure to the new art on display in Montparnasse changed the way Elizabeth saw things, or worked. If anything, the European years deepened her humility about her own talents. She knew she was an *able* artist and came to believe she was not more.

Her landscapes, from the early Monhegan scenes to the later canvases of the Arizona desert, are alive and evocative; her portraits "catch" their subjects, and some are moving; she knew her way in the art world. But when she returned to Deerfield in late 1926 she seems to have decided that was where she would stay. She would find what work there was to do rather than seek a wider arena.

Elizabeth offered her services locally as a portrait painter, and she entered the local cultural life. She was a founder of the Deerfield Valley Artists Association, and she played violin in the Pioneer Valley Symphony based in Greenfield, as well as in its chamber music ensemble. In effect, she re-established her Deerfield identity, but she longed to get away from the long winters.

There is no evidence that Elizabeth took HBF's 1929 advice to visit Duff in Arizona, but in 1931 she did travel to Oracle, Arizona, a tiny village some forty miles from Tucson, to join her brother Alfred and his wife Anne, who were living there in a dirt-floored cabin for the winter. The trip was to be fateful.

Three years younger than Elizabeth, Alfred had graduated from Amherst College in 1924 and had gone to work for the New England Telephone Company. At the same time, Mary, for whom the family's artistic tradition was of utmost importance, urged him to paint.

That same year Mary sold the studio-gallery Williams family house on Albany Road to Deerfield Academy, now a private, nonprofit institution. Frank Boyden, who, fresh out of Amherst College in 1902 had become the Academy's headmaster, had by 1924 raised the enrollment from sixteen to more than one hundred students. From a village-supported high school it had become a boarding school whose strong reputation was spreading. Mary's agreement with Boyden was that, while the house's living spaces would be the Academy's to use as it wished, the studio space would remain dedicated to Fuller family art and Alfred would be the studio's custodian and curator.

Alfred was a tall, heavy, quiet, and "clumsy" man—I am quoting his nephew, Richard Arms Junior. It seemed to Arms that Anne "ran the show."

The couple moved west in 1930 and spent most of several years in La Jolla, where Alfred began to paint the seascapes that became his stock-in-trade, and where another development occurred that would be as important to their fortunes.

Anne was a trained nurse. Working in a San Diego hospital she became friends with a patient, Margaret Lewis, who was heir to a department store fortune and who suffered from a congenital and incurable disorder of the lower spine. Seemingly, Lewis was a lonely, frightened, and needy person. She and Anne became lovers, and a menage a trois was formed.

It seems doubtful that Mary Fuller exactly understood

the Alfred-Anne-Margaret Lewis relationship, but she disapproved of what her son was doing in La Jolla. In a letter to Elizabeth in Oracle in 1932, during the first of Elizabeth's winter returns there, Mary wrote that she was discouraging a friend from visiting "rich and idle friends in California," the Alfred Fullers. In the same letter Mary referred affectionately to Elizabeth as "my archaeology girl in Oracle." This was a misunderstanding but a minor one.

Oracle is a small community on the northern slope of the Catalina Mountains which stand to the northeast of Tucson. Oracle's Anglo history begins in the nineteenth century with the creation of large ranches and the establishment of a stagecoach stop. Mining operations then began that continue today in enormous open pits, just out of sight of the town.

Early in this century William Neel, an African-American who had been a member of Buffalo Bill's "Wild West" troupe, ran a combination dude ranch and hotel in the town.

The town's culture was changed by the arrival in 1924 of Alice Carpenter, a widow with a young son in delicate health, who stayed permanently after her son's death. She became Oracle's postmistress, was involved in all the town's business, and developed a strong and knowledgeable interest in archaeology. Her collection of Native American artifacts is now housed in a small Oracle museum.

During her first Oracle winters Elizabeth lived in a wood-floored, tent-roofed cabin on land that Alice had ceded to Alfred and Anne and that Elizabeth took over from them. She became Alice's great friend and often accompanied her on archaeological digs, but rather than dig, Elizabeth would draw or paint the landscape.

As years passed the walls of Elizabeth's house became

adobe, and the tent roof became tile. A screened front porch was added from which there was a long view of the dry and rugged, red and orange desert mountains.

Today the house, brought up to date in conveniences and with an addition larger than the original structure, belongs to a scientist and academic, Julio Betancourt, who was a boy in Oracle during the 1950s. He remembers the community as being personified by "four independent women. They *were* Oracle." He refers to "Alice and Leslie and Ellen and Em," "Leslie" being Elizabeth. Brother Alfred had nick-named her "Leslie" long ago, had introduced her as such, and she was so known in Oracle and Tucson, where she would regularly go for supplies and sometimes to teach art or to paint a commissioned portrait.

"Leslie" always wore dark clothes and one string of pearls, and she never talked about her life in Deerfield to which she would return every spring.

Elizabeth's attachment to her Oracle-Leslie life was passionate. One day in the 1930s a friend of Elizabeth's drove up to The Bars to take her to the railroad station to start her long trip to Tucson and found Mary at the door saying that Elizabeth was not going and that the friend should leave. From an upstairs window Elizabeth shouted, "I"m coming," and forced her way out past her furious mother. But Deerfield would remain as much a part of her fate as Oracle.

In 1924 Frank Boyden wrote a letter to the founder of the Society for the Preservation of New England Antiquities saying that "somehow there should be found some way of securing money to buy these old houses [on Deerfield's Main Street] as they are thrown on the market," that Deerfield should be preserved "for the whole country." For this quote and much of the information that follows I am indebted to Elizabeth Stillinger's *Historic Deerfield*.

There were indeed good historic and and commercial reasons to save these houses. Deerfield had been attracting visitors for many years, both to see its colonial architecture and to see the evidences of the battles with warring Mohawks that had taken place in 1675 and 1704. The latter episode, known as the "Deerfield Massacre," had been a turning point in the consolidation of European settlements in western Massachusetts. The tomahawk marks on some of Deerfield's front doors were exciting reminders of those times.

But by 1924 many of the old houses were falling into disrepair and abandonment due to their lack of modern heating, insulation, and plumbing. And for Boyden there was a strong reason to save them. In the words of a former teacher at the Academy, Boyden "regarded the whole town as a backdrop for the Academy." He had recently bought one of the old houses and behind its facade had built an Academy dormitory—he was not an historical purist. Boyden sensed the possibility of using the preservationist urge—to which the projects of Henry Ford and the Rockefeller restoration of Williamsburg, Virginia, had then given publicity and impetus—to help expand the Academy. It took him some time to do so, but in the late 1930s he found people to help him realize this project.

They were Henry and Helen Flynt, the enthusiastic parents of an Academy student. Henry had grown up in a small Massachusetts town and undoubtedly responded to Boyden's dry Yankee wit and to the Academy's clear success. Flynt had married the heiress to a Cincinatti milling fortune, and the couple lived in Greenwich, Connecticut.

To outsiders, at least, Boyden appeared to be a good representative of the New England myth. A small man, just over five feet tall, he hewed to some habits of his forebears and expressed conventional wisdom and a belief in rectitude with an even-keyed, laconically humorous delivery. He was open to new ideas, however, and he could be forceful.

On good weather days Boyden drove around the campus and down to the playing fields in an immaculate horse-drawn open carriage. Wearing a black necktie and a white blazer he knocked out grounders to the varsity infielders before baseball games, and at frequent school assemblies he could be both sympathetic and inspirational. He quoted Emerson, "Raise your eyes to the hills, boys!" meaning for us to set our sights high—as he had in developing the school. I can report these things because I was an Academy student during the academic year of 1941–42.

Boyden would never have quoted from Emerson's essay "Self Reliance," however, where Emerson advises that to develop character one should "always scorn appearances." Indeed, Boyden once said to a former student, "Appearance is everything," and he meant it. That was how the Academy was run. Our goal as students was not to become independent thinkers but to become agile climbers of corporate ladders, and we dressed in neckties and jackets accordingly.

While I was at the Academy a fire occurred in the living quarters of the Albany Road studio that Mary Fuller had sold to the school. I was unaware of the fire until Boyden summoned me to his office—a large desk set in an open, central area of the ground floor of the major classroom building where we students would see him several times a day, passing between classes. He asked me—forcefully, I would say—to refrain from telling anyone at The Bars about the event. It would just be better if they didn't know.

Mary and Elizabeth became involved in Boyden and the Flynt's efforts to preserve the appearance of the town in 1945. Flynt wrote to Elizabeth to say, "Your invaluable knowledge, your familiarity with people, events, and things, and your willingness to establish the many contacts that are necessary will be most helpful." Elizabeth had agreed to accept the position of director of research and development at Historic Deerfield, Inc., a new nonprofit corporation.

Travel to Arizona had been impossible during several of the war years, and I believe Elizabeth was grateful for the job and genuinely interested in preserving the best of Deerfield's past. I wonder how she felt about Boyden's narrow focus on the project and what comments she may have made about Henry Flynt's increasingly grandiose aims.

In the late 1940s Flynt wrote that a restored Deerfield would be "an inspiration to future generations," that it would stand for "the spirit of free enterprise, the spirit of New England, the spirit which needs to go out into the Nation now." The Cold War had begun, and Old Deerfield would be a player in it, Flynt wanted to believe.

Stillinger writes, "Over and over [Flynt] speaks of the importance of Deerfield in educating and inspiring all Americans. 'Is it not possible,' he asks, 'to sum up the strength of this Republic, its vigor and idealism and enterprise, in a single American community?'"

As the actual work of acquiring and renovating buildings progressed, another grandiose aspect emerged. When the interiors were refinished and furnished the Flynts' impulse was to upgrade the houses from farmers' and tradesmens' homes to upperclass residences. Rare period furniture was bought for them, and the mannequins placed in the rooms opened to the public were often richly dressed. At parties to celebrate the openings of the houses the Flynts and their friends would come bewigged and dressed in period silks and satins, as though attending a high ceremonial affair. This was image creation rather than re-creation.

Apparently Elizabeth and Mary sometimes said to the Flynts, "That's not right for Deerfield," and the Flynts would take note, but the trend to furnish with increasingly valuable antiques continued. Starting in the 1950s, old houses of particular architectural interest were moved from other towns and rebuilt on vacant Main Street lots.

Today Old Deerfield is almost wholly an Academy surrounded by a museum. Free enterprise has been entirely eliminated—all corporate entities being nonprofit. Rather than "adventurous" and "forward-looking" the mindset is one of conservation—quiet protection of the collected, and sometimes improved, antiques.

George, Elizabeth's brother, died in 1950, and their mother Mary a year later. Elizabeth inherited The Bars and its responsibilities. She resigned from Historic Deerfield and began again to winter in Oracle.

For a dozen years she ran the farm with the aid of hired hands, then simplified the operation by selling off a large portion of its acreage. The pattern of her life became fixed: from May to October, Elizabeth was at The Bars; November to May, Leslie was in Oracle. As a painter Elizabeth mainly did commissioned portraits of children in both places.

A friend of Leslie's in Tucson, Thomas Hubbard, collected a number of her Arizona landscapes and portraits both of children and of Mexican-American adults, some with particularly hard-worn faces, whom she painted for pleasure. This collection now belongs to the Oracle Historical Society.

These portraits are genuine and expressive, and the desert mountains in the landscapes project the remote, untouched, barrenness that attracts one's eyes to them in life. They are among her best works as, too, are those collected at the Deerfield Memorial Hall Museum.

Except in her earliest works, however, it seems to me that Elizabeth would not often imbue her works with her own emotional reactions. Had she been too caught up, perhaps, in the maintenance of her two identities to let herself go?

Elizabeth died in a Tucson hospital in May of 1979 at age eighty-three. The Society of Deerfield Artists later presented an exhibition of her portraits of children, and in 1995 the Memorial Hall Museum held an exhibition of her Deerfield and Arizona landscapes. In both cases her skills were clearly displayed.

Alfred, Anne, and Margaret began regular summer use of the Monhegan Island Fuller house in the mid-1930s. By that time so many painters had used Monhegan for so many years that the island was well-known. It had become a day-trip destination for a steady percentage of Maine's tourists, despite the long and often rough ferry trip from Port Clyde.

The painters had by then organized themselves as "Monhegan Artists" and had begun the custom of tacking up their schedules at "The Spa," a small refreshments and knickknacks store near the ferry landing. The schedule showed that the artists would be present in their studios on certain days and hours to receive whomever would like to see their work and potentially buy it.

The Fullers and Margaret were joined each summer by Clara and Warner and their daughter Lucia. The Taylors had built a cabin toward the north end of the settlement, near the Ice Pond, and they came for stays of more than two months. When they and the other summer people left the island for their winter homes the Alfred Fullers left, too, to live in a succession of places that included Deerfield, where Alfred taught art for some years at the Eaglebrook School.

In 1939 Margaret Lewis's affections shifted, and she moved to Madison with the Taylors, creating a new menage a trois. Warner did not protest this development— indeed, he said he welcomed it—nor did Alfred and Anne attempt to hold Margaret back. She left, but she did not desert them. She bought a house in Port Clyde for the Alfred Fullers' winter use and continued to provide a regular allowance of money.

When Rockwell Kent and the other early Monhegan painters, including Elizabeth, had begun to paint the Monhegan scenes, the fishermen were regularly risking their lives to bring in a catch of fish or lobster to sustain their families' bare livelihoods. There was a felt poetry in what Kent and the others saw in the fishermen's patched and worn equipment. As the island's economy changed to dependence on what "the summer people" spent, and what appetites the tourists brought, the painting of the same artifacts became the painting of quaint things. Alfred found certain subjects and perspectives that buyers liked, and he stuck to them.

The Monhegan Artists organization gradually improved in efficiency. By the 1960s maps were printed showing all the artists' locations, schedules, and phone numbers. Alfred was one of twenty-three painters so listed in 1966 who kept "open" hours. His were noon to two daily and one to three on Sundays. Of the artists' names listed that summer, none have resonance today, a clear comedown from the first third of the century.

Alfred most often painted the sea, usually a rather cheerful sea under a bright sun, whose waves look forceful but not threatening. They curl prettily and, breaking on the rocks, throw pearls of spray high in the air. The gray and black sea under fog that surrounds Monhegan much of the time did not interest him—or he had found that representations of it did not sell.

Alfred's work was likeable. It was shown for many years at the Grand Central Galleries in New York, and at the Gallery of Maine Artists in Wiscasset, Maine. He belonged to several national artists associations.

Relative to other family painters, Alfred enjoyed large measures of physical and economic comfort. He was never burdened by the management of The Bars or forced by money worries to do work other than art. He and Anne were childless. She, as an RN, could earn money more or less when she wished to, and Margaret's support relieved them of anxiety about life's basics.

But these economic freedoms seemed to produce the opposite of artistic freedom. Perhaps he needed sales to justify to himself the title of "Painter." For whatever reason, his work is without much adventure or strong feeling.

In 1972 Alfred sold the Monhegan house, and he and Anne bought a house in Cape Elizabeth, Maine. Alfred died there in 1980, and Anne not long after. After Warner Taylor's death in 1958, Clara and Margaret Lewis used the Port Clyde house for themselves, Clara dying there in 1982 and Margaret three years later. The Taylors' Monhegan house passed on to Lucia Taylor Miller and her husband, Dr. Harry Miller.

Alfred's first cousin and contemporary, Robert and Bessie Fuller's daughter Alice, was born in New York City on August 16th, 1900. During her early years the family lived in Boston, where, according to Alice's daughter, Barbara Goodhue Legler, Alice ingested a double dose of manners—genteel southern attitudes from her mother, a Virginian, and a broad-A, Boston-Brahmin speech and crispness from her Higginson relatives. Alice retained these features of her personality throughout her life, and her daughter believes that not only did they give her extraordinary charm, they provided her with an impeccable facade that allowed Alice's spirit the freest of interior play.

Alice became a tall woman, five feet nine, and was "quick-witted and strong-minded"—those are Barbara's adjectives. No artwork from her childhood has survived, and neither are there drawings or paintings from the years she spent in the Far East in the 1920s with her husband, Charles Goodhue, an engineer.

Alice and Charles married in New York in 1922 and traveled immediately to Manila. He held a job there with the U.S. Department of Commerce and was later transferred to Batavia, now Indonesia, where daughter Barbara was born in 1925.

The Goodhues returned to New York in 1927, where Charles went to work for Remington Rand and Alice became a student at the Art Students League, studying particularly with George Bridgeman. Two years later, Alice decided to become a miniaturist and became a student of Elsie Dodge Pattee's. It is possible that Alice's interest in the genre came from her early acquaintance with her aunt, Lucia Fairchild Fuller.

By the time Alice's work with Pattee came to an end in 1933 her miniatures had already appeared in several exhibitions and had had immediate success. Between 1931 and 1942 Alice's work was included in forty gallery exhibitions, among them the National Gallery of Art and the Corcoran Gallery in Washington, the Los Angeles County Museum, and the Philadelphia Academy of Fine Arts. Her subjects were principally portraits but also included landscapes, some of them Far Eastern scenes. Alice won a number of best-in-show medals, and her work sold with relative ease in what were hard times for most artists.

Her portraits are skilllful, subtle, and witty. One feels from them that Alice has persuaded her sitters to choose the clothes they would most like to wear for their portraits, and that they have arranged their own settings. The chairs on which they sit, the objects by which they are surrounded—a lamp, a toy, a picture on the wall behind them—are the objects they most want to have in the picture. The subjects' attitudes suggest satisfaction. Sometimes the satisfaction seems a trifle self-conscious, but it is a satisfaction nonetheless.

The effect, given the fact that furnishings and clothes are certain to go out of fashion, is both touching and humorous. Alice was not mocking her sitters' tastes, nor their pride in favorite possessions. She seems understanding and gently amused by the prominence one subject wants to give a wall clock and another a party dress.

Alice was one of the most accomplished and appreciated miniaturists of her time, but she stopped painting entirely in 1942, complaining that her eyesight was failing. She never painted again in any genre.

Alice had experienced a difficult and perhaps destructive divorce in the late 1930s after she and Goodhue moved to Buffalo, New York, where he had taken a new job. It could have been with some relief that Alice put her energies into "war work" as she did, starting with "Bundles for Britain" in 1942. She later worked with an organization that shipped packages to American prisoners of war, and she continued in similarly charitable programs after the war's end. These were not volunteer but salaried jobs.

In 1954 Alice learned she had an incurable cancer, but, keeping this information to herself, she continued working in public relations for the Buffalo Children's Hospital for the remaining three years of her life.

Her daughter Barbara, admiring her mother's courage and self-possession, has said, "She did a fantastic job with her life." Many of the letters of condolence Barbara received after Alice's death spoke of her love of laughter.

Lastly in the generation of my parents there is someone I know of only from a brief obituary in an Old Lyme, Connecticut, newspaper, and a photograph taken when Elizabeth Fairchild was, I imagine, in her forties.

This Elizabeth was the daughter of Charles Fairchild Junior, the one described by his brother Blair as a "scourge," the one who took his own life in his early sixties. Charles and his wife May had two children. Lucius, the eldest, had a career as a U. S. Army officer and had a childless marriage.

As a young adult Elizabeth lived in Washington. She became a portrait painter there and developed a specialty—

painting portraits of pets. This she did with a modest, steady success, it seems, for the remainder of her life.

Her photograph shows the deeply lined face and ropey neck of someone either anorexic or otherwise ill. She is smiling for the camera but the implication of her expression is that there is little to smile about. From her features I can imagine that, healthy, she was potentially beautiful. She never married or bore a child.

Elizabeth had been living in Old Lyme during her last years in the 1950s. Chas, her first cousin, was living not far away in Stonington during much of that time. Neither I nor Chas's widow Anne have any memory of his speaking of her. She was the last to bear the name of the once large and prosperous Fairchild family.

During times that were not easy for anyone in the entire world, the generation of the George Fullers' and the Charles Fairchilds' grandchildren found both art and life difficult. Some of their troubles would have been familiar to their grandparents. Some would have been recognizable under new names. There was certainly some novelty in them, too, and cruel novelty in the great bloodletting of the first half of the century. If letter writing had not been replaced to so large an extent by the telephone as the means of private communication I would, perhaps, better understand them.

Of their troubles: although Prohibition complicated its procedures, there was nothing new about family alcoholism. The sexual customs and adventures that drink often lubricated had some novelty in style and openness.

Anorexia was, perhaps, new, as was the diagnosis "multiple sclerosis."

So was "image," as a concept. The pressures of conformity were a very old story, but the growing subliminal notion that an individual *was*, to all extents and purposes, the presentation of an apparent self, consciously shaped, decided on, and maintained—that, I believe, was new. If, after the image had been set, an individual's "character" could be found, it was for the individual's eyes alone, or only his or her closest companion's eyes, to see.

I believe that the growth of image-consciousness—its construction and above all its maintenance—created a new kind of loss of freedom. The possibility and fear that an image might be shattered by unexpected events made for a new sort of human rigidity.

These artists lived through a time of immense human fear. The "radicals" who appeared to act freely may have been at least as fear-driven as any. It should not be a surprise that some artists clung to aesthetic codes, and others to accepted, formulaic art. A self-image as a painter of popularly appreciated seascapes was preferable to feelings of being small and vulnerable. Whatever the success or lack of it of these artists, they were luckier, I think, than those who had been enjoined not to try to make art although they were, at the same time, brought up to revere it. I am thinking, of course, of Clara and Chas.

Chapter Eight

MY CONTEMPORARIES:
BARBARA GOODHUE LEGLER
and JILL FULLER FOX

My sister, Jill Fox, is the youngest of Jane and Chas Fuller's children. Perhaps in part because our older sister Sage "won all the blue ribbons" in school and elsewhere, and I was athletic and competitive, Jill became introspective as a child, recalcitrant in school except on the playing fields. She was a particularly close friend to our cousin, the late Sue Coward Marquand. Sue and a few others knew Jill to be talented, witty, and imaginative.

Both of our parents encouraged Jill to draw and paint. It was clear to them that she had, in family parlance, an original eye, "a real eye," Jane liked to say. In a family in which art was of such supreme importance this praise was no doubt helpful to Jill's spirit as she endured the conventional requirements of ordinary schools.

Jane would sometimes, and memorably, raise her eyes heavenward and exclaim, "Thank God for Grandpa Sage!" he being the maker of the family fortune of which we and a number of relatives were the beneficiaries. Grandpa Sage was the only businessman I can remember her or Chas speaking enthusiastically about.

If I asked what kind of work a family acquaintance did I might be told vaguely by either parent, "I believe he's in business of some kind." Chas would sometimes invent the businesses of men he disliked: "I think he has a corset-making factory," or "He has a hot dog plant in Yonkers, I think," followed by chuckles.

Because I was not talented in art and was interested primarily in sports, Chas once talked to me about "the professions." He was determined to tell me that the professions were respectable, that "professionals" were different from businesssmen. When I asked him to list the professions for me, however, his tone of voice reflected, at best, a decent respect for doctors. Then lawyers made him wince, egineers and scientists bored him, and architect was something I should not, absolutely not, consider becoming because of the disastrous effect of Depressions on an architect's ability to work, witness his own. Finally, accountants made him look a little ill. He said, "There are accountants, I suppose."

Jane's second husband was a publisher. One day I said to her that publishing was a business, wasn't it? She became piqued. "Oh well," she said dismissively, "there's a business side to it as there is to everything."

Thus when, in my adolescence, Jane suggested to me that I should think of becoming a lawyer, I felt disparaged. I asked her what lawyers actually did at work. She replied that she would find a lawyer to tell me about it, and an acquaintance soon explained to me that most of an average lawyer's time was spent on the close reading and writing of contracts. My imagination of this was so dreary as compared to what I knew of artists' lives, that I felt that to choose the life of a lawyer would be to choose unhappiness.

While neither Sage nor I became visual artists it should seem no surprise that Sage became a dancer and I, after some years in business, a writer and teacher.

Jill graduated from Miss Porter's School before she was truly encouraged to apply herself to art, the great profession. She then became a student at the Art Students League and at age eighteen won first prize in a *Seventeen* magazine illustration contest. In 1953 and 1954 she won two National Academy of Design awards, the Mary Henman Carter Prize, and the Julius Hallgarten Prize, both of them for oil painting.

At that point it might well have seemed to her and others that her path to professional recognition had been prepared and would be facilitated in something of the same way Lucia Fairchild Fuller's had been in 1891. But the message Jill got from her League mentor, Chas's friend Louis Bouche, was, instead, discouraging. He told Jill that a professional life in the arts was impossible for a woman unless she abandoned hope for a normal life.

Bouche said she would have to choose. She could pursue an artistic career, and she might have a great one. Or she could marry and have children. But she could not do both.

Without hesitation Jill told him she would marry, and Bouche said, "Good. You've made the right decision."

Jill married the late Random House editor Joseph Fox and soon was pregnant with the first of her four sons.

Jill made little art in the years that followed. The Fox family moved to one of the old houses on the Crowfields property. Her sons left Jill little time for her own work, and, in any case, there was no studio at hand in which to do it. In these years she was missing the period when American art went through its most extraordinary evolution.

As a confident declaration of national artistic independence abstract expressionism may now seem oddly personal and obscure in its aims, but the movement was bold in putting aside any and all recognizable objects as subject matter and in inventing new techniques to express states of mind and feeling inexpressible in words. The fact that these new artists were American—Pollock, Motherwell, and Kline were nativeborn, and de Kooning had been a New Yorker since the 1920s—was joyfully seized on by critics and galleries, and the values and the pecking order of the New York art world changed rapidly.

Before World War II many painters were certainly recognizably American by their subject matter and by their "succession" (Edward Hopper follows John Sloan, for example) or by their regions (Grant Wood and Thomas Hart Benton were Midwestern beyond any doubt). But now in the late '40s and '50s painters from all corners of the country were doing work that bore some relation, each to the other, and it had novelty, freshness, and a vitality that nothing coming from what seemed an exhausted Europe could match.

The strong positive response to abstract expressionism seems to me a recognition that image was not all. As a movement the paintings proclaimed, Here are the depths you are ignoring. The personalities and the behavior of the movement's leaders said, Conformity be damned!

Surrealism was quickly gone from the New York critical mind, and the great market for art was suddenly in New York and for American-made art.

For Jill it was not so important, perhaps, tht she was not frequently seeing the new work. What may have most affected her future art was the fact that she missed the collective New York chauvinism and excitement of the time. She was and felt artistically alone, and in a time of interest and belief in psychological analysis her work became more personal and introspective.

Jill began again to produce paintings in the mid-1960s and showed in group exhibitions at several Westchester County galleries. Later in the decade she and her family left the suburbs for the city, but there was family upheaval and she did not produce art there. After her divorce in 1971 she moved to southern Vermont and has lived since in the town of Peru and then in Londonderry.

She has had one-artist exhibitions at the AVA Gallery in Lebanon, New Hampshire, Thornes Gallery in Northampton, Massachusetts, Beside Myself Gallery in Arlington, Vermont, and Elm Street Arts in Manchester. Her paintings have been included in a number of group shows, and for many years in the annual Stratton Arts Festival.

Jill lives on a dirt road about one mile from Londonderry in a two-story, early nineteenth century farmhouse to which two wings have been added, one containing a spare room and bath and, above it, her crowded studio, which connects by exterior walkway to her bedroom in the main part of the house.

The other wing, constructed to accomodate Jill's quadreplegic son, Blair, who has since chosen to live in easier climates, is sometimes rented out and is often vacant. Although Jill has visits from friends and family she spends much of the year alone.

The setting in which she lives is reminiscent of what the earliest family painters had before their eyes. Across the road to the south of Jill's house is a flood plain created by Utley Brook, a tributary of West River which, twenty miles further on, flows into the Connecticut River at a point perhaps eighty miles south of Cornish and eighty miles north of Deerfield. Wooded mountains rise in the distance beyond the floodplain.

Within Jill's house there are many reminders of our joint artistic heritage. On the walls there is an Augustus Vincent Tack portrait of a wide-eyed, extremely dignified five-year-old girl, a portrait of a fashionable 1920s-dressed woman by HBF, a white marble female torso by Jane, some drawings by Chas, and a small George Fuller landscape, but the house has no feeling of being a museum. Jill is a voluminous reader, and the piles of books are as eye-catching as the art.

More striking than either the books or our forebears art is the spectacle of Jill's energy. Broad-shouldered and trim, Jill works in her garden on the north side of the house, created with the collaboration of her son, Michael: a dammed-up brook has made a pond around which are flower beds, sculptures, an open gazebo for summer meals, and a stone waterfall. She strides long distances on daily walks, works at clearing underbrush from the woods uphill beyond the garden, serves on the local library board, and makes enough art for a yearly or bi-yearly exhibition. She has appreaciated something Robert Henri said to his students: "It is not desirable to devote all your time to the appreciation of art. Art should drive you forth. It should be an incentive to life."

Over the years Jill has produced a succession of "series"

of paintings. Sometimes a series will fill an exhibition, sometimes two of them. When she feels a series has reached what she feels is its natural end she will end it, and, in time, another will begin.

A series is often radically different in tone and and technique from the one it has followed. For this reason there is no "signature" to Jill's paintings, nothing that tells the viewer at a glance they are by her. All of her work, however, is to some extent surreal.

One recent series is entitled "The Lamp in the Window." In landscapes of mostly bare green hills at twilight there is a single light from a window in a dimly seen house. One sees these lights down avenues of trees, or a road, or in a swale between hills. They have in common that no one, no person, animal, or sign of human work is in sight—except the house.

While windows imply transparency, these windows are all opaque. They give out light but provide no hint as to what is inside the house or of what sort of reception one might find there. The window is both inviting and threatening, as a far-off island might be to a person in a lifeboat. It is what one needs—dry land for a castaway or the security of a house for a weary traveler, but the inscrutability gives one pause. It would be hard to commit to entering there.

Another series, "Monkey Island," is related in feeling to "Windows." Creatures that are not monkeys, not apes, not humans, but certainly android and alive, stand and sit "together"—grouped but not in each others' arms, not visibly relating. They seem in some way to share the warmth of each other's coats of fur, but their eyes are so recessed they do not appear to see one another. Something is keeping these creatures stiffly apart, although their impulse to connect is palpable.

On another tack there is a series of "Interior Landscapes," small—very small—ink drawings of common scenes in the street, or within an office or a living space. The pen-work has depicted deliberately hard-to-interpret occurences in these familiar places. Just what is happening between those two people? What is the viewer expected to see?

After struggling to decipher the action, one understands that one is looking into oneself for the answers that the drawings pose. The "trip" is toward one's own memories rather than into the dynamics of what one can literally see. In this respect, the objectives of the drawings are the opposite of George Fuller's stated wish to "bring you in" to the picture. Jill's drawings throw you back into yourself, into your past, quite likely into your discomforts.

A more recent exhibition was of large oil-crayon paintings of magnified roots and vegetable seedpods, imagined, rope-like tendrils and uterine-like flowers. She used models from nature in some cases but felt she had failed if the root of a beet, or any other specific vegetable, was recognized. The colors on the canvases are earth brown, rhubarb red, and dirty green for the objects, and the backgrounds are yellowish, yolky—fecund.

By the angles of vision, and through enlargement, the objects have become abstractions of human genitalia—not simply the outward features but the entire systems—some of them so explicit the gallery owner kept them in a back room, shown only on request.

The generative process Jill presents is dark and mysterious. Seedpods burst at jagged cracks. There is violent growth and decay, pearly seeds becoming husks. There is grit and sweat, and power and ecstasy. Death is in the next unpainted scene.

Jill's exhibition following the 'vegetables' was entitled "What Remains." Rather than the beginnings of life the paintings in this series are postmortems, but, oddly and affectingly, postmortems that keep and display the vitality of the small animals and birds that were her subjects. The attitude of a blue jay's open beak and his grasping talons express the essence of his life's activities. The painting is not a "still life" but is of a life arrested at a moment of intense activity. This is equally true in paintings of a field mouse, a mole, and other creatures. Jill's youngest son is HIV positive and in this period she was, in fact, intensely worried about him.

Jill's pictures sell—not in great numbers, and not for very high prices. She can afford to live as she does because of our parents' mating of art with inherited wealth. In this her life differs greatly from the lives of the early Negus-Fuller painters, who escaped the farm only if they could support themselves by their work. Her situation, however, is far from exceptional today.

The art schools of America have been training ever-larger numbers of students for many years, when only a few of their graduates will ever have an exhibition of their work and far fewer still will be able to support themselves by artwork. In the San Francisco Bay Area there are now said to live 250,000 *self-proclaimed* artists, of whom 50,000 live in San Francisco alone, a city of 750,000.

A small fraction of these artists are making visually pleasing work and succeeding in selling it to households and institutions that want "original" but basically familiar art. An infinitestimally few others, initially championed by established artists or teachers and then endorsed by some combination of critics, gallery owners, museum curators, and collectors, will enter the company of the "hot."

For the past two centuries, at least, there have always been artists-of-the-moment—"God knows how many Corots there may be in Boston and New York by now," George Fuller wrote in 1882. But not before the ascendance of the "pop artists" of the 1960s were there "hots." These were not simply artists whose works were in demand, but artists who became "stars," celebrities whose appeal was felt widely and valued immediately in cachet and in dollars.

"Hotness" is heady, irrational stuff. In the 1970s one New York collector bought up Jasper Johns entire output of paintings over a period of several years and stored the pictures in a warehouse where no one, including himself, could see them. Perhaps the collector's pleasure could be described as hysteric imagination.

A vortex of forces is necessary to create "hotness," and the forces are to be found in New York and, to a much lesser extent in London, Chicago, Los Angeles, Paris, and now perhaps Berlin. The ingredients that "create media" are not to be found in Londonderry, Buffalo, or Minneapolis–St. Paul, where the three contemporary Negus-Fuller artists work. Any artist outside the few great art-market cities is likely to feel baffled and frustrated by the seemingly inexplicable vagaries of who is "hot." My guess is that none of the family artists will be candidates for "hot" partly because the long family tradition precludes the extraordinary excitement of the first-generation challenge.

Why does Jill paint? In answer she paraphrases Robert Rauschenberg, saying that making art is a way of making it possible to get along with herself.

"Art is a way of living a life," she says. She must use her "eye," and she must explore how it might further be used. If she did not she would falter spiritually.

"A way of living a life" has some novelty as a reason to produce art in western cultures. It implies that artistic skill may or may not be used to earn a living, to be the vehicle for ambitions, or the medium through which one may express political or personal passions. It may be a way only of keeping one's psychological and spiritual balance.

That Jill should quote Rauschenberg is interesting. While art always derives partly from immediate perception and partly from preceding art, there are periods when it seems almost entirely derived from other art (the Beaux Arts tradition is an example), and, contrarily, periods when it seems freshly to reflect contemporary living (the "Ashcan School").

The "pop artists," Rauschenberg most prominently among them, made an art predominantly from life but often used art discards and transitory advertising to make its points. They declared through their work that we Americans no longer could see the Eden-like vistas the Hudson River School painters had seen. Instead, what we really saw was the billboard blocking out the mountain, or the mountain framed by the windshields of our cars. We could no longer see the agricultural fields from the edges of our cities. We saw instead gasoline stations and junkyards where stuffed goats and wornout tires were jumbled together. Instead of plowed furrows and barns we saw Campell's soup cans stacked on the supermarket shelves. The fields that produce the contents of the soup cans are perhaps a continent away.

Jill's art, too, is predominantly from life but its imagery is not public imagery. Rather it is personal and psychological.

There are rewards for Jill. There is the appreciation inherent in a sale or, better still, a review like this one by painter and teacher Paul Stitelman in the *Bennington Banner* writing of the "What Remains" exhibition:

"Fox's concerns go beyond the materiality of the images. The animating line creates a kind of alchemy. We are aware that the subjects are dead, but at the same time, the pictures are not lifeless. They are, in fact, suffused with life. Some viewers may feel that this metaphysical speculation is a reach, but the works seems to me to call for this sort of discussion.

"By moving toward a metaphysical program, Fox removes the work from the concerns of so much recent art which so frequently demands a strict materialism. Clearly the work at hand is not meant to be in any sense mainstream, but is a private expression by an artist who has gone her own way."

Barbara Legler, the only child of Alice Fuller Goodhue and Charles Goodhue, was born in Djakarta and returned with her parents to New York at age two.

One of her mother's earliest miniatures, and one that would reman a favorite at the exhibitions at which Alice showed her work, was a portrait of Barbara as a child. Barbara thus grew up as someone involved in her mother's career, and in the house she was surrounded by paintings by her grandfather, Robert Fuller, and her great grandfather, George.

Barbara began her own formal art training in her late teens in Buffalo, studying with Philip Elliot and Isaac Soyer at the Albright Art School, and then with Charles Burchfield at the Art Institute of Buffalo. Initially, she was most interested in portraiture.

Barbara married engineer John Leroy Legler in 1947. Their daughter Jennifer was born in 1949 and sons Jeffrey and Robert in 1952 and 1953 respectively.

I met Jeffrey in the course of researching this book when he, too, was researching family matters. He has compiled the Fuller-Higginson genealogies which trace our family history back to one Rynold de Wyntuwade who was living in the year 1066 in Stafford, Yorkshire. Jeffrey has also made and collected as many slide transparencies of as many of the family works of art as he has been able to find, and both projects have been of the greatest assistance to this book.

As a result of our meeting I visited Buffalo to meet Barbara Legler and see her paintings. I didn't know Buffalo and was interested in it historically and as an influence on her work.

Buffalo surely thought of itself as a city on the cusp of greatness for a period of at least one hundred years, until the "Rust Belt" depression years of the late 1960s and '70s brought much of its steel-fabricating business to a stop. A walk around its older residential sections shows that the fortunes made from the confluence of the metals industries, and from the transportation hub of railways, Great Lakes shipping, and the Erie Canal produced grandiose Victorian monuments and housing, ambitious and pleasing parks, and splendid museums and theaters while, at the same time, blocking the city from the lake with the ugliest of industrial buildings and fouling its air with coal smoke.

Biographers of Mabel Dodge Luhan, who grew up in Buffalo in the 1880s and '90s, a rich period for the city, depict a world of hard-nosed business competition, social pretension, and emotional coldness from which Luhan fled to create, as much as anyone, the bohemianism of Greenwich Village during the first two decades of this century, and subsequently the artistic-refuge atmosphere of Taos, New Mexico. I assume that Luhan created around herself some things she had longed for in her Buffalo provincial childhood—an absence of strict propriety and cultural self-satisfaction and social assertiveness.

Now, in the 1990s, there are aspects of Buffalo that would make Luhan feel more kindly toward her place of birth. There is a downtown attempt to convert the waterfront to more gracious uses. The large State University campus has some exceptionally distinguished departments. The Albright-Knox Museum is one of the nation's finest, and there are parts of the city in which coffeehouses and galleries are common.

Still, it was the old Buffalo in which Barbara grew up and lived her early maturity and the remains of it, including an abandoned Bethlehem Iron Works not far from her home, are sad and oppressive to the eye. I believe much of Barbara's work can be understood as a reaction to the era of coal smoke, clanging metals, and newly-immigrant workers, and of ostentation and tough-minded capital accumulaton among the city's elite.

The Leglers live in the 1950s-built suburb of Orchard Park where their house sits unobtrusively on a quiet street of closely resembling neighbors and where the trees have grown tall enough to obscure the world beyond.

Once the front door has opened, the Legler house is revealed as extraordinary. Barbara, a vigorous and meticulous woman, and her retired husband, are closely surrounded in every room by Fuller-family art, including, of course, her own. Every wall, it seems, is covered top to bottom.

There are three exceptional George Fullers: an 1845 portrait of Elizabeth Dempsey Fuller, a cousin with whom George was said to have been in love; an 1866 portrait of Robert Fuller as a baby; and a late portrait, dating perhaps to1882, of Agnes, but of Agnes as a young woman

Agnes's figure has a certain stiffness—perhaps George worked from an old and formal photograph. She appears to be beautiful, as she always did in George's renderings of her, but his technique is a surprise. Having learned from the Barbizons and having reached Impressionism on his own, George in this picture paints as a pointillist—and successfully.

There is also in the house a portrait of George looking heavy, tired, and old, by his friend Edwin Billings. The portrait could be of a man fifteen years older than the sixty-two at which George died.

Landscapes by both George and Robert seem to have affected Barbara's work most—the former by their soulful quality, the latter by their touches of brightness, of hope, perhaps.

Some thirty years ago Barbara came to an alcoholic crisis. She did no painting for the following thirteen years, and when, sober, she began to paint again, her urge was to do landscapes rather than portraits. Indeed, there is not a human being or an animal in any of her paintings that hang in the house, or in the Buffalo gallery Art Dialogue that

represents her, or in the Members Rental Gallery of the
Albright-Knox Museum, which also handles her work.

Barbara has painted the same landscape for many years
now, "same" in the way that other painters have spent their
lives painting the Long Island potato fields or the desert
mountains of the West. Her subjects are the low, forested
hills of western New York State, a soft and intimate landscape as compared to rocky mountains or crashing seas. Its
hills have rounded with geologic age and its vegetation
grows thick, often warmed, in her pictures, by a tinge of
autumn in the foliage. She is less likely to paint spring
green or winter barrenness.

Typically, a narrow road will go from the picture's fore-
ground up and into a hill, disappearing as the road curves
into a forest. No vehicle will be on this road. Up close, at
roadside, will stand a thick-trunked, sparsely-limbed and
foliated tree.

In the kitchen of her house, Barbara pointed through the
window and said, "See? There's my tree! I mean, it's in my
neighbor's garden, but that's my tree."

In fact, the tree is recognizably "hers." The broadness of
its trunk projects strength and endurance, but its limbs look
foreshortened and fragile. The skimpy foliation makes a
suggestion of pathos. Solidity, too, can be needy. In short,
the emotional complexities of her work are symbolized in
the tree.

Although Barbara's technique is straightforward and
realistic, the effect of the pictures is dreamy and faintly nos-
talgic. I, at least, feel comfortable in these scenes, as though
they are places I have been but have forgotten. High
dramas have not occurred in them, rather they are places

where repose and contemplation are possible. The empty, old, well-traveled road winding into the forest does not beckon one to follow it into new territories. Instead, it turns one inward to memories.

Barbara has written, "Making a painting takes me out of myself to places where I want to be." She adds that she has put "a combination of imagination and memory (with perhaps a dash of escapism)" into her paintings.

So described, her paintings have a clear cousinship to Spencer's, Arthur's, and Robert's landscapes. A world is being presented that the painter believes was the real world not long ago, and may still exist, and this world is likely to look more attractive to us than the world of pop art or the reality of time present.

Jill Fox's "Windows" series and Barbara's lonely roads are perhaps not so far apart and have sources in common—in life as well as art.

Since 1986 Barbara has had four solo exhibitions and has been included in another half-dozen shows with two or three other artists. Her work has won awards from the Buffalo Society of Artists, the Fine Arts League of Buffalo, the Niagra Frontier Art Exhibit, Art at the Site IV, and the Amherst Society of Artists. In 1995 a canvas of hers won the "Best in Show" award in an exhibition of landscape and wildlife paintings in Hamburg, New York.

Barbara's paintings are included in several American corporate collections, including Xerox's, and have been collected in private and corporate collections in England, Germany, and Japan.

Critic Adam Gopnik has described "everything one [is] expected to admire in the major American painting of our time" as "dash, spontaneity, brio, difficulty." Often enough dash, spontaneity, and brio would seem to lag behind difficulty as the outstanding recognizable quality visible in contemporary establishment choices. Explicators need difficulty in order to have something to explain, and by now there seems to be an underlying assumption among a large portion of the art public that art that does not require explanation cannot be interesting art. The motive of Barbara's art runs contrary to this expectation. It wants to be literally and emotionally accessible, although not without mystery.

Although Barbara talks of her own ego in relation to her work, of the gratification of selling it or of hearing it praised, her paintings seem made for the viewer rather than for ego-gratification. She says that "making a painting is a tremendously exciting, intensely personal experience," but she wants the personal to be clear and communicable.

Barbara works at her paintings every day and for long hours, but it is not dedication to her art that pushes her. Dedication would imply that will is required to get her to her easel, and this is not the case.

"I must paint," she says intensely. "I absolutely must."

Chapter Nine

FULLER COWLES and CONNEE MAYERON
until now the last generation

Fuller Cowles was born in 1961 in Minneapolis, my sister Sage's fourth and youngest child. He was a healthy and strong boy, but it became clear from the time of his entrance into kindergarten that reading and writing were difficult for him. While in second grade he was diagnosed as dyslexic.

Fuller became a builder of Lego toys, a maker of basement theaters and environments, and a tinkerer with machines. Those were his dominant interests but he graduated from high school, the Blake School in Minneapolis, and continued to Bennington College, where he found an art department that encouraged and inspired him.

I spoke with Fuller about his art one day in the extraordinary house and studio, built on the foundations of a large barn near Taylor's Falls, Minnesota, that he and his wife, ceramacist Connee Mayeron, live and work in approximately half of each year. During the winter months they live mainly in a converted firehouse in St. Paul, where an industrial-size kiln has been built in a part of the fire-engine garage, and an apartment on the second floor.

Fuller showed me through the barn-studio as we talked, a complex he has created for the use of "collaborators" as well as for himself. Much of the time Fuller prefers to work with others rather than alone.

The main four-story-high building has mimicked the barn's shape but is otherwise not barn-like. The exterior of its southern "house" side is glazed with insulated glass, and its interior contains two floors of living space and an aerie designed with dramatic orginality.

The flooring "floats" around an open spiral stairwell. With the exception of the bathrooms and a second-floor master bedroom and bath, which juts out from the body of the main structure where a silo once stood, there are no walled rooms. Much of the furniture has been made in-house, and a central, broad, but upwardly tapering four-story chimney has been covered with Connee Mayeron tiles.

The major studio area is a single open room from floor to roof, and it appears to be stocked with every kind of equipment a sculptor might require. Suspended from tracks fastened horizontally at approximately third-floor level, a one-ton hoist can bring finished work to a truck backed in through a sliding barn door. Racks of tools for work in metal, stone, and wood are ranged on tables and against the walls, and works in progress are at several stations on the floor.

Two outbuildings contain a photographer's darkroom, a room with print-making equipment, a shop for work in neon, a small kiln, storage spaces, and an office for record-keeping and the management of the enterprise.

Fuller has a restless, muscular energy, and he took me quickly through the entire complex, bounding up stairs and starting machinery and flicking lights on and off with familiar pleasure. His explanations were tossed-off and brief.

The studio stands on what was a farm bought some years ago by Fuller's father, John Cowles, former editor-in chief of the *Minneapolis Star and Tribune,* and later chair of Cowles Media, which owned that newspaper and a number of others and television stations in the upper Midwest and elswhere in the nation. Cowles Media was sold to the McClatchy newspaper chain in 1998.

Fuller's parents have renovated and expanded the old farmhouse to serve as a country home large enough for family reunions, and they ceded the barn area to Fuller for art production, as well as considerable acreage fronting the highway for the creation, in 1996, of the Franconia Sculpture Park, which has become a pemanent site for changing outdoor displays of sculpture by many artists.

Several of Fuller's larger sculptures are usually installed near the studio, but the main display of finished work is in the Park, whose activities are directly managed by a friend of Fuller's and a fellow-sculptor, John Hock. The Park's exhibitions have included work that is various in scale, material, and intention, but much of it has been large and bold.

When I asked Fuller that day what sculptors he particularly admired or had found to be influential he mentioned first Brower Hatcher, one of his teachers at Bennington, then, in this order, Antony Caro, Brancusi, Rodin, and David Smith. In historical order, Rodin, Brancusi, and Smith have taken virtually all contemporary sculptors a long way from the Beaux Arts traditions of one hundred years ago.

Rodin, feeling the decadence of Beaux Arts tradition-
alism, made the emotions of his subjects visible and thus
challenged the conception of what beauty itself was. For
Rodin, John the Baptist's resolute-looking stride and
visionary eyes were his beauty, rather than his features or
his musculature.

Brancusi so simplified forms that they could be seen as
beautiful without being related to deities, ideals, or to specific individuals or emotions.

David Smith (but others, too, beginning with *Dada*) took
a different tack: sculpture would not have human subjects.
What humans had created, primarily through engineering,
would either be glorified (the heroic or romantic pieces of
Mark di Suvero) or parodied (Tinguely), or seen as destructive junk (all of the pop artists).

During this long process, the human body became progressively less attractive, less worthy of any regard.

It may seem an irony that human beings have, in fact,
become better-looking over the past one hundred years.
Our skin is clearer, our teeth better preserved, we stand
taller and stronger. But the few fine-art sculptures that have
been done of humans in recent years have been bitter and
mocking—see the last works of the late Robert Arneson,
for example.

Contrarily, advertising art has continued to present the
human face and figure in such ways that the viewer is
attracted not repelled, and it is not only sexual attraction
that is employed. Empathy and sympathy are also aroused.

It is argued that the attitude of the fine arts expresses
deeper, even metaphysical, truths while advertising creates
illusions. Improvements to facial beauty and physique can

be seen as the opposite of true beauty—as outgrowths of vanity (one of the seven deadly sins, after all). "Improvements" can also lead to grotesque artificiality (see Willem de Kooning's *Marilyn Monroe*).

But most significantly, I believe, we are all more widely and vividly aware of the catastrophes of our history than people have ever been. Film and tape might be said to keep past sins continually before our eyes. The Holocaust is still very much with us and other horrors of World War II have recently been brought before our eyes in film with a vividness never before approached. Cloaks of commercial sentimentalism or romanticism cannot possibly cover the irrefutable evidence of human barbarity. How, then, can we truly be beautiful?

In his sculptures Fuller's aesthetic seems not to be an exception to the harsh self-assessments of our time. It is rare that a work of his wishes to be graceful, although there is often charm in discovered suggestions and resemblances. Some of his pieces, made from discarded junkyard metal, employ what Fuller calls the "miracle of steel," that is, the ability of steel to cantilever from fixed bases so that the form need not be in balance, as work made with earlier material had to be, but the strength of steel serves no purpose in his sculptures—beyond irony. The leftover detritus of an industrial machine has a certain poignance. It suggests productive uses that can no longer be accomplished. But why had the machine been abandoned, if its purpose was of any real value?

The viewer's imagination will attempt to reassemble the machine and imagine its missing parts so that its function can be identified, but the sculpture is too cleverly mysterious. The original (a die-cutter? auto body press?) cannot be reconstructed in the mind, thus one sees the remains of a machine that appears to have been without rational purpose. Decay is a prominent impression—rust is a part of nearly every surface.

Fuller has made two pieces that directly refer to humans, one of which is humorous and winning. The horizantal member of a park bench is held up at either end by metal uprights cast into the forms of mens' business clothes hanging neatly on closet hangers. The jackets and shirts and neckties are carefully and neatly arranged, and they are supporting the real people who might sit on the bench.

Contrarily, his life-size *Hero*, made of welded and painted pipes, plates and tubes is striding forward into adverse winds, it seems. Essentially a stick-figure holding a porous shield, *Hero* is dynamic but blind and perhaps quixotic.

Fuller's other pieces generally reflect a grimmer view: *Ascension,* in which a twisted and broken ladder reaches six pathetic feet or so toward the sky, is an example.

As our planet continues to be toxified, stripped of its ozone, and denuded of its trees, has an art naturally and laudably come into being that not only can't approve of the human face and form, but of any of its productions?

The fact that Fuller uses the most sophisticated tools and devices to construct art that condemns science and industry may at first seem an irony, but is it not perhaps the best possible use of technology to make a strong visual statement against the uses to which technology has been put?

There is another side to Fuller's art that has come about since his marriage in 1993 to Connee Mayeron, whose energy appears to match or even outdo Fuller's. A ceramacist whose work had been sold both through gallery exhibitions and department stores, Connee threw eighty dinner and eighty dessert plates for the guests who gathered in the studio to celebrate her and Fuller's marriage, an evening enlivened by fireworks and a Chicago blues band.

Connee and Fuller have collaborated on a number of projects, and the result has been an art that is lighter, more playful than his solo work. It has consisted mostly of big-scale ceramics: patio furniture, for example, full-scale sofas and armchairs made from clay that are shaped to resemble conventional, "overstuffed" living room pieces. Holes are drilled at the seats' lowest points so that rainwater and snowmelt can exit, and the pieces can remain outdoors in all seasons.

They have made hot tubs in which inset stones of various shapes and colors take on a pleasing brightness under water. One gallery show of their joint work featured wall-hung sconces for outdoor lights and glass-topped tables supported by seemingly chaotically bunched copper tubing that, in fact, held the glass solidly and at perfect level.

In 1995 Connee and Fuller fulfilled a commission for a multilevel, multi-faceted, free-form sitting area, sited outside the entrance to the public library in Stillwater, Minnesota. There are indented seats at the correct height for children, and others for adults, some facing each other, and benches wide enough to be comfortable for two or more. Depressions in the ceramic are deep enough to serve as small flower beds, and the form's eccentricities create separate spaces for the users, so that they find privacy despite their closeness.

In the same year Connee and Fuller, funded by Minnesota's Percent for Art Program and with the collaboration of the inmates, made a remarkable circle of benches for the Shakopee Correctional Facility, a women's prison. The sitting spaces resemble the Stillwater seating, but the surfaces are covered with mosaic tile decorated by the inmates.

Hearts are prominent on these tiles, both bleeding and loving. There are messages both religious and profane, and some so personal as to be touchingly inscrutable. In the words of a commentator for *Arts Board News,* "Looking at them is not unlike poring over old snapshots or reading notes in somebody's school yearbook." Since the benches are in constant use and there are always new inmates, the humanity of the messages should become a memorable sight to many.

Fuller's sculpture has been included in more than twenty group exhibitions over the past fifteen years. The Franconia Sculpture Park has grown in size and in its programs, and Fuller has served on a committee to revitalize the economy of St. Paul through promotion of its arts. He also sits on the board of directors of the nonprofit *Public Art Review.*

Productivity at the studio has been such that a new adjoining area is being planned for a larger studio and more storage space. On a rainy day Fuller dashes back and forth across the site, explaining the locations of its planned features, asking opinions on the placement of roadways, and talking about the construction schedule.

The Cowleses' work appears to have just begun.

Chapter Ten

THE FULLER COLLECTION

In the early 1940s Elizabeth Fuller created the Higginson–Fuller Collection of letters and other family documents at the Memorial Hall Library in Deerfield. Most of her gift was in the form of string-tied bundles of letters, bundles that had been collecting in boxes and trunks at The Bars since Nathan Negus sailed for Savannah in 1819. Elizabeth asked relatives if they had papers in their attics, too, and by the 1990s the collection had grown to more than 30,000 items.

The artists of the family had written a large fraction of these letters. Like Elizabeth herself, they had left Deerfield to find art teachers, to find work, and to try their skills in the great world, but they had kept strong bonds of affection with family members who remained at home. Both artists and homebodies cautioned each other to remember to preserve the correspondence.

In the 1950s Clara Fuller Taylor assembled the boxes of letters and papers that had come into her attic when her mother Lucia had moved to Madison in 1918. This collection was added to during the remainder of Lucia's and

HBF's lives, and sporadically thereafter—letters between Clara and Chas, for example.

These papers created the Fairchild-Fuller Collection in the Special Collections Department of the Dartmouth College Library. Dartmouth and its Hood Museum have taken a continuing interest in the history of the Cornish Colony.

There are some ten thousand items in this collection, most of them letters, many of these written between Lucia and her siblings and mother. The difficulties and downfall of the Fairchild family are documented by them, as well as the artistic and personal travails of Lucia and HBF.

Then in 1995 Richard Arms Junior and his sister Mary Arms Marsh, present owner of The Bars, jointly decided to make a gift of more than nine hundred drawings and paintings to Deerfield's Memorial Hall Museum, which adjoins the library and shares its nonprofit umbrella, the Pocumtuck Valley Memorial Association, founded in 1870. Most of the paintings in this gift had been kept in a downstairs front room in the old farmhouse, some of them since the 1820s. The drawings and watercolors had been kept out of sight inside protective folders and sketchbooks.

The Memorial Hall Museum has been and is today principally a historical museum. Displays include some anthropological-ethnographic Native American material and artifacts reflective of Deerfield's long colonial history as well as a number of works of art, most of them antiques. But now, in the words of Timothy C. Neumann, the PVMA's executive director, the Arms-Marsh gift has "changed the direction of the museum."

The permanent collection includes one of the finest of Nathan Negus's paintings—his self-portrait—as well as Augustus Vincent Tack's portrait of Elizabeth, a number of

George Fullers, and some Spencers and Arthurs. With the Arms-Marsh gift the Fuller Collection was created, and it has received work by Augustus Fuller, Caroline Negus Hildreth, Alfred Fuller, Elizabeth Fuller, Katharine Fuller Arms, Lucia Fairchild Fuller, HBF, Robert Fuller, Chas Fuller, Barabara Legler, and Jill Fox.

Suzanne L. Flynt, the museum's curator, is attempting to collect work by all the family artists and has included in the collection one of whom I have not written, Agnes Gordon Cochran Higginson, the mother of Agnes Higginson Fuller who was not a "professional" but a talented landscape painter, and work by Violet Fuller Tack, whose life I have touched on without discussing the art she stopped producing when she married.

The Fuller Collection has also been enlarged with works by artists who were friends or somehow allied with Fuller artists—Edwin Billings, Henry Kirke Brown, Irwin Hoffman, Ellen Miller, and Margaret Whiting, and by a painting by the mother of Mary Williams Field Fuller, Rebecca Jackson Williams (1799–1883).

At present there is not much available space to display the work in the Museum's old, box-shaped, three-story brick building. One museum room has been dedicated to a series of exhibitions of selected family work—landscapes by some half-dozen of the family painters are hung there as I write—but plans for the collection are ambitious. In 1995 PVMA acquired two buildings whose lots adjoin the Museum and Library complex, and these buildings will be used to expand exhibition space.

One building is Deerfield's former town hall, a nineteenth century Greek Revival building, and the other a more modern brick school building. All of Deerfield's children are now educated in South Deerfield's schools.

How these structures will be reconfigured into a history and art campus has yet to be decided, but the emphasis will be on art. Historic Deerfield has more or less preempted history by building a six-million-dollar repository for historical documents, artifacts, and changing exhibitions only one block away. Neumann expects that the opening of the new complex, including its Fuller Collection "wing," as he imagines it, should take place in 2004, the three hundredth anniversary of the "Deerfield Massacre."

Standing on Museum Street's sidewalk to look at the two "new" buildings I wondered how Frank Boyden and Henry Flynt would react to the new Old Deerfield. Boyden would be delighted, I thought. An all-historic, museum-quality setting had been created for his renowned, clearly prosperous and beautifully maintained school. Devil-take-it that the children of the town no longer attended.

Under the summer leaves of the high shade trees on Main Street every one of the old houses appeared to be freshly painted with its grass mowed and its hedges trimmed whether it was open to the public or not. The "appearances" were as Boyden would have liked them.

I was not so certain of Flynt's feelings. Surely he would be pleased by the town's historic look, but might it not strike him as odd that no local school, apart from the Academy, was operating? Might he not wonder why the town's municipal business had become so minor that it had become more efficient to transfer all departments to South Deerfield?

Flynt, after all, had imagined Old Deerfield as symbolizing a bustling spirit of adventure and free enterprise, and should that not show somehow?

Some teachers at the Academy may be telling students to "raise your eyes to the hills," as Boyden did in his Emersonian moments. The Academy's students must surely be as computer-literate as any, as well-prepared, and as eager to get on. Educationally, they are certainly not lost in an historical backwater.

Nothing, however, that the students can see in the Academy's buildings or grounds, or in the town itself, will suggest to them that innovation can be desirable, or that art can be revealing, awakening in its novelty, or fun. The only new sight I noticed that day on Main Street was a sign at the entrance to one of the old farms. "Conservation Farm," it read, meaning that "organics" are grown there—a Thoreauvian note in what used to be Emerson country.

There is such discretion in Deerfield, such "good taste!" No sign on the highway touts Deerfield's wonders to the passing motorist. Instead there is a super-modest rectangular sign, perhaps twelve by four inches, reading "Old Deerfield," with an arrow under the lettering indicating the turnoff to Main Street.

The Historic Deerfield office displays a discreet "Tours" placard, but it does not describe what the tour-takers will see. The Academy itself does not show its name to passersby—there is no sign at all! This is conservatism gone a little mad. Would it be vulgar to identify this large institution to those who do not know it?

The artists of the Negus-Fuller-Fairchild family have followed an aesthetic trajectory opposite from the town's. They passed from realistic portraiture to impressionism, neoclassicism, symbolism, abstraction, surrealism, and junkyard-material sculpture—and without even being radical! Essentially, the artists' reactions to history have been different from the town's—the differences are only secondarily a question of aesthetics.

For more than two hundred years they have continually made art, which raises the unanswerable question as to whether these seven generations share some genetic disposition to see acutely and thus to find joy and challenge and reward in art, or whether, to the contrary, Joel Negus's eccentric enthusiasm for art, and Augustus Fuller's deafness, and the Hartford Asylum's experimentation to find the special talents of the deaf combined to start a tradition that was too exciting to forsake, so that for succeeding generations of the family's children—whether they were truly gifted or only capable—avenues other than the avenue of art looked drab.

Perhaps art has been a choice for each of them, and perhaps essentially for none. But for all it has certainly been "a way of living a life" that had, and still has, many consequences.

Many of these artists' early rewards came rather easily. They were "brought-along" by their forebears, and applause for young talent was always enthusiastically, gratefully given. The later rewards, the ones that as an artist matures become the only ones worth having, were and are extremely hard come by. If they are achieved, recognition is most probably brief, and disappointment is, practically speaking, inevitable.

Meanwhile, however, true artists have lived their lives "upon the stretch."

Emerson would have approved of that.

Postscript

Years have passed since I began research on this book. Other family members have begun to create art in this period, or to practice crafts.

Lucia Taylor Miller, grandchild as I am of Lucia Fairchild Fuller and HBF, has shown her ceramic sculptures based on the human figure three times at the Evanston (Illinois) Art Center, twice in group exhibitions, once in a solo show.

Until recently I was unaware that Lucia's daughter, Katherine Lynn Miller, had exhibited her handmade paper in two group exhibitions at the Lincoln Center at Fort Collins, Colorado, and had had an exhibition of her pottery at the One West Art Center, Fort Collins.

Lucia's younger daughter, Patricia Claire Miller, is a cofounder of Chicago's Randolph Street Gallery.

Jill Fox's oldest son, Logan, is married to the artist E. Wyeth. Ellie has had four exhibitions of her line drawings and gouaches at the Princeton (New Jersey) Small World Coffee space. She has produced a variety of handmade cards and furniture painted for children. She is the illustrator of John McPhee's *Irons in the Fire*, and painted the cover for the paperback version of that book.

I have developed the hobby of making gable-ornaments, "sunbursts," one of which is shown on the cover of Jim Tolpin's *The New Cottage Home*. It is installed in a house belonging to my niece, Jane Cowles.

Lastly, Jill's quadriplegic third son, Blair Fuller Fox, has created a website from which he offers his "Light Boxes," images juxtaposed three-dimensionally and illuminated from within.

The Negus-Fuller Family Artists

JOEL NEGUS (1768–1816)
m. Basmeth Gould

Aaron Fuller (1786–1859)
m. 1) 1808 Elizabeth
2) 1820 Fanny Negus (1799–1845)

Stephen Higginson (1808–1870)
m. 1831 Agnes Gordon Cochran (1810–1888)

NATHAN NEGUS (1801–1825)

CAROLINE NEGUS (1814–1867)
m. 1844 Richard Hildreth

Francis (1810–1837)

AUGUSTUS (1812–1873)

Horace (1812–1873)
m. 1841
Achaia Burke
(1820–1892)

Elizabeth (1817–1906)
m. 1845
Asiel
Abercrombie
(?–1874)

Joseph (1824–1895)
m. 1845
Lydia White

GEORGE (1822–1884)
m. 1861
Agnes
Gordon
Higginson
(1838–1924)

Elijah Spencer (1827–1859)

Arthur Edmund (1830–1848)

Harriet Pamelia (1832–1879)
m. 1864
Edward Dammers
(?–1884)

Francis Benjamin (1838–1915)
m. 1860
Caroline Munn

John Emory (1838–?)
m. 1) 1867
Ella Melendy
(d. 1873)
m. 2) 1879
Emma Hood

Aaron (1809–1879)
m. 1845
Sophia Smith
(d. 1882)

GEORGE SPENCER FULLER (1863–1911)
m. 1889 Mary Williams Field
(1863–1951)

ROBERT HIGGINSON FULLER (1864–1927)
m. 1895 Bessie Clagett
(1858–1930)

HENRY BROWN FULLER (1867–1934)
m. 1893 (sep. 1905)
LUCIA FAIRCHILD (1872–1924)

AGNES GORDON FULLER (1873–1959)
m. 1900
Constance Trowbridge

ARTHUR NEGUS FULLER (1879–1945)
m. 1920

AUGUSTUS VINCENT TACK (1870–1949)

Agnes Gordon Tack (1901–1940)
m. 1932
Elstner Hilton

Robert Fuller Tack (1904–1949)
m. 1933
Jean Proctor
(?–1987)
she m. 2) Hayden
Kuehn

KATHARINE YALE FULLER (1891–1985)
m. 1927 Richard Arms
(1895–1956)

George Fuller (1893–1950)

ALFRED RUSSELL FULLER (1899–1980)
m. 1924
Anne Connell
(1899–1983)

ELIZABETH BROOKS FULLER (1893–1950)

Frances H. Fuller (1898–1984)
m. 1923
Howard Savage
(1886–1972)

ALICE FULLER (1900–1957)
m. 1922 (div. 1946)
Charles Goodhue
(1895–1983)
he m. 2)
Margery McCutchcon

CHARLES FAIRCHILD FULLER (1897–1960)
m. 1) 1922
JANE WHITE (?–1982)
she m. 2) Canfield
he m. 2) 1945
Anne Jones Thacher

Clara Bartram Fuller (1895–1982)
m. 1916
WARNER TAYLOR (1880–1958)

Jane Sage Fuller (1925–)
m. 1) 1946
E. Flores
m. 2) 1952
John Cowles

Blair F. Fuller (1927–)
m. 1) 1957
Nina de Voogd
m. 2) 1965
Diana Burgess
(div. 1985)

ISABEL (JILL) FULLER (1931–)
m. 1950
Joseph Fox
(div. 1971)

Lucia Fairchild Taylor (1928–)
m. 1947
Harry Miller

Richard Arms (1928–)
m. 1951
Joan Pollen

Mary Chapin Arms (1933–)
m. 1954
Herb Marsh

BARBARA GOODHUE (1925–)
m. 1947
John Legler

Maud F. Savage (1929–)

Cordelia F. Savage (1926–)
m. 1) 1946 W. Allen
(div. 1950)
m. 2) 1952 G. Gaskell
(div. 1975)
m. 3) 1977 Richard
Marche

CHARLES FULLER COWLES (1961–)
m. 1995
CONNEE MAYERON

Selected Bibliography

While the principal sources of documentation for this book are the letters in the Fuller-Higginson Collection at the Memorial Hall Library in Deerfield and the Fairchild-Fuller Collection in the Special Collections Department at the Dartmouth College Library, a number of polished works have contributed to the history, including

"A Circle of Friends: Art Colonies of Cornish and Dublin." University Art Galleries, University of New Hampshire, and the Thome Ssagendorph Art Gallery, Keene State College, 1985.

Archives of the Houghton Library, Harvard University, (letters exchanged between William Dean Howells and Caroline Negus Hildreth while she was in Trieste and he in Venice, early 1860s).

"Augustus Fuller of Deerfield," a lecture by Suzanne L. Flynt, 1992.

Baker, Carlos. *Emerson Among the Eccentrics.* Viking Press, 1996.

Ball, Thomas (1819-1911). *My Fourscore Years: an Autobiography.* Reprint edition, TreCavalli Press, 1995.

Baskin, Leonard. *Iconologia.* Harcourt Brace Jovanovich, 1988.

Blanchard, Paul. *Margaret Fuller: From Transcendentalism to Revolution.* Addison Wesley, 1987.

Blaugrun, Annette (ed.). *Paris 1889: American Artists at the Universal Exposition.* Pennsylvania Academy of Fine Arts with Harry N. Abrams Inc., 1989.

Burns, Sarah. "George Fuller, the Hawthorne of Our Art," *Winterthur Portfolio,* Vol. 18, Numbers 2 and 3 (Summer 1983).

Clark, Eliot. *History of the National Academy of Design, 1825–1953.* Columbia University Press, 1954.

Delevoy, Robert. *Le Symbolisme.* Skira, 1982.

Dods, Agnes M. "Joseph and Nathan Negus, Itinerant Painters," *Connecticut Valley Painters* (1944), and *Antiques* (1959).

Family Tree is based on one prepared by the Memorial Hall Museum, Deerfield, Massachusetts.

Fuller, Lucia Fairchild *Emerging From the Shadows*. Judith K. Mueller Memorial Hall Museum, Deerfield.

Fuller, Robert H. *The Golden Hope, A Story of the Time of Alexander the Great*. The Macmillan Company, 1905.

Furth, Leslie. *Augustus Vincent Tack: Landscape of the Spirit*. The Phillips Collection, 1993.

Garfinkle, Charlene G. "Lucia Fairchild Fuller's 'Lost' Woman's Building Mural." *American Art*, Winter 1993, National Museum of American Art, Smithsonian Institution.

Harding, James. *Artistes Pompiers: French Academic Art in the Nineteenth Century*. Academy Editions, London, 1979.

Hartmann, Sadakichi. *A History of Art in America*. 1902.

Henri, Robert. *The Art Spirit*. J. B. Lippincott Co., 1960.

Howe, Benjamin. "Sketch of the Negus and Fuller Families," Unpublished (1840s).

Kirk and Warburg. *William Dean Howells and the Art of His Time*. Rutgers University Press.

Kluver, Billy and Julie Martin. *Kiki's Paris: Artists and Lovers 1900–1930*. 1989.

Laclotte, Lacambre, Distel, and Freches-Thory. *Paintings in the Musee d'Orsay*. Editions Scala 1986.

Lynes, Russell. *The Art Makers of Nineteenth Century America*. Atheneum, 1970.

McGowan, Susan and Amelia F. Miller. *Family & Landscape: Deerfield Homelots from 1671*. Pocumtuck Valley Memorial Association, 1996.

Meet Your Neighbors: New England Portraits, Painters, and Society, 1790–1850. Old Sturbridge Village Press, 1992.

Middleton, Robin (ed.). *The Beaux Arts and Nineteenth Century French Architecture.* Thames and Hudson, 1982.

Mumford, Lewis. *The Brown Decades: A Study of the Arts in America 1865–1890.* Dover, 1955.

Olson, Stanley. *John Singer Sargent: His Portrait.* St. Martin's Press, 1986.

Revisiting the White City: American Art at the 1893 World's Fair. NMAA NPG; Smithsonian Institution, 1993.

Robb, David M. "American Barbizon Painter (re. George Fuller)," *Art Quarterly* XXIV (Autumn 1961).

Rosenblum, Robert. *Modern Painting and Northern Romantic Tradition.* Harper & Row, 1975.

Russell, Lord Bertrand. *The Autobiography of Bertrand Russell.* Allen and Unwin, 1969.

Saxton, Martha. *Louisa May: A Modern Biography of Louisa May Alcott.* Houghton Miflin, 1977.

Spencer. Laurel A. "Victorian Domesticity in Deerfield: A Case Study (re. Agnes Gordon Higginson Fuller (1838-1924)," Deerfield Memorial Hall Museum.

Stahl, Michelle M. *Elizabeth Brooks Fuller: An American Landscape Painter.* Smith College, 1995.

Stillinger, Elizabeth. *Historic Deerfield: A Portrait of Early America.* Dutton Studio Books, 1992.

Tufts, Eleanor. *American Women Artists 1830–1930.* The National Museum of Women in the Arts, 1982.

Van Rensselaer, M. G. *Catalogue of the Memorial Exhibition of the Works of George Fuller.* Boston Museum of Fine Arts, 1884.

Zea, Philip and Nancy Norwalk (eds.). *Choice White Pines and Good Land: A History of Plainfield and Meriden, New Hampshire, Written by the Townspeople.* Peter E. Randall, Publisher, 1991.

BLAIR FULLER is the great-great-great-grandson of the first of the artists whose stories are told in this book. He is the author of two novels, *A Far Place* and *Zebina's Mountain*, and a collection of short stories, *A Butterfly Net and a Kingdom*. Two of his stories were winners of O. Henry awards. Fuller has been one of the *Paris Review's* editors for many years, has taught at Barnard College, Stanford University, and other institutions, and is a co-founder of the Squaw Valley Community of Writers. He lives in San Francisco and Tomales, California.